A GRUNT SPEAKS

A GRUNT SPEAKS

A Devil's Dictionary of Vietnam Infantry Terms

RAY GLEASON

Erinach LLC

To Sharon Boland Ellis and Bob Craft

Without whose help I would have never dealt with most of what's represented in these pages.
I don't know if they agree with some of the values expressed in this book, but they understand their essential truth.

And

In Remembrance Of Our Fallen Brothers Of 27 September 1968

"We, the unwilling,
led by the unknowing,
do the impossible
for the ungrateful.
We have done so much,
for so long,
with so little,
we can do anything
with nothing."

Also By Ray Gleason

THE GAIUS MARIUS CHRONICLES

From Morgan James Fiction
De Re Gabiniana – The Gabinian Affair (2015)
De Re Helvetiana – The Helvetian Affair (2016)
De Re Suabiana – The Swabian Affair (2017)

From Erinach, LLC
De Re Strigis – The Vampire Affair (2022)

THE GAIUS MARIUS MYSTERIES
From Erinach, LLC
Vindicta a Sanguine – Blood Vengeance (2023)

ALSO

From Unlimited Publishing LLC
A Grunt Speaks: A Devil's Dictionary of Vietnam Infantry Terms
(1st ed, 2009)
The Violent Season (2013)

A Grunt Speaks
A Devil's Dictionary of Vietnam Infantry Terms
2nd Edition (2023)

ISBN PRINT: 979-8-218-19138-2
ISBN EBOOK: 979-8-218-19140-5
Library of Congress Control Number: Applied for

BOOK COVER DESIGN: The Book Cover Whisperer
OpenBookDesign.biz

EDITOR: Jan E. Peyser

INTRODUCTION TO
THE SECOND EDITION
(2023)

When I first wrote this book back in 2009, I had no idea where it would lead.

First, it started a rather "late-in-life" writing career as is indicated by what has been published since 2009.

More importantly, it opened to door to my own past by re-introducing me to many of my buddies from the Vietnam war through the 35th Infantry Cacti Association, the 75th Infantry Ranger Association, and the Company A, 2nd Battalion, 35th Infantry Association comprised mostly of guys from my old 1st Platoon with a healthy participation by members of the other platoons, the medics assigned to our company, and even a few mortar and artillery guys.

These guys are for me the real deal. We experienced the war together, along the same bunker line, on the same patrols. "We band of brothers," as my friend and comrade, Pat Martin, terms it.

We're certainly grayer, our waistlines have expanded a bit and, instead of being able to hump twenty klicks through the boonies, we huff and puff going up a short flight of stairs.

But the fire is still there! The fire we had in the belly to fight that war and take care of each other.

I've often wondered what would make a sane human being commit to such an insane act as going to war. I think the answer is two-fold.

Some go because they believe it's the right thing to do ... fight communist expansion ... defend the right of self-determination of the South Vietnamese people ... or for those who were drafted, the sense of responsibility, duty, and commitment to see it through and not hide in a squat in Haight-Ashbury or hightail it to Canada.

That's only what got us there. But once there and faced with the horrors of combat, we lost our idealism. Our vision was focused on the bunker line ... the next patrol ... a sweep through an area of operations ... digging in ... stringing wire ... filling sandbags ... incoming ordinance ... running up on a bunker complex ... ambushes ... losing friends.

What kept us there, what kept us engaged in the mission, was each other. We became closer than brothers. No one wanted to betray that intimate trust. You go, I go! I got your six! I'm here as long as you need me!

The "Army," Big A, was an indifferent and somewhat incompetent entity that existed somewhere "back in rear," "off the line." The Army worried about shined boots, shaves, filling out forms, and moving us around the terrain like chess pieces on some inscrutable playing board.

Actually, it was somewhat like the game Battleship; they kept dropping us onto various grid squares until we hit something.

The real army, our army, was us ... six or seven of us in a squad ... three squads of us in the platoon ... three platoons of us in the company.

We shared rations; slept three to a hootch; got drenched in the monsoon; listened to the Grand Ole Opry on Saturday night; drank dirty, iodine-lace water;, sucked steaming, brown army coffee through our teeth during stand-to and spit out the grounds; and, when we had to, fought the war and tried to keep each other alive.

So, we may have gone to war because of our ideals, but we fought the war for each other.

This was the bond I was able to recover when I finally rediscovered my A Company brothers down in South Carolina. The connection is still there!

The book has served its purpose for me.

The horrors of that war are still with us lurking in the recesses of our minds. The lucky ones have been able to compartmentalize much of it, so we can function normally.

But the "locks" don't hold. Something we experience can trigger a memory we locked away.

Even on the best of days, these memories whisper to us through the locked doors behind which we have consigned them, trying to influence how we react and behave.

To this day, I cannot walk down a path without analyzing the terrain for threats. "Good spot for an ambush ... that's where the machine gun should be emplaced ... high ground on my flank ... scan the ridgeline for movement."

A couple of years ago, I was training a new employee to do a student-supervision job at a boarding school where we worked; we were essentially the weekend babysitters for over eight hundred teenagers.

We were going through a section of campus called the "bird sanctuary," a large expanse of woods in the northeast corner of campus where, for no sane reason I can imagine, the school issues rifle hunting licenses during deer season. The reason we were back there was to orientate the newbie to the terrain and to be on the watch for teenagers out in the woods doing things we rather they didn't do.

We were riding a golf cart on a horseback-riding trail about thirty meters north of a state highway, when we heard three gunshots to our northeast. My immediate reactions: rifle ... within fifty meters ... that direction ... at least 30 caliber ... not firing in my direction."

While my brain was processing, the newby asked, "What was that?"

My first thought was to maneuver on the shooter's position. Then I remembered this is 2020, not 1968 ... I'm not in Nam, but Indiana ... there are police to handle this stuff.

So, I answered, "We're unassing the area and calling campus security." Which we did. And, my rookie learned a grunt term, "unassing."

For us veterans, if we can recognize our monsters that still lurk in our subconscious for what they are and face them, they can't hurt us. "That was then, but not now!"

So, this book reminds its readers of what they already know, so that what they already know doesn't sneak up on them and cause them to do something that made sense then but makes no sense now.

If you have ever been to a veterans' reunion, you know the most common opening to a conversation is, "Do you remember ..." followed by a war story. If you think about it, most of the stories have become humorous over the years, stripped of the uncertainty and horror felt when the event was unfolding.

"I had the little bastard dead-to-rights in front of me ... I pulled the trigger of my M16 and nothing happed ... not even a f'ing' click ... by the time I realized my safety was on, the dink had didi'd on me ... why he didn't grease my ass, I'll never know ... needed a change of underwear after that one ..."

Sounds funny now ... big joke on me!

It wasn't then!

So, this book also serves to pull the monsters' fangs by poking fun at them. A monster you can laugh at has no power over you ... except of course vampires ... don't laugh at vampires ... use the garlic, then go for the wooden stake.

In a way, these anecdotes that veterans share with each other aren't "war stories"; they're therapy. Get it out ... make it funny ... then it can't hurt you anymore.

So, when I hear from one of my younger colleagues about a family member who served in Nam, I check the pedigree ... where, what unit, what MOS, etc. Many times I get the answer, "I don't know ... he never talks about it."

So, I offer a copy of the book.

Sometimes, I get a response, "He read it and really got a kick out of it."

Once, a young woman told me her uncle had read the book and had used parts of it to share for the first time some of his experiences with her.

That's why I write.

That's why I give a copy of this book to any veteran or veteran's family member who wants it.

INTRODUCTION TO
THE FIRST EDITION
(2009)

I work in the leadership department of a private high school; fellow instructors are veterans of Vietnam, Desert Storm, Iraq and Afghanistan. I am also in communication with buddies from Nam through veterans' groups. When we get together, we occasionally swap "war stories" over a couple beers. As grunts, we've seen some "pretty hairy shit" but tend not to get too maudlin and weepy about it. We release the stress caused by these experiences by reducing terror to humor, albeit a somewhat dry and dark humor. So our stories are about humorous situations: the banana cat who routed an infantry squad; the Orangutans who beat up a Ranger team; the elephant who walked through the kill zone of an ambush in the middle of the night while the FNG, who was supposed to keep watch, missed it ... not about how the brains of some guy were blown into our face when he got shot in the head or the smell of an NVA bunker complex that was smoldering from napalm.

As I worked through the project, I couldn't help noticing that the humor is a little violent, coarse and, dare I say, "anti- social." My first reaction was to "clean it up," but then I realized I would be distorting the "mores" that these reflections represent. When you read these accounts, you are actually sharing the culture of the men and women whose experiences they represent; the infantrymen, "grunts" in army-speak, who fought the Vietnam war, and the men and women who supported, entertained and sometimes literally put them back together.

Many grunts still believe they were trying to do something worthwhile in Nam. Some might articulate it in terms of "freedom" and "stopping communist aggression," others in terms of keeping faith with their buddies. This book reveals what was important to them: hot chow; a warm, dry place to sleep; clean, operational weapons; a few days of dry weather; and guys you could trust with your six. What was repugnant to them: REMFs, lifers, Jody and chicken shit. What they loved: home, loyalty, buddies, and letters from their girls back home—even if she was mom. What was funny: anything that pisses off lifers and doesn't get you killed. Unless these are explained the way grunts understood them, they're distorted.

It's taken quite a while for Vietnam vets to "come home;" that is, reach some sort of peace with themselves about the war. Let me tell you a story.

One time, in graduate school, I was in the student center having a beer with the professor and some students after class. I went to grad school while still in the army, so I was a bit older than the other students (and at least half the faculty) and my hair was a bit too short to be stylish. I know it was October 1986, because we were watching the Mets and the Astros play in the National League Championship Series. The prof and I were both New York ex-pats and Met fans despite the university being a hotbed of Cubism and other futilities. One of the students, a young woman who looked to me to be about twelve, but was obviously old enough to buy a beer, asked me if I had been in Vietnam. I guess the haircut and the twitching gave me away.

I froze! Which in itself was amazing! I was a combat- experienced infantry officer and Ranger. Shoot at me, I don't freeze! Drop artillery on me, I don't freeze! A twenty-something on a college campus asks me if I had been in Nam—I freeze up like a can of beer left in the freezer too long (apologies for the metaphor...too much Raymond Chandler at an impressionable age).

When I got back to the "world" in the early '70s and was finishing my undergraduate degree at the City University of New York, that question was usually the first salvo in a battle:

"You in Nam?"

"Yeah."

"So, how many babies you kill?"

"None! But it's never too late to start ... Baby!"

What the hell, I thought, Vietnam was ancient history to these kids. So I told her I had been there. When I said this, she reached across the table and laid her hand on my arm and said, "I don't think anyone really appreciates what you guys did over there. Thanks!"

I plotzed! I had been out of Nam over fifteen years and this was the first time anyone had shown any gratitude or even tried to make me feel okay about what I and my buddies had gone through over there.

This may be typical of the experience of many Vietnam vets. Many of us went to Nam for what we believed to be a "noble cause"—defend the South Vietnamese from North Vietnamese aggression; stop the expansion of Communism; serve our country. Though, some of us just got drafted but decided to face up to it and not run off to Canada.

We had grown up in the early '60s, when Jack Kennedy said we should do something for our country before we expected our country to do anything for us. Many of us bought it. Vietnam was our opportunity to serve, our cause, our fight to "preserve democracy and freedom" like our fathers had in Europe, the Pacific and Korea.

Whether these beliefs had any validity is irrelevant; we believed it! Many of us went to Nam because of it. When we got in country and found ourselves up to our asses in NVA, the vision of the "noble cause" faded, but still we fought with and for our buddies. We fought a competent enemy under disadvantageous conditions for a nation which seemed to have repudiated us along with that unpopular war. Like every American infantryman before (and after) us, we suffered, we won victories, we experienced defeats, and we lost friends. And most of us did all this before our twenty-first birthday.

But, unlike our cousins who fought in Korea and our fathers who fought World War II and our grandfathers who fought in World War I, we returned home to discover that we were "the babies thrown out with the bath water."

Being a Vietnam veteran in the early '70s was hell. Popular culture portrayed us as murderous, drug-crazed psychopaths. The news carried stories of massacred villages and napalmed children. We were portrayed as "baby-killers," rapists and murderers—" worse than Genghis Khan's horde," as a former presidential candidate characterized us at the time.

When we got back to the world, we quickly learned to keep our mouths shut about where we'd been and what we had done in Nam. I remember coming home through the Oakland army Terminal in the Spring of 1970. We got off the bird from Tan Sun Nhut, kissed the tarmac and were told not to go into San Francisco because we might be attacked! Sounds like advice for Saigon or Pleiku, not an American city! Of course, we ignored the advice, put on our khakis with our CIBs, branch insignia, infantry-blue shoulder cords and decorations and went to town. I wound up in a working-class bar near the ferry building where my money was no good all night. I was underweight, a little dehydrated, and downing boilermaker for a few hours. I got shipped back to the army at zero-dark-thirty in the back of a city cab … barely in time to catch my plane home … thanks, guys!

When we got home, we tried to get our lives back, but we quickly learned to conceal our service. In job interviews, you had a better chance of getting hired if you said you had spent twelve months in detox!

There's a bit of an irony in this. Like the "antiwar movement" which fueled the hostility to returning vets, grunts hated the war. How can you not hate the thing that had done so much damage to you and people you loved?

When I went to Nam, I was a war-movie cliché. I was "engaged" to my "high school sweetheart;" we planned to get married when I got back. I carried her picture wrapped in plastic in my ruck for almost two years. By the time I did get home, that part of my life was gone. My girl-friend had drifted away from our relationship and eventually married someone she met in college. After almost two years of combat, I was no longer a "high school sweetheart, going steady, pin a corsage on the prom dress, holding hands in the movie" kind of guy. She went off to law school and a career. I tried to run a bar in Queens with my father, crashed in a bad marriage (which produced two wonderful kids) and re-upped in the army because it was the only place I felt I belonged. I still have the picture, by the way.

Here's a dirty little secret you don't see in war movies. Wars are fought by children—teenagers—most of us were too young to buy a beer in the corner bar when we went to Nam. I got to Nam at nineteen and left when I was twenty-one (going on fifty). At nineteen I should have been learning how to unhook a bra in the back of a Chevy, not how to set a time-delay fuse in a Willy Pete grenade and arm Claymore mines. At nineteen, I got my first rifle squad and Purple Heart. At twenty, I had a ranger team and lost my best friend. At twenty- one, I won the Bronze Star and Air Medal, but developed a bad habit of vomiting when I smelled helicopter exhaust.

The war wasn't kind to our loved ones on the home front either. My youngest brother told me a story about my mom long after she had passed away. My mom was one of the toughest people I knew growing up in a pretty tough, working-class section of New York. She was a volatile combination of French and Irish; five feet and a hundred pounds of piss and vinegar and she didn't take crap from anybody. I remember in the fourth grade I came home from school crying because some "big kid" was picking on me. Instead of consoling me, she sent me right back out of the house to kick that kid's ass!

While I was in Nam, my mom refused to answer the phone or go to the door. She had my brother, who was not much older than four at the time, answer when the other kids were away at school. One afternoon the doorbell rang and my mom called out to my brother to see who it was. He looked through the front window and saw one of the parish priests at the door. When he told her, my mom collapsed! Priests didn't make house calls in those days unless they needed to explain how one of your children dying in southeast Asia at nineteen was part of God's inscrutable plan. Better than getting a telegram from a taxi driver, I guess.

So, when I say I hate war, or even that war, I don't have to depend on some dreamy theory. I have the "lost love, malarial headaches, scarred body, bad dreams, memories of buddies who never came home" blues fueling my hate.

Although grunts and the anti-war movement shared a hatred of the war, many vets also despised the peace movement. Admittedly part of the reason is that grunts are generally contemptuous of civilians; it's the basic "you send my ass to Nam to do your dirty work while you stay safe and comfy at home, take my job, snake my girl and talk shit about me!" syndrome. But, more than that, the antiwar movement attacked us, slandered us, despised us and repudiated us.

The peace movement didn't seem able (or willing) to differentiate its hatred of war from its hatred of the soldiers who fought it. Vets became a lightning rod for their anger over everything they thought wrong with the war. They certainly did not recognize—or seem to care—about the damage they did to us by encouraging our enemy. The peace movement sent a clear message to the North Vietnamese that they didn't have to defeat us; they merely had to avoid being defeated long enough for the inevitable withdrawal of US Troops. The enemy also understood clearly that they could fuel anti-war sentiment in the US with casualties, which the media reported faithfully every evening to our mothers, fathers, brothers, and sisters who waited and worried at home.

But even worse is what the peace movement did to those of us who made it home and desperately wanted to put our lives back together. Vets had to hide the fact that they had fought in Nam when what they really needed was to be able to get these horrors out...to talk it through with someone who wouldn't attack them as "baby-killers," and psychopaths.

It took me over twenty years to "come home" from Nam. When I first got home I didn't feel like I "belonged" anymore. The world seemed "out of tune;" nothing seemed quite the way I remembered it...people, friends, music...everything was "off." I didn't (or refused to) recognize the effect that over twenty months of combat had had on me. I was "functional." I wasn't doing drugs or staying drunk all the time. I had a job, friends, a home and kids. I mistook "functional" for "okay."

Had I the opportunity to talk about what I had gone through...how these memories made me feel...I may have had an opportunity to start healing. But, I had to keep my mouth shut to avoid becoming an object of derision and vilification, a pariah. There was no one to talk to; it was dangerous to try.

Yet, I constantly saw movies where grunts were portrayed fragging officers, killing each other, burning villages, slaughtering civilians, and getting stoned. Every day I got the daily casualty count on the evening news wondering if one of those statistics was a friend. I was told daily the futility of our sacrifices and heard about another "informed source" with a tale of atrocities committed by the troops. In politics, the party in power lied claiming it had a strategy to successfully end the war — "Peace with Honor!" — while the other side sucked up to the peace movement while propping up the war long enough to use it as leverage in the next election and, when successful, began bellowing the "Peace with Honor" cant ... all the while good people suffered and died in Nam.

Fortunately for me, almost twenty years after the war I did finally "come home." I finally realized that my emotions were so locked up that they couldn't be seen by the people I loved. I was able to get help when someone, a counselor, made it safe to talk about the war, really listened and made me believe that I wasn't a monster. Thank you, Sharon and Bob!

Because of these shared experiences, the grunts who experienced combat and kept faith with each other over the years are bonded. There is no closer and more durable fellowship. It's a brotherhood and sisterhood that goes beyond cultural, ethical and racial differences. Let me tell one more story.

Some years ago I was killing a few unneeded brain cells with pints of Guinness in an Irish bar in Evanston, Illinois. It was Saturday night. The place was packed and I was defending my twelve inches of bar space with elbows, attitude and determination. Suddenly, my space was invaded by a scruffy looking black guy in a dirty, army field jacket, who I thought looked definitely out of place in that "Clancy Brothers, melanin- challenged, porter-guzzling" gin mill...besides he was muscling into my bar space. I can't remember what he said, but I immediately recognized the "grunt-speak." So I asked him the first critical screening question, "You in Nam?" When he said yes, I popped the second critical question, "Who with?" He mentioned some Marine grunt unit (Okay...Department of the Navy...but a grunt's a grunt). After testing his bona fides, I established he was for real...in fact based on his dates of service, we probably chewed some of the same dirt up in I Corps. This immediately trumped all potential racial, economic and bar- space issues...he was a brother ... and there was plenty of room for him at the bar with my arm around his shoulders. We recognized each other because we talked the talk and we related because we had walked the walk...hell, we got so expansive, we even let some ex-Air Force guy drink with us.

So, when you read "grunt-speak," you are entering our world. I can't promise you that you'll find it pleasant or amusing. All I can guarantee is that it's as real as I can remember it.

A BRIEF AFTERTHOUGHT

There's an expression we used in business that goes, "Eat your own dog food;" in other words, practice what you preach.

It's advice I should have observed. Especially since, when I teach writing, I tell my students to write the introduction after the main argument because "you're never sure what you're really going to write until you've actually written it." I wrote the introduction above long before the final draft of the book. So, let me catch you up with how this book actually turned out.

First, in my introduction I slammed the "anti-war movement" pretty hard. Although there is justification for a Vietnam vet to harbor some hard feelings, I'd like to set the record straight on my attitude about that.

When it comes to war, there is no sane position other than to despise it. But, that revulsion should not extend to those who choose to fight in a cause they believe is worthy. Furthermore, I do not despise those who honestly honored their consciences and opposed the Vietnam war from outside the military.

A colleague of mine once said to me, "Oh! You'll probably hate me because when I was in school I protested against the war." But my answer was no.

If you did it out of the courage of your convictions, not only do I not hate you for it, but I applaud you for it. I don't believe it's ethical to tolerate unethical acts. So, if you truly believed that the war was unethical, you were obliged to oppose it!

What I do detest, however, are those who used an "anti- war" posture either to conceal their own cowardice, or to veil their unwillingness to serve their country, or to gain political advantage, or to further their careers. Further, I sometimes suspect that those who used an anti-war position deceitfully and then felt the guilt of their own false pretense allowed that guilt to fuel their vehemence in attacking those who went to Nam and did their duty.

But, for those who honestly opposed the war and did nothing to harm those who fought it, I have no problem.

Another issue is the "tone" of the book. I promised that I would not "soften" any of the language or attitudes in order to honestly represent the "grunt culture." However, that position became obviously untenable if I expected anyone, who was not actually part of the "grunt culture," to be able to read the book without being alienated from its message by its language and tone. I have to accept that there are some aspects of the grunt and civilian values and mores that are simply not compatible.

First, I banished a certain well-known English word, derived from a most ancient Anglo-Saxon verb meaning "to copulate," that is quite common in grunt-speak but not in socially acceptable English usage. It's in the text, but not fully exposed.

I did, however, leave in its companion word, one which the late comedian, George Carlin, used to such great effect. So, anyone, who finds Carlin's humor offensive because of the use of that work, may have a problem with parts of this book.

Finally, grunts rarely referred to their enemy as the "NVA" and never as the "bad guys." The term commonly used in the AO where I served was "dinks;" down in the Delta, they were typically called "gooks." These were terms that grunts considered quite appropriate, even mild, when referring to a group of people whose goal was to kill them. However, when brought over into early twenty-first century American civil usage, these terms seem racist and become impediments to expressing the point of some of these experiences. So, I felt it best to "soften" the tone to preserve the "message."

Finally, the text strayed from its original purpose of a somewhat amusing and satiric presentation of grunt terms and concepts to a bit of a memoir. To tell the truth, I'm a bit uncomfortable with my new role as the protagonist of some of these stories. Like most grunts, I consider what I did in Nam "just doing my job" and not worthy of any special notice. I certainly don't consider myself a "hero" since heroism is merely the normal response of ordinary people to extraordinary circumstances. In a strange way, "heroes" are created by circumstances in which they find themselves but over which they have little, if any, control. I'm sure that any grunt faced with extraordinary circumstances would have had the competence and the chutzpah to do what needed to be done. And most of what grunts did in Nam, they did to do their job and to "be there" for each other, not to boast of in a book.

NUMBERS

1

105.   Pronounced, One-Oh-Five. This is the 105 mm howitzer, artillery, a grunt's best friend in need, indeed! In formal "army-speak" the M101A1, 105 mm Howitzer, a common source of fire support for grunts in Nam.

The 105s provided what's called "indirect fire support," meaning the guns fired from behind the grunts and the rounds went "up, over and down" instead of directly into a target.

The 105s fired H.E. (High Explosive), WP (White Phosphorous, "Willy Pete" or "White Smoke"), Smoke (Technicolor and Black & White), HEAT (High Explosive Anti-Tank) and Flechettes (many nasty anti-personnel darts). The 105 had a maximum range over 11,000 meters.

The 105s were typically deployed on fire bases in battery strength of four guns. Typically, a 105 battery directly supported an infantry battalion.

On the fire bases, the artillery guys built "gun pits" for each gun with a round "blast wall" constructed of sandbags to protect the guns and their crews from enemy "incoming." A "ready" magazine was located in each gun pit to increase and maintain a rapid rate of fire.

The guns in each battery were controlled by the FDC, Fire Direction Control. The gun settings were calculated for a target by the FDC and a senior artillery NCO, the "Chief of Smoke," directed the settings of the guns for a fire mission by shouting them across the battery.

Normally, the 105s provided indirect fire support on specific targets in an Area of Operations (AO) and conducted "Harassment and Interdiction" missions (H&I), random fire on possible areas of enemy activity far beyond where the artillery crews could see.

A notable exception occurred during a battle in the highlands in early 1968. The NVA managed to overrun the bunker line of a fire base and the surviving grunts had to pull back to the artillery gun pits. The bad guys began to mass on the bunker line for a final push through the perimeter when, like a civil war battle when artillery fired canister directly into massed infantry, the artillery lowered their gun barrels and fired flechettes directly into the massed enemy. A single battery of flechette rounds literally transformed the massed NVA into a misty red cloud the grunts could see under the light of the mortar flares. The flechettes broke the back of the enemy's attack on the firebase. The next morning, when the grunts reclaimed the bunker line, there was little left that could be identified as the remains of the enemy.

In Nam, the army also employed the 155mm, 175mm and 8-inch guns for indirect fire support. When the 8-inch guns fired, the concussion could blow out candles at five hundred meters. I still have trouble understanding what my wife is saying to me because I was too close to an 8-inch battery when it was firing (That's my story and I'm sticking to it!).

2

201 File.   Pronounced, "Two-Oh-One File."

This was formally called the Official Military Personnel File (OMPF).

The 201 file was the repository of a soldier's personnel records. It contained all personnel paperwork created about, for or against a soldier.

Hence, it was the primary weapon of the REMF and the center of all their power over grunts. Beneficial paper and medical records could disappear and noxious paper suddenly appear depending on the whims of the company clerk.

In the army-world, the 201 file was the heart of the REMF-centric bureaucracy. If it wasn't in the 201 file it didn't happen, and conversely, if it appeared in the 201 it did happen — whatever it was. Promotion and transfer orders had been known to vanish without even a whiff of smoke while orders for a CIB mysteriously appeared in the file of a REMF who had never gotten closer to the boonies than the bunker line on a division base camp.

The 201 file was absolute proof that the most dangerous thing in the army, other than a 2nd Lieutenant with a map and compass, was a REMF with an attitude, an inferiority complex, a typewriter, some carbon paper, and access to a grunt's 201 file.

4

4F.　Literally, this was the draft classification of an individual judged unfit for military duty.

Figuratively, for grunts it described any loser, sad sack, snuffy, or waste of meat.

There's a bit of an irony operating here. Although "4F" was used as an expression of derision based on the contempt that grunts had for civilians in general and for 4Fs in particular, there was also quite a bit of sub-conscious envy fueling the fervor of its use. If I had gotten a letter in Nam from my draft board saying that a terrible mistake had happened, I was unfit for military service and would be sent home immediately, I'm not sure I'd have been real upset.

To let you know how efficient the SACs (Sorry-Assed Civilians) who ran the draft were back then, I got my draft notice from my New York City draft board when I was already in the army finishing Advanced Infantry Training down in Alabama. The notice to report was even sent to my army address!

Since being drafted usually meant two-years active duty in the infantry, and I had enlisted for three-years active duty in the infantry and was having a bad case of buyer's regret (See the quality of people they give Ph.Ds. to these days!), I asked my Drill Sergeant if I could opt for the shorter option. He wasn't amused in an obscene sort of way.

45.　This is the general grunt term for the M1911A1 .45 caliber pistol, or "Pistol, Caliber .45, Automatic, M1911A1" in lifer-speak.

This was also referred to by grunts as the "noise maker" due to its ineffectiveness in combat. At most, it made the bad guys duck.

The army 45 was infamous for its inaccuracy. In fact, most grunts believed that, unlike other weapons, the 45 had no "maximum effective range," the maximum range at which targets could be engaged effectively. Grunts were sure it had a maximum range, but they knew they couldn't hit crap with it.

The good news about the 45 is it never jammed and, if it did hit a bad guy, he stayed down. The army 45s were made with such loose tolerances that it could be buried in sand, and it would still fire. But, due to these loose tolerances, a grunt couldn't hit a target while standing right in front of it. There was no way of telling where the round would end up.

When I became an officer, I qualified with the forty-five on a ten-meter target. My first round was off my aiming point. Since the sites on a 45 can't be adjusted, I adjusted my aiming point. Another miss! But off in a totally different and unexpected direction on the target. Another aiming adjustment. Another unanticipated hole in the target. So, like Clint Eastwood in a "spaghetti western," I just emptied the magazine in the general direction of the target. Five in the circle! I qualified. (Thank God for No. 2 Pencils!)

45s were greatly desired by grenadiers — grunts who carried the M79 — because they had no effective close-up-and-personal protection. Of course, army TOE did not authorize grenadiers to have 45s. (It's just the way the system works). So, there was a healthy "gray market" in 45s between guys who needed them in order to stay alive and guys who were authorized to have them in order to indicate their status.

The 45 was the weapon of choice for REMFs, lifers, armorers, and supply guys (never know when you might get into a firefight on the way to the NCO club). A "war trophy," an NVA belt buckle or pith helmet, could usually be swapped for a 45 with a base camp commando.

5

50 Cal.   This is the M2 Browning .50 Caliber Machine Gun.

Light-infantry grunts (is that redundant?) didn't see the 50 Cal too often. At over eighty pounds — gun, tripod, traverse & search mechanism, barrel & spare barrel, head space & timing gauge — it was too heavy even for grunts to hump.

Grunts might see them on firebases, base camps or when they were working with Cav or Mech Infantry units who festooned their Armored Personnel Carriers (APCs), M48 tanks, and deuces with them.

In Nam, there was an interesting variation of the 50cal called the "quad 50" which was exactly what it sounds like, four guns that fired in the same direction and the same time. The quad was designed for anti-aircraft use during WWII, but it was used in Nam for perimeter defense. Although it was a very effective weapon for stopping the bad guys, it made body counts both messy and confusing. "Hey! I'm short some parts on this one ... anyone got some spare bits?"

The 50 Cal had a maximum effective range over a mile, which grunts always considered a bit of overkill (Yes! A pun!) because no one could see targets that far away. At a mile, the bullet actually arrived before the sound of the shot. That must have come as a rude shock to someone!

One night we had an M48 tank on the perimeter with a 50 Cal that could fire semi-automatic (i.e., one round at a time) equipped with a telescopic night vision device. That was a reality show!

8

81s.   These were the M29 & M29A1 81mm mortars.

Each rifle company had its own 81 section of three tubes. The 81s shot mostly HE, smoke and illumination.

Although the 81s could deliver HE out over three klicks, a good 81 section (and these guys were really good) firing max elevation, minimum charge during FPF could drop a round right in front of the bunker line ... an unmistakable invitation to the bad guys to go away and leave grunts alone.

I spent a couple weeks as the "guest" of our company's 81 section. I was coming back to the field from the hospital after getting patched up from the firefight where my helmet got killed. The company was out humping the bush and the 81s were on a firebase outside the vi;;age of Duc Lap with the battalion TOC.

That's about as far as I got. I came down with a slight case of dysentery. That's the problem with shamming in a hospital ... too many germs.

When I went to the aid station, not only did the battalion surgeon give me some stuff for my case of Ho Chi Minh's revenge, but he also decided I had ringworm. So, the old man decided I should stay back with the mortars and load supply choppers until I stopped leaking.

Since I wasn't trained as an 11C, a mortar grunt, the section chief put me on radio watch. The mortar guys had built an underground, waterproof FDC where we worked and slept. I would have felt I was in heaven if it hadn't been for the constant trips to the latrine, the nausea, diarrhea, dehydration, and the chalky crap with three quarts of water the Doc was making me drink every couple of hours.

There was one other problem ... the rats had found us.

Rats eventually became a problem on any firebase. No matter how good the food and garbage discipline was, these rodents always seemed to think they were better off living with grunts than out in the bush. The fact that grunts were pretty grubby, ate a lot of C-Rat cheese, and spent a good deal of the time underground, might have made the rats think we were related in some obscure way.

Once the rats did arrive, there was no getting rid of them. So, most grunts and rats tried to work out some modus vivendi with each other ... you don't bite us, we won't kill you.

But sometimes the truce broke down and a shooting war resulted.

We had rats in the FDC. For the most part, we were all ignoring each other and going about our respective businesses until the night one of the rats decided to get a little too chummy.

It was late and I was off shift, all snuggled up with my poncho liner and air mattress in a bunk behind the radios. I was just about asleep when I thought I felt something creeping up my leg.

I convinced myself I was imagining it because I had the willies from all the rats crawling around the bunker. Besides, I thought, rats don't crawl into bed with humans.

Whatever I convinced myself I was imagining seemed to crawl up, settle into the crook of my arm and stop. So, I had two choices: either a rat had just snuggled in with me for the night, or I was suffering from a bad case of rat-induced heebie-jeebies. I opted for the latter (who wouldn't).

Just to confirm my assumption, I suddenly flung my arm out across the bunker. Then I heard a thump, a squeal, and the radio guy scream something about a flying rat!

It took us a little time to get things settled down.

The rat of course immediately disappeared. But the radio guy was a bit jittery and had this idea that I was throwing my rats at him. I soon convinced him that if I had any rats to throw, I'd throw them at the Chief of Smoke, the top-kick of the FDC, who not too many guys liked that much.

Now we had to decide what to do about the rats.

Phase I of the rat counter-offensive was not successful. We located their tunnels into the bunker and sealed them off.

The rats just dug new ones.

Phase II was a bit more aggressive. We got some rat traps down in the village and baited them with unwanted C Rations.

We soon found out that what grunts won't eat, neither will Vietnamese rats; they just ignored the bait.

So, we baited the traps with peanut butter; no rat can resist peanut butter!

We were right! The rats took the bait but didn't spring the traps.

We were obviously dealing with NVA super-sapper-rats.

So we upped the ante and started shoving pieces of mortar charges and C4 into the burrows in an attempt to burn them out.

Again, this had no appreciable effect on the rats ... except they were now eating their food hot. The fumes certainly ran us out of the bunker a few times.

The rats were winning and we had the honor of our species at stake ... to say nothing of sleeping in a nice, warm cozy bunker instead of out in the mud.

So we took one the FDC guys' 45 and emptied out the magazines. We popped the slug and charge out of each round, replaced it with a BB from a claymore and sealed it with wax. We tested the new anti-rat weapon on a paper target and soon got pretty good with it.

Now we had to solve the night warfare problem. The rats only came out when it was dark in the bunker, and we couldn't see them to shoot them.

So, we opted for a high-tech solution. We borrowed a night vision device, a Starlight scope, from battalion.

Now we could sit on our bunks in the dark with the Starlight scope and the anti-rat 45, and snipe at the little buggers as they infiltrated through their tunnel system.

Just to assuage the animal lovers out there ... we didn't do much damage to our little rodent buddies.

The 45 was wildly inaccurate, the BBs didn't have much power, and the damned rats soon learned to avoid the whole set up. Like good grunts, they learned not to bunch up, to stay under cover, and to do their little three-second rushes across the bunker to get at our food.

I don't know how that war ended. My problem finally "dried up" and I was back out to the field. And none too soon ... I was getting a bit too squirrely over this rat thing.

One night, I was sure a rat had "Chieu Hoi'd" to me.

9

90-Day Wonder. Refers to an officer commissioned through Officer Candidate School (OCS).

Although the term is essentially derogatory, it didn't necessary describe an officer's competence. My experience with OCS guys ran both ways ... some were good and others not so much. The term was usually applied as a condemnation of officerial incompetence, "Whadda ya expect? He's an f'ing 90-day wonder!"

The officer-prestige pecking order in the army was 1) "Ring Knockers," West Point Grads; 2a) ROTC, Prestigious Military College, like the Citadel and VMI (The south shall rise again, Suh!); 2b) ROTC, any old school; 3) OCS; 4) "Mustangs," officers commissioned from the enlisted ranks.

There was also a very rare breed of commissioned officer prowling around Nam, the direct commissioned NCO. They were fairly recognizable because they wore Second Lieutenant bars, bronze, while other LTs wore First Lieutenant bars, black.

The army direct commissioning program tried to solve the problem of filling junior officer slots in combat units. It was open to NCOs, E5 and above, with combat experience (CIB), clean records (Good Conduct Medal), and not a total Section 8 case. It was pretty much automatic if a qualified NCO applied.

Since the gift came with strings ... the applicant had to accept an additional 12 months in Nam assigned at the army's discretion ... the general opinion was a guy had to be nuts to apply, or a complete psychopath. So, infantry officers walking around in Nam with 2LT bars were to be avoided.

LETTERS

A

AAR.   This is an abbreviation for "After Action Report," a formalized army methodology of explaining what went wrong and the fond, but somewhat delusional, prediction of how it'll never happen again.

Agent Orange.   This is the code name for the now infamous herbicide used as a defoliant in Vietnam.

Agent Orange contained dioxin, exposure to which increases risk of various types of cancer and genetic defects. Other than that, a great idea!

Shortly after the Vietnam War, veterans began to report various health complications which could be traced to exposure to the dioxin in Agent Orange. But it was not until 1991 that Congress enacted the Agent Orange Act allowing those who served in Vietnam to receive treatment and compensation for these conditions.

The list of "presumptive" conditions, those that are assumed to be the result of exposure to Agent Orange, includes prostate cancer, respiratory cancers, multiple myeloma, Type II diabetes, Hodgkin's disease, non-Hodgkin's lymphoma, soft tissue sarcoma, chloracne, porphyria cutanea tarda, peripheral neuropathy, chronic lymphocytic leukemia, and spina bifida in the children of veterans exposed.

The Agent Orange issue is yet another unfortunate example of the government's "what have you done for me lately" policy when dealing with vets.

Standard government policy seems to be that health-related issues effecting vets as a result of their service are automatically denied and the appeals are buried in the bureaucratic swamp known as the Veteran's Administration.

On a good day, this can be attributed to the inherent inability of a bureaucracy either to be compassionate or to make timely and correct decisions. On a bad day, it seems to be the result of Democrats' antipathy to the military and the Republicans' antipathy to a government agency making medical decisions for free when some campaign donor could be making millions on it.

Fortunately, the government finally did the right thing for Vietnam vets and is now beginning to do the right thing for Desert Storm vets. The next battle is to ensure proper care for Iraq and Afghanistan vets.

Guys and Gals! If you served in Nam, you were exposed to Agent Orange! Register with the VA.

Air Mattress.   A grunt's air mattress was probably his second-favorite creature-comfort in Nam ... right after his poncho liner.

Essentially, this was an OD pool float on which a grunt slept, gently suspended over rocks, branches, mud, biting insects, and cold water ... in other words, heaven!

Before placing the air mattress in the hootch, a grunt was very careful to clear the ground of anything that could puncture the mattress. A punctured air mattress was a domestic disaster! Getting a replacement through channels could take weeks since air mattresses were typically skimmed off the supply chain by the comfort loving REMFs in the rear areas.

"You hear about Snuffy in the third platoon?"

"No! What happened? Did he get ..."

"No! Worse! His air mattress is KIA!"

"The poor bastard!"

Typically, the rucksack was placed at the head of the mattress as a back rest, and the protective mask and holder served as a pillow.

Carrying the army protective mask was required by the TOE. Theoretically, it protected grunts from gas attacks, quite common after a meal of ham and lima beans, and biological agents not carried by the mosquitoes.

The problem with this theory was the persistent damp weather fused the charcoal filters rendering the mask INOP ... a grunt couldn't suck air through it. So, since they had to be carried, they were repurposed as ration carriers, purses, and pillows.

In the dark, it was absolutely necessary for a grunt to know where all his junk was (yeah ... that too). So, critical equipment was positioned in routine spots.

The M16 was either placed to the right side of the air mattress with a bandoleer of magazines, or some grunts actually slept with the rifle between their legs.

Here's a little factoid that will make weapons safety advocates pale. The M16 was not cleared at night. Grunts kept it in Condition 1 – magazine locked, one in the tube, safety on.

The sound of an M16 bolt going forward was unmistakable, and it gave away a grunt's location in the dark. No way we were giving the dinks a chance like that! We preferred the slight click of the selector switch sliding from "Safe" to "Fire."

The web belt was also positioned where it could always be located in the dark. This is where a grunt strapped his frags.

One of my evening routines was eyeballing my frags to make sure all the cotter pins were properly bent open. The pop and ping of a frag's charging handle being activated was not something I, or my hootch-mates, wanted to hear in the dark.

Grunts also slept with their feet at the opening of the hootch. To wake a guy up for bunker duty, the guy being relieved would grab an ankle and whisper some sweet nothing like, "Get your ass out on the bunker so I can get some sleep."

To this day, I could be in the deepest sleep; as soon as someone touches my ankle, I'm wide awake ... time to get out on the bunker or we have uninvited guests.

Wet or dry, in the field boots never came off at night. Finding, fitting, and lacing boots in the dark, while the bad guys were getting frisky, was not a recommended practice. Remember the scene in the movie, *The*

Longest Day; the German officer who had his boots on the wrong feet? Think about it!

For a grunt, sleeping without fully laced and often wet boots was a luxury, a luxury that could only be practiced safely in a rear area, like Hawaii.

Guys sleeping in a three-man hootch pretty much spooned. After a few weeks together, it was customary to give your hootch-mate at least a friendship ring.

Air Mattress Bug.   This was a grunt name for a rubber-eating, nocturnal insect indigenous to the Central Highlands of Vietnam.

This was a particularly perverse termite-like creature with large mandibles that attacked air mattresses only when occupied by sleep-deprived grunts. The bug was rumored to be in the pay of the NVA.

Air mattress bugs even conducted a PSYOP against grunts. They announced their imminent attacks by rattling dead leaves and twigs as they approached in the dark. Their arrival at the objective, some poor grunt trying to catch an hour or two of sleep, was typically marked by the hiss of escaping air, the moan "Oh, Shit!" and a splash.

The bugs were also rumored to be monitoring US Admin-Log nets through over-sized antennae in order to coordinate their attacks with the arrival of fresh air mattresses back-logged for months in the quagmire the army called logistics.

These bugs were of course especially active during the monsoon when they could drop their victims into cold mud.

AK.   This is an abbreviation for the Kalashnikov AK-47 Assault Rifle.

This was the basic tool of the bad guys and greatly respected by any grunts who encountered it.

The AK was a very reliable (rumored to be able to shoot underwater—a desirable feature during the monsoon), 7.62mm assault rifle, capable of semi-automatic (one bullet at a time) and automatic (lots of bullets at a time) operation.

In Nam, it came in two basic flavors: the Chinese version which was made of flattened-out beer cans — but somehow still worked well — and the Czech version which, if you pulled the trigger on Monday, would keep the bullets coming until Friday.

The AK was fed by a thirty-round banana clip (A magazine, Drill Sergeant!) which was considered very cool among the Che Guevara—look–alike set.

You knew you had arrived in gruntdom the first time you heard the "whip crack" of a 7.62-short breaking the sound barrier as it went by your head (Thank God!).

The AK came in a folding stock version, the AKM. This was a very cool, primo war trophy. For this, a REMF would fix you up with his sister (perish the thought).

Ambush.   The favorite tactic of NVA, VC, army rangers, divorce lawyers, and the Apaches in the old John Wayne cavalry movies.

An ambush is a deliberate, surprise engagement by fire on a moving or temporarily halted enemy from concealed positions. The purpose of an ambush is to destroy the enemy force or to cause significant casualties.

Ambushes come generally in two flavors: close and far.

A close ambush is one in which the kill zone is well within the effective range of the small arms fire of the base element, usually no more than fifty meters or so. In other words, you can smell them.

A far ambush is usually beyond the capability of the small arms of the base element to engage effectively the target. Far ambushes usually include the use of crew-served weapons, rockets, like the dreaded RPG, mortars, snipers, and artillery.

Immediate action for a far ambush is to deploy smoke and get your ass out of the kill zone.

Immediate action for a close ambush is a completely unnatural act – at least for normal human beings who believe they have a life ahead of them. The element in the kill zone immediately attacks into the base of fire and through the base element. Don't worry about smoke ... you don't have time.

The best way to counter an ambush is by not walking into it.

1. Don't walk on trails
2. Don't return the same way you left
3. Don't pass through narrow valleys
4. Don't trust high ground on your flanks or to your front
5. Don't announce your arrival – talking, equipment noise, cigarette smoke, etc.
6. Recognize ambush terrain, i.e.
   Blue lines, streams and rivers, are usually in valleys. The kill zone is the water and the base element is on the high ground either front or rear
   On hills and ridgelines, expect a U-shaped, high ambush, to the front climbing up, to the rear climbing down.
7. Don't go out on patrol with a FNG LT fresh out of OCS

If you're walking point in the middle of the boonies and, all of a sudden, get a strong whiff of fish, stop! Your about to trigger a NVA ambush. They all had Nuoc Mam breath.

AMF.   Abbreviation for "Adios, Mother F'er!" "Goodbye" with attitude! A synonym for DEROS.

Ann-Margret.   Ann-Margret Olsson is an American actress, singer and dancer who entertained U.S. servicemen in remote parts of Vietnam and reputedly still refers to them as "my gentlemen."

When I was in high school, probably fifteen years old, I went to see the film version of *Bye Bye Birdie* at a theatre in downtown Scranton, PA. My teenage-boy libido imprinted on Ann-Margaret during her performance of the reprise at the end of the flick.

We are now and forever honored by you considering us "your gentlemen"! Thank you for your service! We love you!

AO.　　　This is an abbreviation for "Area of Operations."

An "AO" is defined as a geographical area assigned to an army unit. An AO has lateral, front, and rear boundaries which define it within a larger tactical area.

The AO constitutes a formalized demarcation of a grunt's not-too-private hell.

It's smaller than a "theater" (Southeast Asia) but large enough to contain a grunt, a couple dozen of his closest friends, a few hundred well-armed, pissed-off bad guys, lots of exotic scenery like elephant grass, "wait-a-minute" bushes, triple canopy jungle, millions of stinging, biting, creeping, crawling, venomous critters, and a liberal dosage of cold water and mud. But there's plenty of room for everyone to play together.

Ao-Dai.　　　Pronounced OW-Dzai.

This is the Vietnamese national costume for babysahns; a high-collared, tight-fitting silk dress, usually white or brightly colored, split up to the waist and worn over white or black silk pantaloons.

I may have been becoming a bit "Asiatic," but after close to two years in-country, I thought these things were *tres sexy* (then again, I may have been too long in the company of men at the age of twenty).

We were on a firebase outside a Vietnamese village during Tet 1969. The village women dressed up in their ao dai and brought us gifts (on the up and up ... not a water point story). We were most impressed ... and greatly appreciative!

Arc Light.　　　"Operation Arc Light" was the code name given to the tactical use of B-52 strategic bombers in Vietnam.

For a grunt "Arc Light" just meant a B-52 Strike.

If you looked "apocalyptic" up in a dictionary, you'd see a picture of an Arc Light — dozens of B52s, flying so high they can't be seen or heard, dropping boocoo high-explosives across the real estate, while bunkers miles from the strike point collapsed from the concussion. It almost made you feel sorry for the bad guys ... almost.

Let me give you an idea of the scale of destruction.

When an 8-inch HE artillery round, the largest piece of artillery fired by the army in Nam, hit the ground, it left a scorched, six-inch deep hole in the ground and blew the leaves off the surrounding trees.

When a B52 bomb hit, it left a hole the size of a house, converted the surrounding trees to toothpicks, and blew them into the next province.

Tunnels? They couldn't dig 'em deep enough.

The closest I ever was to an Arc Light strike was sitting on a firebase over a klick from the target. Believe me! For these babies that's "danger close"! It felt like we got hit by an earthquake; my ass was bounced off the bunker I was sitting on.

The next morning we sent a patrol out to the strike site. We couldn't get into the target area because of the downed trees. The trees were lying across each other like sticks in the early stages of the game "pick up sticks," but the branches were almost woven together into an impenetrable barrier. For over an hour we tried to get through to the objective and just gave up.

For all the crap grunts gave Air Force guys about their easy lifestyle, we loved them for this, close air support, and Spooky.

Article 15.　　　　This is also called "Non-Judicial Punishment" (NJP) and is a key element in the oxymoron known as Military Justice.

Article 15 of the Uniform Code of Military Justice UCMJ) allows for certain limited punishments to be awarded for minor disciplinary offenses by a commanding officer in lieu of Court Martial.

Under Article 15, the accused waives the right to a court martial and essentially pleads guilty to the charge. In return, the accused receives a lighter punishment than that which could be imposed by a court martial.

Also, at some time in the future, based on the behavior of the accused, the Article 15 could be removed from the soldier's record.

Typical punishments resulting from an Article 15 are reduction in rank, loss of pay, extra work details, and company confinement.

Article 15s were not too common in Gruntdom. It was difficult for a grunt to screw up in an "Article 15" way. Want to go AWOL? How? You're on a firebase, in the middle of the boonies, surrounded by bad guys.

For most "offenses," a grunt NCO would just take the miscreant out behind the bunker line and kick his ass till he got the message. Saved on the paper work and was usually more effective.

However, back in a base camp, this was one of the primary tools of a lifer for keeping order and maintaining authority.

The difference, at least for a grunt, was not the use of the Article 15, but the occasional pettiness of its use.

When I was in LRRPs, we had a weekly "touch" football game against the CIA guys, who weren't there. This was pretty rough for touch football! I was "touched" a couple times ten feet into the barbed wire. But we all understood this, gave it and took it.

One day, a brigade staff-weenie, a captain, joined the game. This guy liked to give it but not to take it.

On one play, he blind-sided me and knocked me on my ass pretty hard. No problem! It's part of the game.

A couple plays later, I returned the courtesy.

Well, he didn't like that at all and said, "You better watch yourself, Sergeant!"

I explained to him in terms I thought were consistent with reasonable military courtesy that all rank was left on the sidelines.

A couple of plays later, I again had the honor of knocking him on his ass, and this time it was, "I told you to watch yourself, Boy!"

Okay! I understood that to mean that the military-courtesy gloves had just come off. So, I told him what he could do to a boy, if he could find one around. He left the field and I considered the matter closed.

Wrong guess.

The next day, the brigade Command Sergeant Major informed me that I had been charged with assault, insubordination, conduct unbecoming, homosexual advances, mutiny, being out of uniform, not wearing underwear, adultery, and not being left-handed by the good captain. Did I demand a court martial or would I take an Article 15?

I discussed the situation with the Brigade JAG (Judge Advocate General) and, although the JAG characterized the charges as "bullshit," the captain was insisting on pressing them.

The JAG warned me off a court martial. Hell! Theoretically I could be shot for some of the crap this captain was charging me with. We decided on a brigade-level Article 15 and hoped the colonel had a sense of humor.

Came the day, I was frog-marched over to the brigade TOC by the Command Sergeant Major and reported to the old man.

First thing he asked me was, "What happened?"

"Well, sir, we were playing football over behind ...

"Wait a minute, Sergeant! This happened during a football game?"

"Yes, Sir!"

"And the captain was participating in the game?"

"Yes, Sir!"

"So when you allegedly assaulted the captain by knocking him down, it was part of the game?"

"Yes, Sir!"

"Then explain to me why you told the captain to ... uh ... fellate you?"

"Sir, I didn't actually tell the captain to ... uh ... whatever you said ... he called me a 'boy' and I suggested he ... uh ... that word you used ... any 'boy' he could find on the football field."

"But the incident happened while you and the captain were playing football?"

"Yes, Sir!"

"Would you say it happened during the 'heat of the moment'?"

"Uh ... Yes, Sir ... I had just knocked the captain on his ass to get at the quarter back."

"Okay! Sergeant, would you step out for a minute and ask the captain to come in here?"

I left the old man's office. Our dear captain was waiting outside with a bit of a Cheshire cat smirk on his puss. "Sir, the colonel wishes to see you," I told him.

I'm not sure exactly what the old man said, but I have heard artillery barrages quieter than what was going on in his office. The captain finally exploded out of the colonel's door like a cat with its tail on fire.

The Sergeant Major gestured me back into the colonel's office.

"Sergeant! I'm tearing up this God-damned Article 15! I want you to go out there and apologize to the captain for telling him to fellate you and never tell one of my officers to fell ... Oh the hell with this ... Don't you ever suggest to an officer that he blow you or anyone else! Do you understand me, Sergeant!"

"Yes, Sir!"

That's one of the only times in my army career I thought I saw a Command Sergeant Major actually grin.

American Forces Vietnam Network (AFVN).   "Gooooood Morning, Vietnam!" This was the radio station of choice for US Forces and the NVA.

Essentially AFVN provided the soundtrack for the war.

In that era of portable transistor radios, rock 'n' roll was almost always playing somewhere on a firebase. It wasn't unknown to be in a firefight and hear the music of the Doors or the Kinks playing in the background from some guy's transistor.

Talk about OPSEC! Not only could the bad guys find any firebase by following the music, I think they showed up for the music!

"Grand Ole Opry" every Saturday night on the bunker line ... Yahoo! Thanks, Guys! Keep the music coming!

APC.   This is an abbreviation for the M113 Armored Personnel Carrier.

The M113 looked like a muddy, dented Olive Drab box on tank treads.

The basic point of an APC was to be a combat taxi. It carried grunts to and from firefights; that's the "personnel" and "carrier" part. It also offered some protection from small arms and shrapnel; that's the "armored" part.

There were a couple of tactical concerns with the M113.

First, the early models used gasoline instead of diesel and the metal used in the chassis was flammable. So these, like the WWII Sheridan Tanks, became known as "Zippos." Later models of the M113 converted to diesel, but the damn tin still burned.

Second, the M113's heaviest piece of armament was a 50cal machine gun. More unfortunately, it was mounted on the top of the vehicle, so a grunt had to expose his head and most of his upper body to fire the thing ... not a job with a lot of future in it, especially since the bad guys figured this one out really quick.

Third, the M113 was an RPG magnet and the armor didn't stop anything much bigger than a 30cal round. Most grunts rode outside the APC figuring if the thing got lit up by an RPG, they had a better chance being blown off it than being trapped inside it (Remember the flammable tin).

The good news about the M113 — it was fast, versatile, scared the crap out of the bad guys, carried a lot of stuff, became a virtual bunker in a perimeter defense, provided shelter from the rain and a dry place to sleep in the rainy season (strictly forbidden by lifers), riding one was a damn sight better than humping, and the thing could "swim" — cross bodies of water like a little OD water bug (although I never met anyone in Nam who had the balls to actually try it).

The presence of APCs on the battlefield created the oxymoronic concept of "mechanized" infantry, grunts who commuted to work in armored vehicles, as opposed to "light" infantry, grunts who commuted to work in combat boots.

The question sometimes asked was, "Are mech infantry guys really grunts?" All I know is the mech seemed to be chewing the same dirt as the rest of us; we sure loved to see them come rolling over the hill when we were in the crap; and they sure as hell weren't REMFs, lifers or civilians.

Talk among yourselves ... I'm verklempt.

ARVN.   Pronounced AR-vin.

This is an acronym for "Army of the Republic of Viet Nam;" "Good Guys" according to the "Rules of Engagement," but not according to attitude or competence.

This was also the day job of the Viet Cong ... Hey! financing a revolution, taking care of a family, making the payments on the fart cart and a tin hootch ... a guy needed two jobs to make ends meet.

ARVN was also the primary collection agency for the South Vietnamese government. The US Army had a lock on the protection racket.

This was Uncle Sam's favorite charity in the '60s & '70s.

ASAP.   Pronounced AY-sap.
An acronym for "As Soon As Possible."

Despite what the words actually say, "possible" has no relevance to timely completion.

This was an emphatic euphemism for: NOW!, IMMEDIATELY!, TOUT DE SUITE!, GET YOUR ASS IN GEAR!, WHAT THE HELL DO YOU MEAN IT AIN'T DONE YET!"

Ash and Trash.   The formal army terminology was "Administration and Logistics."

This was the natural habitat of the REMF, the lifer, and the realm of the XO. Therefore, to a grunt this was the seventh circle of hell.

This was the land where papers were typed in triplicate, signed only in black ink, stapled, stacked, filed, and lost. The fumes from the mimeograph machines and carbon paper were overwhelming.

The goals of army administration and logistics were seemingly to lose things in an orderly manner and to ensure that anything that would give comfort, ease, or a sense of coziness to grunts never reach them in the field ... it wasn't part of the TOE.

And these goals were accomplished so very well!

AWOL.   Pronounced AY Wall.

An acronym for Away Without Leave, in other words, leaving an assigned duty post or assignment without permission (see also, *didi mau*).

Going AWOL in Nam was almost impossible, but I managed to do it.

When I went to the LRRPS, I took a six-month extension in Nam to get the assignment. If one were a bit suicidal and pissed off – I was both back then – it wasn't a bad deal. For taking a "burst of six," the army offered the in-country assignment of choice plus 30 days leave anywhere the Air Force wasn't currently bombing. The leave started on arrival at the destination and ended when you turned yourself in.

In order to do this the army-way, I had to report to the S1 section, personnel, of the 4th Infantry Division on Camo Enari, the REMF capital of the central highlands.

So I reported to a SEA-Hut full of 71 Limas, sat down at a desk with a Spec 4, and filled out enough forms to start a landfill. After every i was dotted and every t crossed, the clerk gave me the arcane and sacred army S1 blessing, and I was on my way.

I decided not to take my leave until I was a month into my extension, so I went up to LZ Oasis, joined my unit, and ran operations until my basic tour was over, and I was a month into my suicide pact with the army.

Then, I bid farewell to my platoon sergeant to enjoy a month of hot food, clean sheets, and cold beer in exotic places.

When I got back to our orderly room in Pleiku, they didn't have my orders. No panic. This was typical of army foreplay ... the tease, the search, the hassle, the satisfaction. My first sergeant suggested I check in with my former unit.

I trudged across the basecamp to my former infantry company. Again, *nada*.

They sent me up to battalion ... *nada*,

Who sent me up to brigade ... *nada*.

By midafternoon, I found myself in the same damn SEA-Hut where I filled out my original extension. I spotted a PFC sitting at a desk playing with his pencil and said, "I'm Sergeant Gleason ... 3rd Brigade sent me up here ... I'm looking for my leave orders."

Before the 71 Lima could respond, I heard a voice from behind a plywood partition yell, "SERGEANT GLEASON!" Immediately a First Louie wearing Adjutant General insignia burst out of the office with fire in his eyes and marched at me like Sherman courting Georgia.

Before I could imagine how I had managed to piss this REMF off during the mere four hours I had been on post, he began ranting,

> "SERGEANT! Do you have any idea how much trouble you've caused the army? We have been looking for you for weeks! You were AWOL from DEROS, and now you're AWOL from Germany! No one misses their freedom bird! Where the hell have you been hiding?"

Hiding? I was dumbfounded. Hiding from the dinks, sure! But not from the army! I'd been up country with K/75 since March! I was on their morning report, for God's sake!

I tried to explain this to the LT, but he wasn't buying it. In his fuzzy, narrow little REMF mind, it made sense that I went AWOL to run LRRPs with the rangers up in the highlands just to complicate his life. My obvious endgame was to put my ass on the line to go stomping around the Ia Drang valley in order to ruin his career.

Finally, I pointed to an empty desk. "I sat right there with a Spec 4 and filled out the papers!"

My inquisitor's mouth slammed shut. He turned to the PFC who had become the audience for our administrivial melodrama and asked, "Wasn't that Mc Gillicuddy's old desk?"

The 71 Lima answered in the affirmative, sir.

The LT walked over the desk and opened the middle drawer. I could see a pile of paperwork inside. The LT snatched it up and his face went paler than a Norwegian in February.

The LT muttered, "Oh shit ... this is bad ..."

Then to the PFC, "Didn't Mc Gillicuddy DEROS the end of March ... Oh, Christ ..."

It seems that, right after I had had performed the secret, army, administrative rites with the now departed and infamous SP4 Mc Gillicuddy, he got the nod to get the hell out of Dodge. Instead of complicating his out-processing and risk missing his flight to the world, he stuffed my paperwork in his desk drawer and left.

So, the LT was technically right. I was AWOL from some unit in West Germany.

I got my leave orders in record time and, by the next day, I was on a bird winging to paradise.

My only regret is that I couldn't be a fly on the wall when that Admin-Commando had to explain what happened to the Division S1.

B

B52.　　This is the Boeing B-52 Stratofortress, a long-range, jet-powered strategic bomber flown by the United States Air Force from Guam and Thailand, which is Air Force code for "the land of perpetual R&R."

The B52 is the grunt version of "Big Bird," not yellow and not especially friendly, but grunts loved them for their ability to drop boocoo large exploding eggs on top of the bad guys.

Ba Moui Ba.　　Pronounced BAH-Mee-Bah.

　　"It was Ba Mi Ba, Ba Mi Ba, Ba Mi Ba, Wah Oh!" (Barry Sadler).

Vietnamese for either "Panther-Piss" or "Thirty-Three;" we were never quite sure which. This was proof that the concept of "bad beer" was feasible.

Ba Moui Ba was the brand name for very cheap (10 – 15 pi a bottle on the black market), very available, very domestic, very scary Vietnamese beer with the clarity and "body" of a bad urine specimen.

In the field (and where else would you drink this crap?) it was usually drunk warm so the full potential of its sassy, yet flat, body could be savored.

Ba Moui Ba was rumored to be made from embalming fluid and formaldehyde. This was never proven (nor seriously questioned); grunts didn't care as long as it got them high.

I was in Washington, DC on business a few years back and I met up with a buddy who worked for the Department of Defense. We had actually joined the army together when we were teenagers growing up in Queens, New York.

"First thing tomorrow, we'll go down to the recruiter over on seventy-fourth street ... join up ... airborne."

"First thing, buddy, airborne, first thing."

Of course, the next morning I woke up with a flaming hangover and was praying that Tony didn't remember a thing we talked about. Alas, he showed up at my mother's house around ten in the morning to pick me up and off we went to the recruiters.

The recruiters were in a little kiosk under the El on 74th Street in Jackson Heights. It was a smorgasbord of all the armed forces — army, Air Force, Navy and Marines — I think even the Coast Guard was skulking around in there somewhere (but no one could get into the CG in those days unless a blood relative of a Congressman).

When we walked in, the army recruiter, whom we'll call "Staff Sergeant Waters," greeted us.

"Hey, Guys! What can I do for you?"

"Uh ... we want to join ... uh ... the army..."

"Great! Tell me a little about yourself."

"Uh... sure... whaddya want to know?"

"You guys ever arrested?"

"Uh... cops slapped around me around a bit when I wised off ..."

"You ever in jail?"

"Uh ... no ... not overnight."

"Ever been before a judge?"

"No."

"Great! How about school!"

"Graduated High School ... my buddy here went to college..."

Great! Drug use?"

"Does beer count?"

"Hell, No! Okay... let me tell you what the army can offer ..."

"We want to go into the paratroopers."

"The paratroopers? That's great! But, when you join, you can choose what you want to do in the army. For example, the

Before I get into the Ba Moui Ba story, let me answer a question which, after reading my brilliant insights expressed in such elegant prose, I'm sure you're asking yourselves, "How did such a brilliant and articulate urban sophisticate as myself become a grunt?"

Actually, that too is a beer story.

In 1966, after having finished my first year of college, I decided to take some time off to clear my head. My timing, of course, couldn't have been worse. The war was on and my draft status changed immediately from "student" to "just call me cannon fodder and take me now."

Other than that, life was good. I had gotten a job in a local grocery store and was dating a neighborhood girl who was going to Hunter College. My best friend through high school (we'll call him "Tony") wasn't in school and was getting increasingly frustrated playing draft board bingo while trying to find a job. In the late 1960s, employers were very reluctant to offer a draft-eligible guy a "serious" job if he didn't have some sort of deferment.

One night, Tony and I decided to kill some brain cells at a neighborhood bar and, as commonly results from flooding the brain with beer, we immediately developed an acute case of "dumb" — an almost terminal case as it turned out.

About one in the morning, we stopped by a diner on the way home. Over the "Hamburger Deluxe Platter," our conversation went something like this ... Tony begins:

> "I'm tired of all this shit, waiting to get called up, can't get a decent job; I'm just going to join up."

> "Tony ... you're my best friend ... if you join, I'm going too!"

Did I mention we had consumed a lot of beer?

> "I'm not just going to join the army; I'm going into the paratroopers ... jump outta planes."

> "You're my best friend, man, if you're gonna jump outta planes ... me too!"

> "Gotta volunteer for Nam; there's a f'ing war goin' on ... gotta do our part."

> "You're my best friend ... you goin' to Nam, I'm with ya!"

army has a great aviation program. You guys can learn to fly helicopters or fixed wing ..."

"That's great, but we want to go into the paratroops."

"That's great, guys, you can go to jump school if you want. But the army offers many career choices for guys like you who volunteer. Like the Signal Corps; it's doing a lot a work with computers ... you could use that after you get out ..."

"Thanks, Sarge, but we want to go airborne; we want to fight in Nam."

"Okay guys, you understand that means you'd go into the infantry ... when you join that's three years active ... you guys got some education ... there's a lot of other stuff the army can offer ..."

"Thanks, airborne infantry is what we want ... can you fix that up?"

We finally convinced the good sergeant, despite his best efforts, that we wanted to join the paratroopers and go fight in Nam. He got us through the paper work and told us we'd hear from the army in a couple of weeks.

We left the recruiters and were headed down Roosevelt Avenue when we ran into a friend of ours, whom we'll call "Pat."

"Hey! I heard you guys were joining the army!"

"'Tis. We're just comin' back."

"What the hell, guys! What about me! I thought we were friends! If you go, I don't want to be left behind."

"Look, man ... we joined the paratroopers and volunteered for Nam."

"So what! We're friends, right! We stick together! You're not leavin' me back here."

So Tony and I did the first "about face" in our army careers and took Pat by the arm back to the recruiters. When we walked through the door, Sergeant Waters looked up from his desk, and said, "Lemme guess. Airborne, right?"

A couple of months later in basic training at Ft. Jackson, South Carolina, we were having a bit of "buyer's remorse." One Saturday night, we were up at the EM club on Tank Hill, about as high as one can get on army three-point-two beer.

Tony said, "You know, I really didn't want to do this. When I picked you up at your house, I was hoping you didn't remember what we said. But you did and I had to go through with it."

Luckily, the MPs arrived before Pat and I could do any real damage to Tony.

To bring an end to this section of my incessant narrative on the evils of beer, we all went to Nam and we all made it back. Tony got his wish and did a combat tour with the 101st Airborne; Pat was a platoon leader with the 9th Division and won the Silver Star.

I told you that story, so I could finish this one.

Years later, Pat and I got together in DC; we went out for dinner and few brews. We had both retired from the army as Infantry officers, and I was having a ball giving him crap about his having gone over to the "Dark Side" — DOD LOGCOM — the very "heart of the Ash & Trash" — the "navel of REMFdom."

I don't remember how it came up ... probably a general "remember when" comment, but we started talking about how awful Ba Moui Ba was. I think I was the one who mused, "I wonder if they still make that shit over there?" Then Pat countered that he knew a bar a couple blocks away that claimed to have every beer in the world.

So, off we went arm-in-arm through the darkened streets of DC in search of Ba Moui Ba. We got to the place, and sure enough they had it!

You know how we are cautioned against nostalgia by the maxim, "You can never go home again"? Well, the Ba Moui Ba was a complete bust. It looked and tasted like any American beer. For all we knew, someone filled the Ba Moui Ba bottles with Miller or Bud! Then Pat noticed the word "Export" on the label.

"I bet those damned commies don't export the real stuff. This shit is just some commie propaganda! They're probably re-labeling bottles of Miller over there. 'See, Yankee Capitalist-Pig!

The peoples' brewery of Vietnam makes beer just as good as you!'"

I had never contemplated Marxist theory as it applied to bad beer, but it made sense to me! (Have I mentioned that we had been drinking beer most of the evening?)

So, somewhere in the dark alleys of Ho Chi Minh City, I'm confident that "real" Ba Moui Ba is still being served. Enjoy!

Oh, Barry! Those snakes on the jailhouse floor ... I've seen them too ... they go away after the Ba Moui Ba gets out of your system.

Babysahn.   Pidgin for any Vietnamese child, but usually a young female; the opposite of Mamasahn.

Babysahns typically came in two varieties down at the water point — "Coke Girls" and "Boom-Boom Girls."

"Coke Girls" screwed you by charging you a hundred pi for a ten-cent soda on the black-market.

"Boom-Boom" girls actually screwed you, but normally charged more than a buck; five bucks MPC or 500 Pi was the going rate at the water point or in town between paydays.

If you went to Vietnam today and saw a young Vietnamese girl, a modern-day babysahn, you'd probably think she looks angelic, like the children you see here in the States. But she would be atypical of every babysahn I ever saw in Nam.

This is whom war devastates! It's not just the soldiers who fight it, but the children who are trapped in it. Instead of being in school, playing silly games with their friends or being fussed over, loved and nurtured by their families, those babysahns were forced to hump ammo for the Viet Cong or to be out plying a trade at some water point.

The fact that we could do nothing for these kids tore a lot of us up. Just because we were grunts in Nam didn't mean we stopped being brothers, husbands and fathers.

Today, as a father and grandfather of babysahns, I thank God I live in a country where men and women willingly put themselves in harm's way to keep my babysahns safe.

Banana Cat.   This was an exotic mammalian member of the Vietnamese fauna said to inhabit banana plantations. This critter was about the size and shape of a cat and had the face of a raccoon.

Like grunts, banana cats could be easily domesticated if obtained as kittens and fed a steady diet of C-Rats. They proved very useful in pest control on fire bases — rats, snakes, lifers and large ... very, very large ... spiders.

According to grunt lore, they were related to the mongoose, and since the little critter took no crap from cobras and other shoulder-less reptiles, this was generally accepted as quite a creditable claim as far as grunts were concerned.

They didn't purr much, but were quite fond of being petted, sleeping in poncho liners, and eating C-rats ... in other words, good grunts ... except the petting part.

I had a close and rather unconstructive encounter with a banana cat on a firebase in July of 1968.

My platoon was actually enjoying a "sleep-in." We had humped some thirty klicks the day before and had taken a raft ride down a monsoon-swollen mountain river chasing some intelligence officer's delusion about enemy ammo caches on little islands in the middle of a monsoon-flooded river. So, the old man gave us the morning off to get the water out of our lungs.

I was sleeping in a three-man hootch with my buddy, Jimmy, and Larry, our squad leader; three grunts, butt to butt, boots off, on air mattresses wrapped in poncho liners out of the rain with no bunker duty ... it didn't get much better than that in gruntdom.

I was awakened by the sound of something scratching around on top of the hootch. When I mentioned it to my slumbering hootch mates, I was told to shut up and take care of it myself. They wanted to sleep. So, I dragged my ass out to take a look.

There, sitting on top of the hootch, was a little critter. It looked just like a cat with a raccoon face. I thought, "Ah! Some poor primeval forest creature has wandered into our perimeter ... it's probably looking for food ... it's more afraid of me than I am of it."

Did I mention I'm a New York City boy who watched a lot of Walt Disney as a kid?

So, I tried to shoo it away. The critter obviously thought this was a fun game, and I must be a great guy to play with. So it jumped off the hootch and came bounding over in my direction.

Now as a city boy. I know nothin' 'bout no jungle critters except stay the hell out of their way. This critter might be small, but it must have what it takes to survive in the jungle, some secret and devastating powers I don't know about ... venom, claws, teeth or speed ... and now it's coming after me! So, naturally I panicked and started shouting, "Get back! Get back! Stay away!"

My panicky shouting disturbed my slumbering hootch mates! "God damn it! Quiet down,! I'm trying to sleep in here!"

The critter stopped, turned toward the hootch thinking "Ah! These guys sound like fun" and dashed inside.

A silent pause ... then a scream, "Oh my God! It's a giant rat!" Then a poncho with legs exploded out the back of the hootch and ran across the firebase screaming.

In the meantime, while the critter was distracted terrorizing my hootch mates, I went and got my rifle for protection.

The critter, confused and somewhat hurt by this apparent rejection, came back out of the hootch and decided to play with me some more.

But now I was armed!

I pointed my M16 at it and ordered it to halt.

The little critter seemed to love this game and kept coming.

Again, I ordered it to halt or I'd shoot, back-stepping to maintain my supposed advantage in range.

I noticed a crowd was beginning to gather and was wondering why no one was trying to help me. In fact, I noticed that a couple of the guys seemed amused by this savage attack on me by a ferocious jungle creature.

"Get back!" I screamed pointing the rifle.

The critter had me backed up against a tree and had obviously decided that I was the most succulent morsel on this fire base. With no apparent concern, it sauntered past the business end of my M16 and started using cat-like claws to crawl up my leg.

There was quite a crowd by this time, but no one was helping me. In fact, I'm sure a couple of guys were laughing!

The critter clawed its way up my leg and onto my shoulder. It was going for my throat, I thought!

I was braced against the tree with a now useless M16 in my hands and the guys watching were in hysterics. The critter reached my shoulder and, as I was wincing for the kill, it started licking my ear!

Finally, one of our mortar guys broke through the crowd of giggling grunts. "Thank God!" he said, "You found Chauncy!"

He pulled the critter off my shoulder and carried him away. "We thought you ran away, you naughty cat! Come on! We have a nice can of ham and lima beans for you in the FDC."

We later found my buddy Jimmy skulking in a bunker on the other side of the perimeter still wrapped in a poncho babbling something about giant, mutant rodents.

Base Camp. This is a term describing any large, semi-permanent army installation where large units located their ash and trash, hence a potential center of REMFism and lifers, in other words, chicken-shit central.

The good news for a grunt was that he was relatively safe from the bad guys and could be comfortable in a base camp, even sleep on a mattress with his boots off.

The other news was that a grunt in a base camp became a lackey for the clerks, jerks, and lifers ... burn that shit, police that area, pull that guard, shine those boots, stand that formation, shave that face, press that uniform, cut that hair.

All this crap quickly made a grunt quite nostalgic for the boonies ... and maybe that was the point.

Beehive.   Although this described a very popular hairdo in the '60s, the "Beehive" that grunts were most familiar with was a particularly nasty, therefore greatly esteemed, anti-personnel round. (Odd expression when you think about it ... I don't know of any "pro-personnel" armaments).

The "Beehive" round, which was fired from artillery pieces, tank guns, and recoilless rifles, was packed full of metal darts, "flechettes," which are released when the round bursts. I'm told the name was attributed to the "buzzing" sound the darts make when flying through the air. I imagine confirming this theory, would require being on the wrong side of the round ... therefore dead ... and therefore unable to confirm anything. I'll take this one on faith.

One of the real nasty features of beehive rounds was that the range at which the flechettes deployed could be set on the fuse.

In late 1968, my battalion was running a daily truck convoy from the combat trains out to its firebase where the TOC was located. There was only one route in and out, so the convoy was vulnerable to ambush, which strangely, and happily, never happened.

But there was a pontoon bridge over the Ia Drang where a sniper used to take pot shots every time the convoy crossed. He was as regular as a lifer's attitude and always situated himself near a tree on the top of a hill overlooking the bridge on its far side. He was so inaccurate that he was a joke among the deuce drivers, but one day he got close enough to shatter the windshield of a truck.

So, he had to go.

We "borrowed" a 106mm recoilless rifle and gun jeep from another battalion. The 106 was an interesting piece of equipment. It was designed as an infantry anti-tank weapon, but modern Soviet armor had pretty much made it obsolete. Besides there weren't many NVA tanks or armored vehicles knocking around the highlands in late 1968.

The gun's high profile and slow rate of fire pretty much disqualified it from being a practical weapon for perimeter defense. It was an oxymoron of current weapons technology and the tactical situation, so we had no problem "borrowing" it.

Another oddity about the 106mm was that it was aimed by an optical sight and by firing a "spotting round," 50cal rifle which sat on top of the main gun. The gunner fixed the target in the sights then fired a 50cal tracer at the target and, with the assistance of the assistant gunner, adjusted his sights until the 50cal round hit the target. Then the main 106mm gun was fired.

One last piece of obscure information. The reason the 106mm was recoilless — like its little brothers the 90mm recoilless rifle, the 3.2 Rocket Launcher and the M72 LAW — was because the firing gases were expelled out the back of the weapon. This was called "back blast."

The good news — no recoil on the weapon.

The other news — don't stand behind this puppy ... it will toast you.

Did you see the Sly Stallone movie — I think it was Rambo (fill in the sequel number)— where he fired the LAW out of a slick? No way! The back blast would have toasted that bird.

One of the worst days of my army career, outside combat, was as the Officer-in-Charge (OIC) of a 90mm Recoilless Rifle orientation range. We were live-firing sabots at a bunch of wrecked trucks down range.

As some sort of perverse lifer joke, someone sent the Division Band to me for orientation fire. I have no idea why. The last time the command, "Drop your piccolos and grab a weapon!" was heard was probably at the Little Big Horn, and I don't think it worked out too well.

But "nature abhors a vacuum" as "lifers abhor idleness," so the band was sent down to me on the 90mm range!

Now, not only am I dealing with the problem that, due to the back blast, there's no safe spot on this range, but I also have to deal with soldiers who are not too comfortable with the concept of weapons and loud noises. E-Minor chord, fine; things that go bang, scary.

I spent the entire day standing in the middle of the firing line, nose-to-nose with one of the firers, holding on to the firer's web gear for dear life.

"Ready on the right? The right is ready!"
"Ready on the left? The left is ready!"
"The firing line is now ready"

"Assistant gunners! Load one 90mm Sabot round and lock the breech!"

"Gunners! Find your targets! Disengage your safe ..."

BOOM!

"Cease fire! Cease Fire! Gunners! Wait for the command to fire!"

"Gunners! On my command! Fire!"

BOOM! BOOM! BOOM!

I had one young piccolo-playing PFC collapse when the weapons exploded. Luckily I was holding on to her web gear and caught her and the weapon before either hit the ground.

That convinced me to close the range due to inclement weather ... 78 degrees Fahrenheit, sunny, 40% chance of back-blast ... seemed damned inclement to me.

So, back to my story.

We borrowed the 106mm and found a heavy weapons grunt, an 11H, who knew how to work the dingus. We zeroed the gun with string and a couple of 50cal rounds behind the water point, threw some 106mm beehive rounds into the jeep, and off we went just before sunup.

We found a good position overlooking the bridge and sighted in on the tree where the sniper liked to hide. On our map, we located our position and the hill, so we knew the range almost to a centimeter. We set the beehive round to deploy its flechettes about twenty meters from the tree.

And we waited.

A couple of hours later, the convoy came rolling down the road and across the bridge. Sure enough, good time Charlie started taking his pot shots from below his tree.

Bang! The sighting round flew straight and true right to the tree.

The spotter commanded fire.

BOOM!

We could see the 106-round fly across the valley right at the tree. Just before it hit, the round seemed to dissolve into thick black smoke. The tree leapt into the air and fell over.

All we could do was stare in amazement.

I don't know if we got the sniper ... I tend to doubt it. But he never shot up our convoy again. In our after-action report, we wrote, "Sighted sapling; sank same!"

Betel Nut.   Betel nut was what Bloody Mary chewed,

> "Bloody Mary's chewing betel nut / She is always chewing betel nut...Now ain't that too damned bad" (Rogers & Hammerstein, South Pacific).

I had to go all the way to Nam to figure out what a show tune lyric meant!

Actually, what grunts thought was "chewing betel nut" was areca nuts chewed with betel leaf and tobacco. Like coffee, this is a mild stimulant and the drug of choice of mamasahns.

Chewing this stuff stains the teeth a deep brownish red, which means mamasahn ain't getting kissed any time soon ... there ain't enough Ba Moui Ba in the world!

The areca nut and the betel leaf are important symbols of love and marriage in Vietnam.

The Vietnamese phrase, *chuyn tru cau*, "matters of betel and areca," refers to the parents' chewing betel nut while negotiating their children's marriage.

Reminds me of an old parody of an Ogden Nash poem, "Candy's dandy / But sex doesn't rot your teeth."

Obviously not true in Nam.

Personally, I prefer the American custom of sneaking away and making out. It didn't turn your teeth brown, and, despite what the nuns told us, didn't make you go blind or grow hair on your palms.

Bic.   Pidgin for "understand."

Thanks to English being universally understood if shouted loud enough, enunciated deliberately enough, and repeated with an attitude, the phrase "YOU BIC?" was understood by all Vietnamese as either "Do you understand?" or "This is an order!"

Especially effective when emphasized by shoving the muzzle of an M16 into the conversation ... YOU BIC?

Bird Shit. A somewhat sarcastically affectionate grunt term for the airborne, since they dropped from the sky out of the ass-end of a bird and made a mess when they landed.

Black Horse Code. This was a grunt "field expedient" code used to encrypt numbers for transmission over the radio.

The army in Nam wasn't too swift with its "SIGSEC" — Signal Security. Grunt units often ignored parts of the CEOI, the Communications and Electronics Operating Instructions.

The official transmission frequencies, "pushes," as they were called, had to be used, but units had their own standard call signs.

Any call sign ending in "6" designated a leader, and at times the unit designation was included in these home-made call signs. For example, "Alpha Charlie Two Six" might be a call sign used to designate the second platoon leader of A Company; not too swift on the SIGSEC hit parade, unless "hit" referred to enemy artillery.

Almost eight months in the Rangers and my call sign never changed: "Romeo Two Eight." One of the CIA guys who wasn't there showed me an intercepted NVA transmission that referred to me personally by this designation in very unflattering terms.

The benefit of this home-grown CEOI was that grunts always knew who they were talking to; the problem was so did the bad guys.

Part of the CEOI were numeric tables used to encrypt numeric information, "shackle" in army-jargon, and confirm stations as friendly, "authentification."

At times, grunts didn't have access to the official tables, or they didn't know how, didn't have the time, or didn't have the inclination to use them correctly. In fact, at times units gave out the coordinates of their locations in the clear, e.g. "Reporting Night Logger Niner Two Four Seven Six Niner", which made the Bad Guy's job — if they really did want to find us — just that much easier.

Rangers and small infantry units often used the "Black Horse Code" to encrypt numbers since it offered a ten-digit code that most grunts could remember even under pressure:

0	1	2	3	4	5	6	7	8	9
B	L	A	C	K	H	O	R	S	E
L	A	C	K	H	O	R	S	E	B
A	C	K	H	O	R	S	E	B	L
C	K	H	O	R	S	E	H	O	R
K	H	O	R	S	E	H	O	R	S
H	O	R	S	E	B	L	A	C	K
O	R	S	E	B	L	A	C	K	H
R	S	E	B	L	A	C	K	H	O
S	E	B	L	A	C	K	H	O	R
E	B	L	A	C	K	H	O	R	S
1	2	3	4	5	6	7	8	9	0

Like any shackle code, in a radio transmission letters represent numbers. Since the code was used informally and "on the fly," usually in critical situations like when a grunt didn't have the time, or the light, or the flashlight batteries, or the official codes to use, the trick was to signal the receiving station which variant of the code was being used.

Units usually had a TSOP covering this, e.g. "Bravo Hotel Zero Lima Break Hotel Break Romeo Echo Lima Break Lima Hotel Kilo Over = Blackhorse Code, Zero Low, Line 'H' 245598".

Like most "field expedients," this didn't "protect" the transmission; it merely slowed the bad guys down. So, if a grunt transmitted his unit's position in the Blackhorse code, it was a good idea to move a few klicks in an unexpected direction before he found out what caliber of artillery and rockets the bad guys had in the area.

Black Label.   America's attempt at recreating Ba Moui Ba.

This was a cheap, US domestic beer left over from Prohibition that seemed to have had no other application besides being exported to grunts in Nam.

Black Label was usually consumed warm, but it was rumored to be capable of being cooled on ice. Due to a combination of the suspected chemical instability of the formula and a complete lack of ice, this was never demonstrated.

Bad taste before, during, and after consumption, but — at ten cents a can — who cared?

The Black Syph.   A Vietnam urban legend about an incurable strain of venereal disease which one would contract if one were to as much as look at an indigenous female when money's exchanged for the privilege.

This was one of many army contagious diseases with a moral conscience. It wasn't caused as much by the unsafe sexual behavior as it was by the immoral intent.

This one, though, was allegedly the "mortal sin" of STDs. If you caught this, you were staying in Southeast Asia forever.

The following is a briefing given to FNGs in the Repl Depl (as best as I can remember it).

"Good MOORNin', Men. I'm Staff Sergeant Jones of MAC VEE and I will be your principal instructor for the next half hour of training where y'all learn about the Black Syph-AH-lis."

"Sergeant! Is there going to be a quiz on this?"

"No! Sit yo' ass down 'n' shut yo' mouth!"

"Back in the world they told you men all about VEE-nereal diseases: the ones that make you drip; the ones that make you burn; the ones that make you itch; and the ones that rot your brain. But over here we got one that'll make your sorry little peckers turn black and drop off. We call it the black syph."

"Ya'll get the black syph same way ya'll get any VEE-nereal disease ... by stickin' yo' sorry little peckers where they don't belong … now you mens going get some pay in your pockets and be wantin' to go cattin' 'round them bars in Saigon or Vung Tau, or just trying to get you some down at a water point … and these babysahns' gonna start lookin' real good t'ya'll … but remember … the French was here before y'all and left a few souvenirs and real nasty surprises. And some of these babysahns' VC and their job is t'infect yo' ass with this shit."

"The black syph can't be cured, people! Penicillin and all them miracle drugs they got back in the world can't do shit for y'all. Once you got it, you got it! And once you got it, y'all ain't goin' back the world t'infect all your girlfriends, your wives, your sheep, or whatever the hell else you think you got waitin' for yo' sorry ass back there in the world.

"If y'all get the black syph, th'army's gonna put yo' sorry ass on a rocky little island they got off the coast of the Philippines where you're goin' sit for the rest of yo' sorry lives weavin' baskets and watchin' yo' sorry little pecker rot off."

"To spare your folks the shame, th'army's goin' tell 'em y'all got killed! They even goin' pay out your GI insurance cause y'all ain't never comin' back … ever, hear!"

"Questions?"

"Yeah, Sarge! About those bars?"

Blue Line.   A river or stream; any flowing body of water.

On military maps, bodies of water were represented by the color blue. Rivers and streams were seen as squiggly blue lines, hence the term.

When I was an FNG, I was stuck out on flank security during a company-sized sweep through the hills.

Flank security is tricky even for a vet. You need to be far enough out to be of any practical use detecting an ambush or enemy recon, but you still have to keep contact with the main body.

But I was an FNG. I was out on the flank. I was alone in the woods. I was not terrified; I was intensely concerned.

I had no visual contact with the main body. I was paralleling them by sound, normally not a difficult thing to do.

Grunts moving through the bush make a racket – equipment clanging, combat boots tripping on tree roots, jungle fatigues ripping along wait-a-minute bushes, branches breaking, plastic M16 parts slapping brush, and the occasional cussing – sort of like the circus coming to town.

Grunts cold also be detected by smell: insect repellant, cigarette smoke, aftershave, and BO. Quite a distinctive bouquet.

So, although I had about as much business being out on the flank as a vegan has in an slaughterhouse, I thought I was doing a pretty good job tracking with the column.

Then I came to a blue line.

We were high in the hills and the rainy season hadn't yet gotten serious. So, this stream was an ankle wetter at best, maybe two strides across.

But right at my intended crossing point, a tiny fish was seemingly hovering in the flow contemplating my sudden presence.

First thoughts ... fish ... tiny ... no threat.

Second thoughts ... why isn't it swimming away? Shouldn't I terrify it! I mean, I'm Catholic! My people devour its relatives every Friday!

Third thoughts ... maybe in its tiny fish-mind, I'm not the potential devourer ... maybe I'm the putative devouree!

Are there piranha in Nam?

No one mentioned that during in-country orientation ... but they wouldn't, would they ... holding back that little factoid as a surprise.

Finally, I tried to leap the blue line. Almost made it, too. Wound up on my ass in six inches of piranha-infested water.

I vaulted up before the little bugger could sink his fangs into my nether regions (or worse) and got to the other side of the blue line.

At first I thought I was home free. I made it to the other side of the blue line, and I hadn't been eaten by the fish. The only downside seemed to be my soaking-wet butt.

Then I realized I couldn't hear the column any more.

I remained still and listened. Nothing!

I sniffed the air. Nothing!

I was out in the jungle!

Alone!

No one for company but a Vietnamese piranha, who hated me because I had spoiled his lunch!

I had visions of my wandering around the mountains, lost for years, until I finally meandered back into civilization in the year 2000 looking like some WWII Japanese holdout in the Philippines!

I moved toward where the main body should be. I cut their trail, but I saw no one there! I still heard no movement.

I won't say I panicked … I was just intensely concerned.

I decided to signal the company by popping off a round.

As soon as I did, a grunt rolled out of a brush in front of me … wide-eyed and, when he saw me and figured out I had shot the round, about as intensely irritated with me as I had been intensely concerned about the piranha.

The company had stopped for a break along the trail.

Mine was a three-echelon screw up. My squad leader, my platoon leader, and my company commander made me wish the piranha had gotten me.

This was the closest I came in my army career of being assigned to the catering corps.

It was also the last time I was put out on flank.

Boat People.   Refers to the refugees who fled Vietnam by sea following the end of the Vietnam War in 1975.

According to the United Nations High Commission for Refugees, an estimated 800,000 "boat people" arrived safely in other countries between 1975 and 1995, but an estimated 200,000 to 400,000 Vietnamese died at sea (Nghia M. Vo, *The Vietnamese Boat People* (2006).

Why, you might ask, did so many flee the "workers' paradise" established by the benevolent Socialist Republic of Vietnam out of the ashes of the fallen imperialist, lacky, running-dog Republic of South Vietnam?

Any South Vietnamese who were too closely aligned with the former government – politicians, bureaucrats, police, military and their families – or any Vietnamese who were "politically unsound" were offered three choices:

1. A quick death, a bullet behind the ear and rolled into a pit;
2. A slow death, a "reeducation" camp, starvation, beatings, a bullet behind the ear and rolled into a pit; or
3. get in a boat and take your chances with the sharks and pirates.

The United Nations' estimates of South Vietnamese who lost their lives during the transition to benevolent socialism in the south approaches one million dead.

The blame for enabling this holocaust to happen rests partially with the Congress of the United States.

But not the US military.

While there were US combat troops on the ground, the NVA and the so-called Viet Cong could not prevail.

For over ten years, the US military fought North Vietnam to a standstill finally forcing the communist government to sign the Paris Peace Accords, recognizing the legitimacy of the government of South Vietnam. In return, the US recognized the political legitimacy of the National Liberation Front and withdrew its combat troops from the Republic of South Vietnam.

Despite its agreeing to the Paris Peace accords, in early March, 1975, with US combat troops no longer on the ground, North Vietnam launched an offensive to annex South Vietnam. ARVN was quickly pushed out of the central highlands, then Hue and Da Nang.

US President, Gerald Ford, pleaded in vain with the predominately Democratic 93rd Congress for additional military financial aid to bolster South Vietnam's struggle.

The Democratic Congress, like most of their supporters on the political left and in the so-called anti-war movement, washed their hands of the US commitment to the survival of the Republic of South Vietnam and the sacrifice of over 58 thousand US service members.

In April, 1975, the government of the Republic of South Vietnam collapsed, and Saigon fell to the North Vietnamese without a struggle.

To say that the Democratic 93rd Congress caused the collapse of the Republic of South Vietnam by refusing to provide additional military aid would be an overstatement. There is no surety that South Vietnam would have survived with the additional defense funding because it never happened.

What is a fact is that the additional funding never happened.

Two take-aways from this sordid morality tale.

First, the United states did not lose the *war* in South Vietnam; it lost the *peace*.

While US combat troops were on the ground, the North Vietnamese were unable to prevail. US military involvement in *war* ended when the communist government signed the Paris Peace Accords.

The Republic of South Vietnam fell only after the US withdrew its combat troops from South Vietnam, in accordance with its treaty commitments.

North Vietnam initiated a military offensive against the Republic of South Vietnam, in violation of its treaty commitments.

The 93rd US Congress refused to come to the aid of a US ally, despite the commitment of the United States to defend South Vietnam against communist aggression, and the sacrifice of over 58 thousand US service members to uphold that commitment.

Second lesson: Don't shed the blood of US service members in a cause, then abandon it when the cause becomes a political liability.

The shedding of my brothers' and sisters' blood is a lasting commitment made!

A commitment to the memory and the sacrifice of those who fell in what they believed a just cause.

A commitment to the people of the Republic of South Vietnam whose self-determination the US promised to defend against communist aggression.

Although my knowledge of criminal law is limited to what I learned from Jack McCoy on *Law and Order*, I indict the members of the 93rd Congress, who refused the additional defense funding of the Republic of South Vietnam, as accomplices in the murder of a million South Vietnamese.

Body Bag.   A body bag is a non-porous bag designed to contain a human body.

Body bags were used for the transport of KIA's from the field to graves registrations and storage in a morgue. This is a black, zippered army baggie for the unfortunate ... I don't want to say anything more about this.

Body Count.   This is a count of the enemy dead after a firefight to provide statistics for the Lifers' Daily Media Score Board: NVA-6, US-O. We win ... yea!

This was a necessary phase of any firefight:

1. get shot at,
2. simultaneously crap in pants, return fire, and get to cover and concealment,
3. light up the little buggers and call in fire support,
4. realize they're not there anymore,
5. clean out your pants and advance on suspected enemy position,
6. find nothing,
7. do body count,
8. derive a high number based on bits, blood trails, imagination, and actual bodies,
9. report body count to command,
10. declare victory,
11. continue the mission,

12. repeat step a,
13. continue 'til you DEROS or become a statistic.

Since most firefights were the result of "meeting engagements" and ambushes during which neither side "holds terrain," and the NVA like us did not leave their dead and wounded on the battlefield, doing a body count was like gift shopping for an irritating relative — just give the lifers something that will make them happy and will cause them to leave you alone for a while.

BOHICA   Pronounced boh-HEE-kah.
This is an acronym for "Bend Over Here It Comes Again."

This is an expression used to describe certain dreaded but inevitable events in the life of a grunt, like the unexpected and simultaneous arrival of a staff weenie, a chaplain, and marmite cans filled with steaks and baked potatoes at what was until that point a tranquil tour of palace guard.

Anytime the padre arrived on the same bird with a hot steak dinner ... BOHICA ... it was time to check your GI insurance and get in line for general absolution.

Boocoo.   Pronounced BOO-koo.
Pidgin for "many," "a lot;" from the French, *Beaucoup*: "I boocoo love you, GI!"

Boom Boom.   Pidgin for "sex," a water point quickie; probably a delusional onomatopoeia.

Boonie Hat.   The headwear choice of the style-conscious grunt in the field.

The army actually had an "authorized" boonie hat, which made a grunt look like Minnie Pearl without the price tag. The army boonie hat had also a bad tendency to shrink when it got wet and was then exposed to direct sunlight — which was essentially the Southeast Asian experience.

Due to this and, since the whole point of the boonie hat was to establish and express one's individuality and panache (while avoiding wearing the steal pot) and communicate one's contempt for all things lifers' held dear, these official, authorized boonie hats were typically shunned by grunts.

The boonie hat was a symbol of the ongoing and perpetual culture war between grunts and lifers.

Grunts knew boonie hats offended the lifers' sense of propriety, so of course grunts displayed the most ornate, outrageous and un-army-like boonie hats they could find without making targets out of ourselves for the bad guys.

The boonie hat of choice was one sent from home or gotten on the economy (i.e. the black market). Favorites included berets, Aussie hats, cowboy hats, hillbilly hats ... anything that didn't look "army."

The official army baseball cap, or the "Charlie Brown Hat," was rarely used as boonie hats — unless it was that of a major league or college team — since the baseball cap was then part of the standard, army fatigue uniform, therefore an issue left best to lifers.

Boonies.   This was the grunt term for the jungle, the "field," the "bush."

The boonies were anyplace outside an urban area, a base camp, or a firebase.

This was a place typically full of North Vietnamese, thorny plants, bad water, exotic tropical diseases, poisonous reptiles, and biting insects, but a place actually preferred by grunts due to the absolute lack of REMFs, lifers, and most forms of chicken shit.

Break Squelch.   Breaking squelch was caused by pushing the "Push to Talk" key of a PRC (pronounced "Prick" ... of course) 25 when the radio was out of the "squelch mood."

In this setting, the radio would receive constant "white noise" — static — and, when the handset was keyed, the static would go momentarily silent.

This was a technique used to signal SITREPS without talking, usually at night, e.g.

The network control station transmits:

"Romeo Two Eight; Negative SITREP, break squelch twice; Over."

The control station hears:

Hiss, Silence, Hiss, Silence, Hiss.

This confirms the "negative sitrep;" i.e., "Nothing happening out here, boss!"

The network control station confirms:

"Romeo Two Eight; Confirm Negative SITREP; out."

The Brown-Boot Army. A metaphor describing the way things were in the good old days before the army went soft, e.g.

"You guys have it soft. They wouldn't put up with crap like that back in the old brown-boot army where I'm from."

The metaphor is based on the fact that, for most of the twentieth century, the army issued and wore brown boots, but sometime after the Korean war, in some misguided fit of free- thinking liberalism, the army changed to black boots.

And things have never been the same since.

Actually, this is the traditional "Golden Age Myth" harking back to when men were men — back when things were "better," "stricter," "tougher," "women more beautiful and virtuous," "men stronger and more honorable," "snow deeper" and "bullshit browner" — before the younger generation came along and screwed the pooch.

We still use this on kids today —

"Back when I was your age, we didn't have air-conditioning, cable TV, Cell phones, and computer games. We went out, hunted down our own food, beat it with sticks, and ate it raw! That's how we got where we are today. Now eat your brussel sprouts, dang it!"

Nowadays, grunts wear nylon boots, body armor, and eye protection ... Hell! They wouldn't get away with that crap back in the old Black-Boot army!

Burning Shit.   This meant exactly what it says, burning shit.

This was the manner in which the army disposed of human excrement and, a fact typically not known by civilians who flush shit, it does burn with the aid of diesel fuel.

On permanent or long-term fire bases, human waste would be a problem if it were not properly disposed.

Number 1 was handled through "piss tubes." A small dry well was dug and filled with stones. A tube, usually fashioned from the shipping casings of 81 or 105 rounds, was propped at an angle over the dry well. Piss tubes were usually dug within the bunker line.

"Shitters" were fashioned to handle number 2.

These were basically out-houses of benches with butt-sized holes carved through them situated over half a fifty-five-gallon drum.

Sometimes, that was it ... a grunt sat on a bench suspended over half a fifty-five-gallon drum out in the open.

On more civilized installations, an actual outhouse was built with walls, overhead cover, hinged doors, screens and millions of flies.

The trick to getting shit to burn properly was coating the inside of the drum with diesel fuel before use. When the drum was full, it was dragged out from underneath the throne, drenched in more diesel, and set aflame preferably down wind of the bunker line.

The smell of burning, diesel-drenched shit is one that any grunt would recognize immediately, regardless of how long he's been out of Nam.

Shit burning was a detail reserved for FNGs and whoever was on the First Sergeant's shit list (maybe that's where the term comes from).

The problem with sitters was that they were built outside the bunker line for reason obvious to the most casual reader.

So, if a grunt got the call at night – and with dysentery-like symptoms rife in the ranks, this was not uncommon – coordinating the trip was about as dangerous and complicated as flushing a toilet in a submarine.

First, a grunt had to coordinate passage of lines ... outbound and hopefully inbound. An M16, a flashlight with a red lens, a copy of Stars & Stripes or the division newspaper, and a wad of C-Rat shit paper were necessary equipment for the trip.

The shitter, if enclosed, had to be cleared like an enemy bunker. A grunt didn't want to surprise an NVA sapper who was dealing with the same problem he was. Also, in an enclosed shitter, a grunt had no idea who might be creeping up on him.

Before sitting down, the hole had to be cleared for snakes, spiders, scorpions, and other bits of pernicious, shit-eating Vietnamese fauna (the flashlight with a red lens).

The M16 was situated within arm's reach preferably to the grunts left.

The paperwork was deposited to the right.

Trou down.

Business.

Cleanup with C-Rat paper and pages of the newspaper (you didn't think we actually read it, did you?)

Trou up.

Grab flashlight (now off) and M16.

Exit.

Start yelling "Chieu Hoi" while approaching the bunker line.

Another tactical problem with shitters was they seemed to be the targets-of-choice for RPGs and sappers with a perverse sense of humor.

I imagine blowing American excrement all over an American firebase was worth extra points to them.

Burst of Six.   In M60 machine gun training, grunts were trained to engage targets by firing "a burst of six;" in other words, six rounds per burst of fire, in order not to overheat the gun yet stay "on target."

To get the proper timing, a grunt would press the trigger, say "fire a burst of six" and release the trigger ... it actually works!

"To take a burst of six" was also a metaphor meaning "to re-enlist" because

1. the basic period of enlisted service was six years, and
2. re-enlistment for a grunt was considered the equivalent of being machine-gunned.

Butter Bar.   The term used to describe a second lieutenant, who wore a gold bar (bronze when "subdued") as an insignia of rank; in other words, a naïf, someone frequently lost despite (or because of) the map and the compass.

In Nam, infantry platoon leaders were typically promoted to First Lieutenant when they got into country and wore silver bars (black when "subdued"). So, infantry second lieutenants were very rare in Nam.

If one were to be encountered, odds were he was a veteran grunt NCO who decided that a commission as a way of getting more money and better treatment for the same work, in which case everything said about 2nd Louies above does not apply ... don't even try to go there.

Butterfly.   Pronounced "But Tah Fry," every time I heard it.

Pidgin for "unfaithful," "false," "perfidious," usually in matters of the heart (or of the pocketbook down at the water point).

I have no idea where this one comes from. My best guess is that either the water point babysahns knew something about Puccini's *Madame Butterfly*, or it was a metaphor based on the beauty and ephemeral nature of the bug that flutters from flower to flower ... either way, pretty lyrical.

"You Numbah Ten, GI! You boocoo buttah fry!"

C

C123.   This was the C123 "Provider," an Air Force two-engine cargo and tactical troop transport known for its ruggedness and reliability.

The C123 used jet assist for takeoffs on short runways with heavy loads which felt like riding a roller coaster up the "big loop" at about a hundred and fifty miles an hour.

Grunts strapped into the red nylon personnel "seats" back in the cargo area loved these takeoffs ... so did the crew chief cleaning up the semi-digested C Rats and other odiferous souvenirs remaining after the grunts disembarked.

C130.   The Lockheed C-130 Hercules is a four-engine, turbo-prop, transport aircraft from whose ass-end many airborne troopers won their wings; hence the affectionate nickname, "Bird Shit."

> "C130 rollin' down the strip
> Airborne daddy gonna take a little trip
> Gotta jump up, buckle up, shuffle to the door
> Jump right out and count to four
> If my chute don't open wide
> I got a REE-serve by my side
> If that chute don't open too
> Hit the ground and go right through
> Bury me in the leanin' rest
> Tell my girl I done my best
> Am I right or wrong
> You're right
> Am I goin' strong
> You're right

Sound Off
ONE, TWO
Sound off
THREE, FOUR
Bring it on down
ONE, TWO, THREE, FOUR,
ONE, TWO, THREE, FOUR!

If you're still double-timing in formation, you only have about 5.9 miles to run before you get breakfast.

Welcome to Jump School, Fort Benning, GA!

C4. This was a substance commonly used for cooking rations ... quickly. It was rumored to be also a plastic explosive.

It was typically found in one-pound bars that could be bartered from engineer units for C-Rations, war trophies, or protection. C4 was also cleverly hidden in claymore mines by unfeeling army contractors, who didn't care if grunts had to eat their C-rats cold.

The art of cooking C-Rats with C4 is based on the understanding that only the contents (notice the avoidance of the term "food") in the bottom of the can needed to get hot ... really, really hot. If not properly stirred during cooking, the stuff on the bottom gets incinerated and the stuff on the top stays cold.

Also, if properly stirred during cooking with the standard C-rat plastic spoon, all body hair was permanently removed from the knuckles, lower arm, and face.

The army actually had a more "civilized" system for heating rations in the field, "heating tabs," which were compressed trioxane fuel bars. They came in boxes of three tabs, and half a tab could heat a large C-Rat can or a canteen cup of water for coffee. These tabs gave off a blue light, which was supposed to be "tactically sound."

The problem with heating tabs was that they rarely made it all the way out to the grunts in the field. They were mysteriously "absorbed" by some magical force in the logistics chain ... along with flashlight batteries, air mattresses, poncho liners and field sweaters.

There was a third alternative for cooking rations in the field, but this one pushed the edges of rationality ... even for a grunt ... artillery charges.

Don't try this at home! Or anyplace else for that matter!

Artillery charges were basically bags of propellant for the artillery rounds ... gun powder in the old days. The higher the charge the further the shell goes.

After a few fire missions, there were usually bags of surplus charges, which the artillery guys would give to grunts, I think, just to watch what they did with them.

This was not a good way to heat Cs but if a grunt wanted a quart of hot water for coffee or washing up, this is what he could do.

Put the water in a large can, take the can and the artillery charges outside the bunker line, pile the charges around the can, and light the charges (This was the tricky part ... especially if one caught fire easily. This was also a great application for the proverbial ten-foot pole).

The charges flared up like Moses' pillar of fire in the Sinai, but the process wasn't quite over.

The charges heated the can to the point where it glowed. About a minute or so after the charges flared out, the water would start boiling heated by the glowing can.

I tried this ... just once! It only took me about six weeks to re-grow my eyebrows.

IMPORTANT ... one last word about cooking with C4 ... never NEVER inhale the fumes or stomp out the flame!

The former will give you enough brain damage to re-enlist, and the latter will get you high ... as in blown ten feet into the air.

C7A. This was the de Havilland C-7A Caribou, a Canadian-designed and produced cargo plane with short takeoff and landing (STOL) capability.

These things could land and take off almost anywhere a helicopter could, and they could carry about thirty grunts with their luggage.

The thing that made passengers a bit nervous was that the Caribou literally flapped its wings in flight.

"Hey Sarge! Are those wings supposed to be movin' like that?"

"I don't know, but as long as the air force guys ain't screaming, I think we're OK."

We rode one of these birds from Pleiku to a small airstrip near Duc Lap.

Landing in Duc Lap, the bird descended through the mountains in the monsoon. We started bouncing up and down as we descended through the clouds, no horizon out the windows, guys screaming, puking, praying, wings flapping up and down, no idea which way is up.

BANG!

The wheels hit the runway, the bird stops, the rear cargo ramp drops, and thirty grunts run out into a raging mortar attack and consider it a blessing.

Thank you for flying Air Grunt.

C Rats.   Pronounced SEE-rats (for reasons obvious to the casual diner).

Also called Cs.

This is an acronym for "Canned Rations" or "Canned Rat."

This was the basic food group of the grunt, and the reason why God created hot sauce.

C Rats came in cases of twenty-four meals, divided into:

B1 Units — Small meat serving, large fruit serving, candy (Beware! Peanut Butter, Ham & Lima Beans lurk here).

B2 Units — Large meat serving, cheese & crackers, cake; source of the high, Pound Cake, and low, Fruit Cake, of the C Rat "cake" experience.

B3 Units — Small meat serving, jam but no crackers (go figure); white bread in a can, and cookies;(cookies and bread went extinct along with Lucky Strike Green cigarettes around 1968 when the surplus Korean War rations ran out).

Since in each squad the Alpha Grunt selected his meals first and so on down the grunt food chain, C Rat selection was an indication of the pecking order among grunts.

A recent article in *Army Psychology and Other Oxymora* argues that the reason for the short life expectancy of FNGs was that the constant diet of Ham and Lima Beans, Fruitcake, and Peanut Butter caused a state of depression leading to suicidal rage: "I'd rather be dead than eat another can of this shit!"

The C-rat hit parade:

> **C rats normally avoided:** Ham and Bullets (Lima Beans); Tuna anything; Chopped Ham and Eggs (affectionately known as "chopped puke"); Beefsteak, Potatoes and Gristle; Fruit Cake (if you threw this to a Vietnamese, you'd immediately get it back ... probably in the back of the head); Peanut Butter (only an army contractor could screw up peanut butter to the point where a grunt wouldn't eat it).

> **C Rats normally pursued:** Franks & Beans; Spaghetti & Meat Balls; Sliced Pork; Pound Cake; Peaches, Pears, and Mixed Fruit.

A C-Rat "Accessory Pack" came in each box of Cs. It was wrapped in a small brown plastic bag which was perfect for wrapping a wallet or an instamatic camera and extra rolls of film during the wet season (i.e. all year round).

Included in the accessory pack was a plastic spoon, salt & pepper, instant coffee, a packet of sugar, a packet of non-dairy creamer (rumored to be made of crushed, dehydrated monkey glands), two Chiclets, four cigarettes, moisture resistant matches, and toilet paper (indispensable, unless a grunt had a subscription to Stars and Stripes or was very good at identifying toxic plants by their leaves).

When the C-Rat gods smiled, there was also a package of cocoa powder.

Typical C-Rat rumors:

- The meals were laced with saltpeter to control grunts' contextually unnatural natural urges.
- C Rats were laced with embalming fluid and other preservatives to make graves registration easier.
- C Rats made you sterile.
- C Rats made you horny (like a nineteen-year-old guy needed chemicals for this).

Since the cans were stamped with the date and place of canning, C Rats actually had a "vintage."

"Ah! Franks and Beans, Camden, New Jersey, June, 1953 ... a rare but zesty vintage ... a hint of the pine barrens with a slight after taste of the turnpike ... pass the hot sauce!"

Here's the tale of the indestructible wristwatch and the use of C Rats as body armor.

I had a wrist watch when I came into country — a cheap Bulova of some kind — and, by the end of the rainy season, the thing had rotted away, band, face, hands, the works.

So, I wrote home asking for a new one, and a few weeks later one arrived. And with my shiny new watch came an unconditional lifetime warranty!

We had a pretty good laugh over that! We were sure whoever came up with this guarantee had no idea what this watch was about to go through in Nam.

A couple of weeks later, we were going out on a "sweep" — army talk for humping the boonies. I packed three days rations; that's nine C-Rat meals pared down to the stuff I'd actually consider eating.

Like most grunts, I packed my rations in a sandbag and secured it on the top of the rucksack; that put them right behind my head when I was wearing the ruck. The intended reason for this is so I could grab a can of fruit or a few crackers during a ten-minute break without having to do a major unpacking.

I was about to learn another altogether unintended reason for packing cans of food behind my head.

We were humping through a little valley when we got hit with incoming mortars. We weren't sure whose they were but, since mortars are essentially a "for whom it may concern" weapon when they're falling on you, we took immediate action, which was moving our asses out of the impact area as quickly as we could.

I didn't get too far when something hit me right in the back; it felt like a giant fist slammed me into the ground.

I was a bit dazed, but lying there on the ground I started to do a post-trauma inventory —

"Legs? Legs OK!"

"Arms? Arms OK!"

"Pain? No Pain!"

Then I felt something thick and wet behind my head. I thought,

"My God! I'm hit! The back of my head is gone!"

I felt no pain, but a thick, wet goo was slowly oozing down the side of my head.

Then I felt bits of something flowing along with the goo.

I imagined bits of my brain were oozing down the side of my head. I think I started fading into shock. I could still hear the incoming and the rest of the guys running, but it all seemed far away ... dream-like.

My buddy, Jimmy, grabbed the top of my ruck and was shouting at me to move my ass ... but my mind was far away ... I almost resented the interruption ...

"Leave me alone... Can't you see I'm killed..."

Finally, some of the goo made it to my mouth ... it tasted ... good! It tasted like ... tomato sauce!

Tomato Sauce!

I was bleeding tomato sauce!

My brains were floating in tomato sauce!

I got to my knees, then to my feet. Jimmy and another guy half dragged me out of the impact area.

When we got clear and I could take inventory, I dropped my ruck. A piece of shrapnel had hit me high in the back, just below where I had packed my Cs. It ruined a perfectly good air mattress, a field sweater, a paperback novel, and blew a can of Franks & Beans all over the back of my head.

Wrong time, wrong place ... almost.

The guys certainly got a kick out of it.

A can of beans almost greased a grunt!

Who wouldn't see the humor in that?

And I got to walk around the bush for a couple of days with a head full of hotdog shrapnel, tomato sauce, and sweat bees.

But! I was also missing my new lifetime-guaranteed wonder watch!

When we got back to the firebase, a guy from another squad gave it back to me. He said he found it imbedded in a tree. He had pried it out with his boonie knife.

Of course, it wasn't working. In fact, it wasn't quite round any more.

So just for grins and giggles, I sent it back to the watch company with a brief explanation of what had happened, asking if the warrantee covered mortar attacks and trees.

A couple of weeks later I got a package from the watch company with a new watch. There was a letter from the company president saying no, the warranty didn't cover mortars and impact into jungle flora, but he was sending me a new watch as a way of thanking me for me for my service.

I really felt grateful to him for that, but I did notice that this watch did not come with another lifetime warranty.

C-Rat Stove. This was a field-expedient (meaning designed and built by grunts with scrounged materials) device used to heat C Rats.

It was extremely dependable and satisfied its intended application perfectly because it had no moving parts, was not manufactured by an army contractor, and did not move through the army logistics system.

Essentially, it was a small C-Rat can, open on one end with holes for ventilation punched through the can along both rims either with a P38 or a church key.

It was only functional when there was fuel available — either heat tabs or C4 — and when the tactical situation allowed for such a degree of luxury — in other words, you weren't too busy morphing into a webbed-footed creature living in a foot or so of muddy water, actually had C Rats to heat, fuel to heat them with, and the bad guys weren't efficiently and creatively trying to ruin your dinner by killing you.

Strangely, grunts were very protective about their C-Rat stoves and their P38s. They were more likely to dump their C Rats than their C-Rat stove, but that may have been just a matter of taste.

Ca Ca Dau. Pronounced KAH—ka—dow.

Pidgin for "kill," "grease," "send to the great rice paddy in the sky," usually accompanied by drawing the index finger across the throat.

Although an unfortunate occupational hazard for a grunt, this term was never directed at another grunt. It was a term reserved for the bad guys.

Call for Fire.   This was a systematized, orderly and efficient procedure of inviting the artillery guys to a firefight and having them land ordinance on the bad guys in a fast, accurate, and effective manner; hence, very important to grunts to get right.

Since in most firefights the bad guys were "danger close" and since artillery was a "for whom it may concern" armament once it left the tube, grunts wanted it landing in the right place at the right time.

Although there is a very precise procedure for these things, a grunt call for fire went something like this.

First, the grunt got the radio on the fire support push:

"Romeo Oscar Five Five; this is Alpha Sierra One Six X-ray; fire mission, over!"

"Alpha Sierra One Six X-ray; this is Romeo Oscar Five Five; authenticate Charlie Quebec, over!"

"I authenticate Mike Mike, over!"

"Affirmative, One Six X-ray; Go!"

"Troops in the open; location Niner Seven Seven Three Four Niner Two Eight; Danger Close, over."

"X-ray, Troops in the open at Niner Seven Seven Three Four Niner Two Eight; danger close, over."

"Affirmative!"

"Wait one!"

"X-ray! Shot, over!"

"Shot out!"

"Splash, over!"

"Splash, out!"

The first round was a smoke round for spotting. From the splash point, the grunt on the ground then adjusted the fire onto the target, i.e., the Bad Guys.

"Five Five! Drop five zero; right two five, over."

"X-ray, I have drop five zero; right two five, over."

"Affirmative."

"Wait one!"

"X-ray, Shot, over."

"Shot out!"

"Splash, over!"

"Splash, out!"

Usually, another smoke round...right about now the bad guys have figured out what is about to happen to them.

"Five Five. On Target! Fire for Effect! Battery Five, Hotel Echo, over."

"X-ray. Copy, on target, over."

"Affirmative."

"Shot out!"

Boom!!!

An experienced grunt working with a good FDC (Fire Direction Control) could get ordinance on target in less than five minutes.

I always considered it good policy to describe the effect of the fires to the artillery guys — vicarious combat for them — and send a couple of cases of beer around to the battery when I got back to civilization, which for a grunt was essentially anywhere cold beer could be had.

CEOI. An abbreviation for "Communications and Electronics Operating Instructions," a document which designated radio pushes (frequencies), call signs, authentication and shackle codes, and signs/countersigns, which changed every twenty-four hours.

This was a very sensitive document; grunts actually tied these things to their bodies. If a grunt lost one of these in the boonies, he and his entire unit would be sent back out to find it, then they'd shoot him.

When some lieutenant lost his CEOI, I had to conduct a police call across a klick of boonies with a rifle squad looking for the damned thing, because it could compromise just about every push and call sign in the AO.

A very important part of the CEOI was the "authentication" and "shackle" tables.

0	1	2	3	4	5	6	7	8	9
k	okm	gbq	lyt	zaw	cpi	vrsn	dxh	jue	qf
n	xmp	rhv	ing	ltq	zub	oca	wjy	sde	kf
e	bhi	ujy	kac	nfx	tdz	sro	epl	qgv	wm
d	gea	ehq	pfm	tcr	kls	xzy	njv	uwb	oi
u	wcp	yfv	mqr	oeb	zhx	sgn	uit	adl	jk
a	zjp	odg	vbr	snu	max	yko	hte	lfc	iw
c	alm	xqp	gjh	ivy	neu	tcf	wdr	kzo	sb
l	uzr	dvm	skt	lhj	bwn	axc	epg	ioy	fq
t	yjd	qol	afn	ktw	pgj	sxh	vbm	cru	ze
z	dxz	whi	ecu	bkv	opm	anq	tsl	yfr	jg
x	nho	czv	ptq	gxm	ise	lfw	ukd	jbr	ay
w	mbq	xnp	tgo	ulc	ari	fjv	hkz	bws	ye
v	pxz	jei	blu	dch	tfn	smw	agq	ovr	yk
h	hnd	ywg	fql	avs	jek	otp	rcm	uzb	ix
o	tyc	aqd	jsw	uop	zvr	kmb	eng	lhx	if
b	wzv	fqg	dcs	rub	mij	tle	npx	hko	ya
y	zqi	pva	jch	dts	log	euk	yfm	rbw	nx
m	spj	zoa	vuk	wbx	rhq	ecl	dmn	igy	ft
q	gzm	fxb	owh	eil	cpa	srd	tuk	jvn	qy

	0	1	2	3	4	5	6	7	8
f	kfw	azc	grh	ptv	obs	nqy	iem	udx	jl
j	fja	coh	zru	ils	kny	mvd	qet	bwx	gp
g	kqd	epg	lwy	vas	ixb	rhj	zut	cfn	mo
p	lgi	qou	abf	zrh	pds	ekj	cxm	yvn	tw
i	dqh	bes	kfy	amc	lop	utr	ngx	zjw	vi
s	icv	fjn	bqw	hdp	rxe	kls	uzo	tma	gy
r	ogk	hsa	dnf	xlc	zrj	peb	tmw	iyu	vq

Since the army didn't want the North Vietnamese calling for fire support from us on us, "Authentication" was the process though which a station or a transmission on a radio network was "authenticated" as valid and friendly.

Using the authentication table, the challenging station would challenge by giving out two letters; the first would indicate the row of the table as indicated in column "0;" the second letter was a letter within the indicated row. The challenged station would authenticate itself by responding with the letter immediately to the right.

For example, using the sample transcript below:

"Alpha Juliet Two Seven, this is Sierra Mike One Six X-ray, over."

"Sierra Mike One Six X-ray, Authenticate November Lima, Over."

"Alpha Juliet Two Seven, I authenticate Tango, Tango, over."

"Sierra Mike One Six X-ray, Affirmative, Over."

A second use of the table was to "shackle," or encrypt numeric information, like grid coordinates, casualty reports, and logistic information.

Now this gets a bit screwy, so try to stay with me on this!

The letters in the table are grouped into numeric columns, so any letter in a specific group of three could represent the number of the column in which it is found — pretty straight forward so far, right?

The trick was indicating to the receiving station which row the sender was using to shackle the information.

The security guys considered it too simple to simply announce the row by its letter, so most of the time the row was indicated in the same manner as an authentication — so for example the letters Mike X-Ray would indicate row Romeo, by the "one right method."

But, since the security guys assumed that bad guys knew how grunts did this and, since they were never sure if the table had been compromised, they'd try to throw the bad guys a curve every now and then.

Instead of the "one right method," they'd designate that the letter above or the letter below indicated the row, the "one up method" and the "one down method."

So, under the "one up" scheme, Mike X-Ray now indicated row Sierra.

Finally, since there were potentially three letters to represent each numeral, letters were not repeated in a single data set even if numerals had to be.

Confused?

Well, imagine how some poor grunt out in the boonies, in the dark, and up to his kiester in bad guys felt.

Anyway, here's an example of shackling using the "one right" formula:

"Romeo Two Eight, Romeo Two Six, Night Laager, Over."

"Romeo Two Six, Romeo Two Eight, Wait One, Over."

"Romeo Two Six, Romeo Two Eight, Ready to Transmit, Over."

"Romeo Two Eight, Romeo Two Six, Ready To Copy, Over."

"Romeo Two Six, I Shackle Alpha Zulu Bravo Mike X-Ray Oscar November Echo."

"Romeo Two Eight, I Copy, Alpha Zulu Bravo Mike X-Ray Oscar November Echo."

"Romeo Two Six, Affirmative, Over."

"Romeo One Six, Out."

If both stations were using the same table and the same shackling method, then the control station understood that the unit whose call sign is Romeo Two Eight had just checked in for the night at the "Motel Bush" located at grid coordinates 868257.

The location and numbers of enemy troops and installations was typically transmitted in the "clear;" that is, grunts just used numbers to represent themselves. Grunts figured that the bad guys already knew where they were.

Still confused?

That was in some perverse measure the point, but this clever deviousness on the part of the security guys also had the unfortunate tendency of confusing the hell out of the grunts shackling or unshackling the information. That and the fact that a CEOI may not be available when it was needed caused grunts to create "field expedient" shackle codes, like "Blackhorse."

Another potentially confusing part of CEOI usage was coordinating when to change codes.

The standard was every twenty-four hours and the conventional way should have been to change at midnight ... sorry! 0000 hours ... but security guys never like to do the "expected." Besides, it's pretty dark out in the boonies at midnight. Even if a grunt could see the hands on his watch to know it's midnight, he didn't want to be trying to read and memorize new call signs and pushes and trying to change all the radios over in the dark ... which should remain dark if a grunt didn't want to announce his presence to the bad guys.

So the CEOI would expire at various planned and announced times during the day hoping the units effected remembered ... again, confusing the hell out of grunts in the field.

The US lost entire infantry companies for hours because the grunts were too busy or distracted by the bad guys to remember the CEOI had changed and were wondering where everybody went until they figured it out.

This is the true story of how the "lost battalion" got lost.

Charlie. This is a generic name for the "Bad Guys"!

The term was derived from the designation "VC" for Viet Cong which in the army "phonetic" alphabet is pronounced "Victor Charlie."

The antiwar movement essentially lionized these guys as the fearless, cunning, freedom fighters of the South Vietnamese liberation movement, but it just wasn't so.

That's not to say there might have been some well-meaning and patriotic members of the movement ... God only knows the South Vietnamese government stank like a dead fish left out in the sun for a week (See "Nuoc Mam").

The VC were also the guys who stuffed bicycle frames full of C4 and blew it up in crowded markets, when a couple of US MPs walked by.

The VC were also the guys who would attack US soldiers from behind a crowd of school children.

The VC were also the guys who would murder Vietnamese civilians whom they thought were fraternizing with US troops,

The VC were also the guys who would take a Vietnamese peasant's last bits of rice as "tax" and let his family starve.

In short, the VC were terrorists and gangsters with an ideology.

"Real" VC were pretty scarce by the end of the Tet '68 counter offenses in late 1968. The last thing the North Vietnamese wanted were "idealists" and "revolutionaries" hanging around after their putative takeover of South Vietnam.

So, in early 1968 the North Vietnamese pushed the VC into a fight they couldn't win and let the US army do their dirty work for them.

There were "VC" units after Tet '68, but they were manned by NVA regulars.

So, as North Vietnam claimed, and the US anti-war movement gleefully trumpeted, there were no "NVA units" in South Vietnam; just bands of merry, freedom-loving revolutionaries in the green wood, from the movie, *Ho Chi Minh, Men in Black Pajamas*.

If you buy this, I got some swamp land in Jersey or a bridge in Brooklyn you'll love too.

Cheap Charley.   Pidgin for "cheapskate," "miserly," "scrooge."
A term often used at the water point when negotiations had broken down, e. g. "500 pi?!? You numbah ten cheap charley!"

Chicken Man.   "He's everywhere! He's everywhere!"

This was a very popular, comic serial on Armed Forces Radio. Chicken Man was a radio series spoofing comic book heroes like Batman.

Since Chicken Man worked Monday through Friday as a shoe salesman in Benton Harbor, Michigan, he could only fight crime on weekends. He traveled around in the Chicken Coupe, a yellow, two-door crime fighting vehicle.

In those simpler, golden days before multi-tasking, this program could stop a fire fight because grunts were too busy listening to it to engage in real mayhem.

"Come back later! We're busy!"

"No sweat, GI! Turn up radio ... we like hear too!"

Chicken Plate.   In the world, a "chicken plate" is two fried chicken breasts; your choice of baked, mashed or fries; vegetables du jour; soup or salad.

In Nam, it was an armored, steel plate worn by helicopter door gunners and short timers who didn't like to move around much.

This was an excellent thing to grab when the crew chief of a slick was tossing your ass, sixty-pound ruck sack and all, out of a slick hovering ten feet above the elephant grass onto a cold LZ.

Where the chicken plate goes, the ass is sure to follow.

Chicken Shit.   This was a vicious miasma exuded by south end of north-bound lifers, similar to a fart in a phone booth, but of less use than a fart since, unlike farts, it was against the Regs to set lifers on fire to entertain at parties or to impress a lot of drunken grunts on stand-down.

Examples of chicken shit are the following activities in the boonies: shining boots, close shaves, weekly haircuts, starched uniforms, personal inspections, wearing steel pots (with clean camo covers) & flak jackets, and formations — issues very precious to lifers but of no earthly good to grunts in the field.

Excluded from chicken shit and practiced by all self-respecting grunts at all levels were clean, serviceable weapons; competence and experience among grunts, NCOs and officers; dry socks; and deep, dry, well-sited fighting positions.

One of the benefits of being in the boonies was almost a complete lack of chicken shit due to having to concentrate at all times on what was mission critical and a complete lack of lifers who, when the shit hit the fan, remembered they had a dental appointment back in base camp and didn't return until the smoke cleared.

My sincerest apologies to self-respecting chickens the world over.

Chieu Hoi.   Pronounced CHEW-hoy.
Vietnamese for either "I surrender!" or "Please shoot me now!"

This was a US sponsored program that offered money, forty acres and a mule to communist defectors.

A GSA study has found that the average chieu-hoier chieu hoied an 3.67 times.

Eventually, this program became the most common source of financing for dry cleaning stores and Chinese take-out places in Southern California.

Choy Oy!   Pidgin; an exclamation; "Wow!" "No Shit!" (in a good way).

The favorite expression of Vietnamese mothers,

"So! You're out all the time doing what? Insurging? For this you can't come visit your poor, old mother? Choy oy! Mrs. Nguyen's boy ... he's a doctor! Married a nice girl from Vung Tau! Mrs. Vong's boy, a lawyer. And you? You got some meshuga schtick that keeps you out all night, every night, and makes you dress up in black pajamas! What kind of son wears black pajamas outside the hootch? You don't call! You don't visit! When are you going to meet a nice girl and give me some grandchildren? Choy oy!"

Church Key. This was the name of a beer and soda can and bottle opener.

Its name was more irony than functionality ... unless you were some sort of back-slider.

Due to the rapid advance of can and bottle technology, this is going to take some explaining to non-boomers.

Back in the day, there were no pop tops and screw-offs (I'm talking about bottle caps here). Cans and bottles were sealed; you couldn't get in without an opening device unless you had a really good set of pointy-sharp teeth.

The church key had two functional ends (which made them superior to most lifers). One end was rounded for removing bottle caps and the other was pointed for opening cans. Each end had a hooking tab that would latch onto the rim of a can or a bottle top.

Opening cans was a bit an art. A grunt had to make one large hole on one side of the top of the can for drinking and another, smaller hole opposite for venting the can. No vent hole and a grunt couldn't suck the beer out; too big a vent hole and the beer ended up on the grunt's forehead, which would leave a clean spot that the bad guys could use as an aiming point.

Of course, this was in the days of the old "Black-Boot Army" when a grunt needed some skills to open a beer can. Today, anyone can pull a tab! Bah!

CIB. Abbreviation for "Combat Infantryman Badge."

This is the principal insignia of the "Grand and Illustrious Brotherhood of the Grunt." It's an award presented to soldiers who participate in active ground combat while assigned as a member of an infantry or special forces unit.

In other words, it's an award that indicates that a grunt has "seen the elephant," "embraced the suck," fulfilled the ultimate purpose of sixteen-weeks army training and was now a fully qualified 11B.

When I got my CIB, it was like graduating from FNG-school to grunt-dom. The other guys, being grunts, didn't come over to shake my hand or pat me on the back. But, it may have been my imagination, they did seem to look at me differently. And they finally learned my name.

The CIB is worn on the uniform above all other awards: above all medals, PX ribbons, jump wings, ranger tabs.

Once a soldier earned one of these, he became a life-time member of the infantry brotherhood.

Claymore.   In formal army-speak, this was the M18A1 anti-personnel mine.

The claymore fired steel balls out to about a hundred meters across a sixty-degree arc in front of the mine. It was used primarily in an anti-infiltration device for fire bases, night laagers, and in ambushes.

The claymore had an OD plastic casing with the words "Front Toward Enemy" on the front (convex side) for grunts who were a little fuzzy about the principle.

Inside the claymore were 1.5 pounds of C4 and 700 steel balls (I never counted them, but there were a bunch of large BBs embedded in the plastic).

The claymore stood on two sets of little, folding, adjustable legs and was equipped with a fixed plastic sight but, since it was more of a "to whom it may concern" than a "this one's for you" weapon, most grunts just pointed it in a general direction making sure it was level and the blast radius wasn't obstructed.

The claymore was carried in a bandoleer which normally outlived the claymore and was re-purposed as a bandoleer for ammo or just a general, carry-all bag when the ruck sack got too full ... kind of a grunt purse.

The claymore served two critical, but somewhat mutually exclusive, functions in gruntdom: blowing up the bad guys and keeping a grunt's C4 dry until ready for use to heat up some Cs.

The claymore played a central role in an ongoing grunt ritual while on palace guard: putting out the claymores in the evening and bringing them back in the morning.

The bad guys were rumored to sneak into the wire at night, turn the claymores around, make some threatening noises, and watch the fun when some poor unsuspecting grunt blew the mines. So, grunts came up with all sorts of ingenious (and pretty dumb) strategies for countering this insidious deed.

Here are some other ways of preventing the bad guys from f'ing with the claymores (see if you can pick out the lifer strategy).

1. Put the claymores out at right angles to the bunker line so, if the bad guys turned them around, it wouldn't make much of a difference. The problem with this technique was that the claymores were only effective when the bad guys were already well into the wire ... not a desired situation.
2. Put the claymores out backwards facing the bunker line so when the bad guys turned them around, they were actually aimed back at themselves. The problem with this theory should be obvious even to the casual reader. It only worked if the bad guys had *actually turned the claymores.* If not, a grunt was shooting himself and, if a grunt could see which way the claymores were pointed in the dark, they were much too close.

If you guessed "2," congratulations! You win!

What made the most sense was not leaving the claymores out during daylight, placing them in different spots each evening, emplacing them after dark, and camouflaging them.

Cluster F'ck.   Look up SNAFU, FUBAR, and Lifer; then mix in Murphy's Law and a lot of bad guys ... and you got it.

Combat Trains.   This had nothing to do with railroads and choo-choo trains, and its connection to combat was at times tenuous.

The combat trains was the facility that provided "combat service support" for the forward tactical elements. The combat trains normally consisted of ammunition, petroleum, vehicle maintenance and recovery, and the battalion aid station ... in other words, a forward concentration of Ash and Trash.

The trains was the army, combat shopping mall of Vietnam. Mostly it was run by guys who knew their stuff and gave a damn. They got grunts what they needed when they needed it ... even if they had to fudge the paper work, steal it (this was known as "re-allocation"), and schlep it themselves. These guys, be they clerks, cooks, drivers, mechanics or whatever, were "grunts."

But some other guys spent their time justifying why grunts weren't authorized to have what they needed in the boonies and making grunts fill out forms in triplicate for the stuff they did get, while skimming off all the good stuff for themselves ... these were the REMFs.

The trains were the realm of the "S4"— the staff logistics officer. This was typically a hard-nosed, smart, and aggressive senior Lieutenant or junior Captain, who was never in a good mood and whom a grunt never wanted to cross.

Another character who usually lurked around the trains was the "XO," the "Executive Officer," the "number two guy" in the battalion after the old man. The XO was typically a senior Major.

If there ever was someone in the army who was omniscient, it was this guy! He knew what you did before you did it and had already prepared the paperwork to reduce you in rank, fine you a half-month's wages, take away your beer ration, and transfer you to permanent point. He was absolute death on sham artists and shirkers.

One of the completely idiosyncratic army practices that emanated from the trains was "ration accountability." In other words, the army felt the obligation to account for every meal it served by individual name. If a company commander were issued eighty "Class A Ration" meals, in other words, real food, eighty names would have to be entered on a mess form.

authority for managing this process was delegated to a trains
e called the "Battalion Mess Officer." This was usually a lieuten-
no had survived his six months with a line infantry unit. This
: collected all the unit mess rosters, tallied the signatures, and the
balanced the numbers with the ration issue.

Since, the system was rife with benevolent fraud, as long as the
numbers balanced, the Battalion Mess Officer ignored certain abnor-
malities and idiosyncratic entries on the mess sheets.

Most of it was unintended.

Say, a company commander's "foxhole" strength was eighty. So,
eighty Class A rations were ordered when the unit was on a firebase.
But, due to wounds, injuries, illnesses, patrols, appointments in the rear,
and general shamming, only sixty grunts made it to the chow line.

Sometimes, the overage was planned.

A good commander knew that the worst thing that could happen
when serving Hot-A's was to run out of food before everyone was fed.
Better to order more than was needed and be able to offer "seconds."

So, how's a guy to "account" for all the rations issued?

Usually, a directive was given by the commander, "Sergeant, I need
eighty signatures on the mess roster!"

And the assigned mission was executed.

If the army were ever to audit the mess sheets from Nam, they would
be surprised at who was fed: multiple Smiths and Jonses; a not a few M.
Mouses and D. Ducks; a Ho Chi Minh or two; I even saw a SP4 Man,
Super, PFC Man, Bat, and a PFC El Zorro.

But, as far as the Battalion Mess Officer was concerned, the numbers
balanced, therefore the meals were all accounted for.

Contact.   A euphemism for "hitting the shit," a firefight, a
meeting engagement.

To quote General Sherman's complete philosophy of war, "War is
hell, but making contact is a mother-fer!"

CONUS. Pronounced CON-us

1. What Robert McNamara did to get us to stay in Nam.
2. An acronym for "Continental United States;" in other words, "home," "the world."

Cover and Concealment. This is a basic principle of all combat maneuver and defense.

"Cover" is protection from armaments — small arms, artillery, mortars, rockets, kitchen sinks, and nuoc mam.

"Concealment" is protection from detection — camouflage, noise and light discipline, restricted movement — "If they can't see you, they can't shoot you!"

In other words, dig a deep hole and pull the rest of the world in around you.

A grunt had to practice both cover and concealment to stay alive.

This concept caused grunts to believe at times that they were on some perverse and low-paying construction job. They dug everywhere they went! Even a night laager, a one-night stand at the "Motel Bush," required the digging of fighting positions — at least prone shelters.

It was a grunt rule of thumb that fighting positions were improved every day. So, a long stay in one place — like palace guard on some firebase — saw some pretty sophisticated construction projects, basically in this order:

1. Digging of individual prone shelters.
2. Digging of two-man fighting positions.
3. Fortification of fighting positions with sandbags.
4. Conversion of fighting positions to bunkers with overhead cover from sandbags, logs, lumber, and engineer stakes.
5. Digging of communication trenches between bunkers.
6. Fortification of trenches with sand bags.
7. Digging of communication trenches within the perimeter.

8. Begin work on officers' swimming pool and sauna, etc.

Integrated with all this digging and sandbag filling would be the preparation of "secondary" fighting positions — those to be used to cover secondary fields of fire — and "alternate" fighting positions — those to use if the primary fighting positions were not tenable, in other words, overrun.

So, even on palace guard, grunts did a lot of construction work and fed the sweat bees.

The trick to an enjoyable palace guard was not being the first unit in — they had to do most of the work building the palace — but to relieve them and take advantage of all their good work. Of course the downside was that, once the palace was secure, the lifers started showing up.

Ironically, the longer grunts stayed on a firebase, the less attention they paid to concealment. With all the construction work, patrolling, choppers going in and out, and the artillery and mortars doing their thing, if the bad guys didn't know grunts were there, they had to be deaf, blind and dumb — and typically they weren't.

If the dinks cared, by just observing they probably had a pretty accurate map of the firebase marking the bunkers, crew-served weapons (machine guns and mortars), TOC, gun positions, etc. So growing bushes around the defensive positions didn't fool anyone and just obscured a grunt's field of fire.

Now, if the bad guys could hit crap with their mortars and rockets, this would be a problem.

Quite the contrary, we seemed to have a "hit me with your best shot" strategy in Nam. Since the US had a significant advantage in fire power, anytime the bad guys concentrated their forces to attack a US position, they took horrific punishment. As a Marine commander is reputed to have said, "We got the poor bastards right where we want them; all around us!"

So, encouraging the NVA to attack a firebase was usually a winner tactically, but not a good day for the grunts holding the perimeter.

This is a good spot to mention the "drug" issue that Hollywood likes to harp on.

One of the many ways of classifying grunts was into "heads" — guys whose drug of choice was marijuana, and "juicers" — guys whose drug of choice was alcohol.

When a grunt unit was in the rear on stand-down, everybody was left to do their own thing within reason ... the lifers would still bust you for "drunk and disorderly" and would lock your ass up and throw away the key for smoking pot.

When the unit was in the field, including palace guard, intoxication, regardless of its source, was not tolerated ... and believe me, getting busted by some lifer in base camp and losing a stripe or two was much preferable to getting busted by a grunt NCO for being wasted on the bunker line at night.

A significant exception was this ... pot grew wild in Nam ... and one of the necessary tasks in preparing a defense was "burning fields of fire" — literally burning off all the weeds, elephant grass, and other various flora that obstructed lines of sight in front of the defensive positions.

When this was done, you guessed it, a persistent cloud of pot-saturated smoke wafted across the fire base, and unlike a former US president, grunts inhaled it.

Double up on the C Rats tonight, boys, suddenly it all tastes good!

D

Dai Uy.   Pronounced DA-wee.

Vietnamese for "boss," "captain," "you who look like you're in charge around here and would kick my ass if I don't recognize it."

Also, it was the generic title for any "S5" or "civil affairs" officer, a somewhat burned-out grunt platoon leader at the end of his combat tour who has now shifted gears from orchestrating mayhem in the boonies to attempting to "win their minds and hearts" with smiles, candy, cartons of cigarettes, and rolls of piasters.

Danger Close.   This describes any situation where something very dangerous is too close to a grunt for comfort.

Technically, "danger close," when included in a call for fire support — artillery, mortars, close air, gunships — meant there were friendlies (that be us) in close proximity to the target (that be them), usually within six hundred meters for artillery or mortars.

This was also a warning to grunts to take proper precautions; i.e. get underground, start digging, hump mother earth, or pull yourself up into your helmet (I actually attempted this a couple of times!).

Finally, it was also used to describe other undesirable situations, like the proximity of North Vietnamese, lifers, and REMFs (notice the grouping).

Deep Shit.   Well, by this time you should be pretty much able to figure this one out for yourselves.

"Shit" is a metaphor for "bad" because it stinks and you don't ever want to find yourself in it. As far as being in shit goes, "deep" is worse than "shallow." So, "deep shit" was a grunt metaphor for any bad ... very, very bad ... situation.

When a unit reported it was in "deep shit," it usually had something to do with encountering more, pissed-off, well-armed bad guys than it knew what to do with.

"Deep shit," like FPF, gave a unit priority for supporting fire.

In Nam, being in deep shit was a somewhat self-perpetuating condition, which is one of the reasons grunts didn't wear underwear.

Demilitarized Zone, aka, the DMZ. The so-called demilitarized border between the Republic of South Vietnam and the not-so Democratic Republic of Vietnam, established in 1954 roughly along the 17th parallel after the French Indochina war, and therefore, littered with dropped French rifles, empty wine bottles, smoked-down butts from Gaullist Gauloises, *pour la gloire de La France*, worn down Edith Piaf records, and pinups of Brigitte Bardot, *pour la gloire de La Brigitte*.

Partitioning countries was quite popular in the post-colonial twentieth century. And why not? It worked so well for the British Empire in its withdrawal from its empire; think of Ireland and India just to mention two stellar examples of British diplomatic legerdemain.

After World War II, the world was being divided up between the Soviet Union, aka, "The Commies," and the western European democracies, aka, "The Imperialists." East vs. West; Socialist vs. Capitalist; Left vs. Right. More specifically, East Germany vs. West Germany, North Korea vs. South Korea, North Vietnam vs. South Vietnam, East Cincinnati vs. West Cincinnati.

The essential problem with the theory of partitioning a nation is twofold.

First, the expectation that a nation, who see themselves as a single people, especially after enduring decades of oppressive colonialization by a hostile power, are going to accept partition because someone else said so was, at best, unreasonable. So, Mother England, don't expect the Irish people to accustom themselves with your continued occupation of six counties of Ireland.

Second, the expectation that the Soviet Union, and later the Peoples Republic of China, whose *raison d'etre* was the global expansion of communism, would accept being confined to its assigned partitions, was at best delusional. Think of Korea.

Geographically, the very concept of a demilitarized partitioning border across the 17th parallel dividing Vietnam was ludicrous. Compare the Vietnamese DMZ with that of Korea. In Korea, both ends of the DMZ end in very deep seawater making it somewhat difficult to circumvent. Despite this, the not-so Democratic People's Republic of Korea, with the aid of Soviet rubles, equipment, and advisors, managed to sledgehammer hundreds of thousands of troops across its DMZ in 1950 without getting their feet wet.

Although the eastern end of the Vietnamese DMZ terminated at the South China Sea, deep saltwater controlled by the US Sixth Fleet, the western end terminated in the mountainous jungles of Laos, which the North Vietnamese soon developed into that infamous, eight-lane, limited-access throughway affectionately dubbed the Ho Chi Minh Trail or Highway Ho.

The DMZ was irrefutable proof that politicians, like lifers, cannot read a map or analyze terrain.

In theory, the DMZ was "demilitarized," hence the name, e.g., no military operations, bases, troops, tanks, artillery, etc. on the ground.

The US Rules of Engagement dictated no entry for US troops, no firing into the DMZ, and no expansion of Dollar General stores north of the 17th parallel.

The NVA, on the other hand, went over, under, around, and through the DMZ at will. The marines occupying positions in I Corps south of the DMZ had to act like prom queens on a Friday night. Don't do anything! Just look pretty until the doorbell rings.

And ring it did!

The NVA used its positions within the DMZ to support its operations against US and South Vietnamese troops in I Corps.

I can remember some discussions among the grunts of my platoon – a tactically proficient albeit strategically challenged bunch – about the disposition of the DMZ.

The consensus was to push the NVA out of it, bring in the engineers, plow it, pave it, turn it into a parking lot, and charge the dinks for parking there.

There was even some mention of setting up rest stops to serve Highway Ho. The money made off parking and concessions would help finance the war, after we capitalist running dogs took our cut.

Dengue.   Pronounced, DENG—ee.

A Spanish attempt at the Swahili phrase *ki denga pepo*, meaning "cramp-like seizures caused by evil spirits and lifers."

This was the typical state of a grunt in the field during the rainy season, a flu-like condition caused by feeding the non-malaria-bearing mosquitoes with a grunt's blood.

Symptoms of dengue include fever, severe headache, muscle and joint pain, rash, abdominal pain, nausea, vomiting and diarrhea.

My most pronounced symptom, other than a low- grade fever, fatigue and headaches, was the feeling that red hot needles were being stuck into my back — about as kinky as life in gruntdom got — especially when you realized you can't scream in the dark!

But a slight case of dengue would not get a grunt out of the field. Go see Doc, get some aspirin and GI gin, stop bitchin', and drive on.

Deuce.   To a grunt, this was one of two things.

First, a very low hand in poker if this were his high card. Mathematically impossible with five cards, you say. You should have seen the deck our platoon medic played with! It seemed to include negative numbers, square roots and pictures of US Presidents, "I have a pair of Millard Fillmores."

More commonly, this was a two-and-a-half-ton truck, also called a deuce-and-a-half. The formal nomenclature was "Truck, Cargo, 2 1/2 Ton, 6x6, M35."

Typically the deuce was much beloved by grunts, since its arrival usually meant a ride, re-supply, hot food, mail, or something good ... "Ah! I love the smell of diesel fumes in the morning! Smells like ... mail call!"

Di Di.   Pronounced, DEE dee.

This was pidgin for "leave," "depart," "get the hell out of here."

For example: "Here comes Top. Time to didi!"

Another example: "In six days and a wake up I'm going to didi my ass out of this hell hole."

Di Di Mau.   Pronounced, dee dee MAU.

An emphatic form of Di di, e.g., "Di di mau, babysahn; I'm broke."

Dien Bien Phu, Battle of.   From 13 March to 7 May 1954, the decisive battle of the First Indochina War between the French and Viet Minh.

When I was assigned to Fifth Army staff for planning, the ongoing joke was that the army was always preparing itself to fight the last war. Even worse, in planning to confront the Soviet Union and its Warsaw pact stooges in Europe, the army had skipped over Vietnam and Korea, and was planning for World War II Rédux, this time without the French.

In modeling Corps-level logistics orders and annexes, I was using tech manuals to forecast everything from casualties to toilet paper usage based on statistics which hadn't changed since the 1950's.

I hope the grunts in Desert Storm got good use of the Lucky Strike Green cigarettes included with their C-Rats. Unfortunately, the Andrews Sisters weren't available.

I believe this same strategic myopia affected the NVA. They were looking to recreate Dien Bien Phu under the guise of the Battle of Khe Sanh. However, they made one fatal tactical error; they mistook American Marines for the French.

I guess this screws my hopes of book sales in France.

Dink.   A derogatory and arguably "racist" term for any Vietnamese, but especially for the bad guys. Synonyms were "gook," "slant," "zipper head," "slope," etc.

In late 1968, after cleaning up the mess popularly known as the Tet '68 offensive, "political correctness" was not in vogue with most grunts. They saw no point in being polite, or "correct," to or about the NVA who were regularly trying to kill them, or the ARVN who were not very interested or effective in defending their own country. e.g.:

"Sir! Sir! The dinks are in the wire!"

"Sergeant! That term is racist, and I won't tolerate it in this unit!"

"Great! Fire me and send me home!"

Dink Gunship. This wasn't a piece of enemy equipment, but another example of the myriad and marvelous diversity of the Vietnamese bug fauna.

This was a large, black, flying beetle that made a deep whirring sound when it flew (hopefully) past a grunt's head. The sound was so loud and the breeze of its passing so strong, that guys would return fire thinking that a large projectile just flew by their heads.

The bug itself was rather benign — it didn't bite and wasn't poisonous — as long as it didn't collide with anyone which would require an NTSB investigation.

We were being convoyed down Highway 14 from Pleiku to Ban Me Thuot. My squad was riding in the back of a deuce, the bed of which had been lined with sandbags for protection against landmines.

According to the SOP, one grunt was standing over the cab as a "look out" and the others were supposed to be watching the sides of the road. We did have one guy up, but the rest of us were napping, bullshitting, or just generally screwing around and working on our dirt tan.

The road was in such lousy condition that it was difficult for the trucks to get any speed up without breaking an axle. We did hit one stretch, though, where the trucks were doing around forty and our "lookout" was leaning on the driver's cab enjoying the breeze like a poodle hanging out the window of a BMW in Miami.

Suddenly, his head snapped back and his body flew backward.

We could see no targets but were screaming, "Sniper!" "Ambush!" "Sniper!"

The truck sped up to get out of the kill zone almost tossing us out on the road as it plowed through the pot holes. When we got out of the assumed kill zone, we went to check on our buddy.

The way his head snapped back, we had written him off; no one survives one to the head like that. But there was no blood! He was a bit groggy but okay ... except for the giant smashed bug right in the middle of his forehead.

Indeed, this was the first, and perhaps only, US "casualty" caused by a dink gunship.

Dinky Dau.   Pronounced, DEENK-ee DOW.

Pidgin for "crazy," "insane." The basic cause of the effect of becoming a grunt. "You JOINED the army! What are you ... dinky dau?"

Shades of *Catch 22*. You had to be crazy to do what a grunt did in Nam. If you were crazy, though, you could be discharged out of the army — "section eight." But, you had to request a discharge on grounds of your insanity. But such a request indicates rational thought. Therefore, all such requests were routinely denied... Thank you, Joseph Heller!

"You boocoo Dinky Dau, GI!"

DIP.   Pronounced, DIP, surprisingly enough.

This was an acronym for "Die In Place." It was a term used to describe a highly undesirable assignment or the mental capacity of anyone who'd willingly accept such an assignment.

I was once a DIP, but it was after Nam in Mr. Carter's army.

This was a bit like serving in the Continental army during the revolution, except for the complete lack of political leadership. Like the guys at Valley Forge, though, we had no support for recruiting, no funding for training, couldn't get updated or functional equipment, missed a couple of paydays at the end of each fiscal year, and were up against reputedly one of the largest, best equipped armies in the world, the Soviets and their Warsaw Pact allies.

While the Carter administration eviscerated the defense budget leaving almost no conventional forces on the ground in Western Europe, the Soviets and the rest of the Warsaw Pact boys were staging a massive military buildup and were making threatening gestures toward Austria and that part of Germany they hadn't taken over after WWII.

I was a platoon leader in a light infantry unit in the States whose CAPSTONE mission was to defend some high ground along a ridgeline in the Fulda Gap.

During the "Cold War," the Fulda Gap was a strategically important region between the industrial areas around Frankfurt and the East German border. Since it was an area of low and open terrain, ideal for large-scale operations by armored forces, it was an obvious route for a hypothetical Soviet armored attack against West Germany. The fact that the Russians used to line their T55, T62 and T74 tanks tread-to-tread along the East German border during their maneuvers was a pretty obvious hint of what they were planning.

(We didn't know then that they had drunk so much of their own jet fuel that they couldn't move the things safely or competently).

Under the CAPSTONE concept, the defensive positions for units stationed in the US were already prepared in West Germany. In fact, the units' "heavy" equipment — which for light infantry was mostly trucks, mortar tubes, and anti-tank weapons — was duplicated and stored in warehouses in West Germany. All a unit had to do to deploy was grab personal weapons and hop on a commercial jet.

The downside of this was, since the defensive positions were pre-prepared, they were undoubtedly marked on every Soviet artillery map ever printed.

Then there was the question of what the role of a light infantry company in a Soviet Tank army's axis of advance was!

I actually asked that question during a mission briefing. Here's the Cliff's Notes version of the answer I got from the staff weenie giving the briefing:

1. Since the US TOW anti-tank missile had at least a one klick stand-off advantage over the main guns of the Soviet tanks, we could shoot them and they couldn't shoot us.
2. The main guns of the Soviet tanks could not elevate high enough to engage our positions on the high ground.

This reasoning makes perfect sense if the following apply to the situation.

1. The Soviet tanks will remain stationary beyond the maximum effective range of their own main guns but within the maximum effective range of our TOW missiles. The fact that such a phenomenon had never been observed was obviously not a reason to assume it wouldn't happen during this putative invasion of West Germany through the Fulda Gap. "I sit here, darlink! I no move. Please blow me up!"
2. The rules of ballistics would not apply in this situation. In other words, the Soviet tanks would not situate themselves in a stand-off position where their main guns could in fact engage US positions on the high ground using "indirect fire" techniques.
3. The Soviets would not employ artillery, close air support, and mechanized infantry to support the advance of their armor.

See that! Piece of Cake! Bring on those damn tank armies!

Later, over a few cocktails, I got the staff weenie's jeep driver to spill his guts.

We weren't supposed to win the fight in the Fulda Gap. Our Cav units were supposed to fight a retrograde action back to the Rhine.

We light-infantry types, who could neither defend, nor get out of the way, nor retreat, were expected to be overrun by the Soviet advance. The resulting US casualties were supposed to convince the voters back in the States that they had to get involved in yet another European war.

This would also give the Carter Administration time to build up the armed forces it had depleted in order to fund its domestic programs and ship fresh units over to Europe in time to stop the Russians at the Rhine.

Oh! Did anyone discuss this strategy with our West German allies?

And that, my dear readers, was a DIP mission.

Dog Tags. An informal but general term used to describe a soldier's identity tags.

A dog tag was a metallic rectangle on which was stamped the grunt's name, service number, religion, and blood type. Two dog tags were worn around each grunt's neck suspended on two chains. The longer chain went around the grunt's neck and held one tag; a smaller chain was connected to the longer chain and held the other dog tag.

For OPSEC reasons, grunts taped the tags together so they wouldn't clink when grunts were stealthily moving through the jungle ... as if the clinking of dog tags could be heard over all the other racket they were making. Stealth was not an attribute of a bunch of grunts moving through the bush.

Dog tags were problematic. Their purpose was to identify a KIA. The medic kept one tag and left the other with the KIA. So, dog tags were a constant reminder of what might happen.

Grunts understood clearly the dangers of their jobs and, if the worst happened, they wanted their loved ones to be notified. Despite the anonymous notoriety, no one wanted to end up in a marble tomb in Arlington because they lost their dog tags.

Then again, the dog tag chain was a perfect place to hang a P38 so it wouldn't get misplaced and positioned it perfectly should a can of C-Rat peaches stumbled into a grunt's clutches.

Just be sure the P38 blade didn't open while being worn. I have a few scares from that particular mishap.

Dog tags took on s special significance to grunts once they got home. They meant the grunt survived! So, they were reverently stored in a special place, like a sock drawer or a jewelry box. Every time a grunt saw them it meant, "F' you, Nam ... I made it!"

Domino Theory. A cold-war, geopolitical fantasy of Robert McNamara ... or not?

The domino theory stipulated that if one country in a region came under the influence of communism, then the surrounding countries would follow.

More specifically applied to the war in Vietnam, if the Republic of South Vietnam were to fall to the communist north, the other nations in the region, such as Laos, Cambodia, Thailand, Indonesia, and Malaysia would also succumb.

The domino theory was forwarded by the US government as the predominant strategic reason for the US involvement in the Vietnam war, containing communist expansion into Southeast Asia.

Today, the domino theory is generally sneered at, especially by the left and, I'm sure, by many Vietnam veterans, as a complete charade perpetrated by the Johnson administration, the military, and the "military-industrial complex" to frighten the US into committing resources to Vietnam.

Even good ole Robert "Conus" McNamara has backed off the scheme.

Why?

South Vietnam fell to communism, but none of the other dominoes fell.

Well ... that's not exactly a complete and accurate analysis.

In support of the domino theory, the USSR, China and regional communist governments had a history of supplying aid to communist revolutionaries in neighboring countries. The Soviet Union provided Sukarno with military supplies and advisors; China supplied North Korea and the Viet Minh with troops and supplies; the Soviet Union supplied the North Vietnamese army with rubles, advisors, tanks, and heavy weapons; China supported the Malaysian Communist Party in its insurrection; the North Vietnamese supported the Pathet Lao and Khmer Rouge.

So, the communists were certainly trying to push over the dominoes, but the western democracies were pushing back.

In fact, some have argued that the containment of communist expansion, as explained by the domino theory, eventually contributed to the fall of the Soviet Union and its communist satellites in eastern Europe ending the Cold War.

For the ten years of US involvement in Vietnam, the resources of the Soviet Union and China were focused on that war. A former Prime Minister of Singapore, Lee Kuan Yew, has argued that U.S. intervention in Vietnam, by giving the members of the Association of Southeast Asian Nations (ASEAN) time to consolidate and engage in economic growth, prevented a wider domino effect (*From Third World to First: The Singapore Story - 1965-2000*).

So, perhaps the reason that the dire predictions of the domino theory did not materialize in Southeast Asia was not because the theory was flawed, but because the US bled the Soviet Union and China white in Vietnam.

The fall of Saigon can then be looked at as a Pyrrhic victory for world communism.

For a grunt, this stuff is pretty ethereal and academic.

Some of us might have gone to Nam influenced by the domino theory and the fear of communist expansion.

But that's not why we fought.

We fought for each other.

Donut Dolly.   This was a term to describe female Red Cross volunteers; in other words, a "Red Cross Girl."

The term "donut dolly" has to do with their traditional role since WWI of passing out coffee and donuts to the troops. But, if coffee wasn't enough, they'd also play a hot game of Checkers or Parcheesi.

Grunts only saw their distinctive light blue uniforms on palace guard and in base camps, but donut dollies were always a welcomed sight and truly appreciated by grunts. These were young American women who voluntarily went to Nam to raise the morale of the troops and show they cared, which they did by their very presence.

The grunt rule of thumb for donut dollies was, "Treat her like you'd treat *my* sister, or I'll want to know why you didn't!"

Thanks for your service, Ladies! It's deeply appreciated.

Dragon Lady. An allusion to a character in the comic strip, "Terry and the Pirates," a beautiful but deadly Chinese villainess; this described any somewhat menacing, usually oriental, villainess; e.g. an ex-wife with a good lawyer.

The ultimate Vietnamese "dragon lady" was Madame Nhu, or Tran Le Xuan, who was reputedly pulling the strings of the Vietnamese government from her exile in France. (Did I say "exile"? I'm an American chewing dirt in the central highlands of Vietnam fighting the war while she's a Vietnamese sipping pink champagne in Paris manipulating the war. And she's in exile?).

Another infamous "dragon lady" was "Hanoi Hanna," who made propaganda broadcasts on Radio Hanoi. She was typically more amusing than demoralizing, "They will give you medal, G.I., but only after you ... dead! Mwaa Ha! Ha! Ha!"

Her playlists introduced grunts to the music of Joan Baez, Bob Dylan and many of our other ardent supporters in the entertainment industry back in the world. Her elocution was most impressive — she rarely mispronounced her Rs and Ls — a subject of many bets and betting pools on the bunker line.

Finally, a "dragon lady" was any betel-nut beauty vending her wares down at the water point who had particularly nasty dental hygiene, hence, "mamasahn."

DROS. Pronounced DEE-rohss.

This was an acronym for: "Date of Return from Overseas Service."

For a grunt, this was better than Christmas, better than his birthday, even better than the day he climbed into the backseat of his old man's Chevy with Mary Lou. This was the day he went back to the world; stopped drinking warm beer and iodine-laced water; stopped eating C Rats, canned peanut butter, and tropical chocolate; it was the day he stopped living in a hole, digging, filling sandbags, digging, stringing wire, digging, feeding the sweat bees, digging, putting up with lifer's' chicken shit, digging, cleaning his weapon daily, humping the boonies, digging, going out on LP, putting out the claymores and trip flares, going out on patrol, bringing in the claymores and trip flares, humping a ruck, digging, standing in the rain, getting fried by the sun, yelling back at the F-you birds, wringing out his socks and putting them back on, burning shit with diesel fuel, sleeping in a hootch spooned with two other guys, getting cut to shreds by elephant grass, digging, sleeping with his rifle between his legs, walking point, picking select members of the indigenousness fauna out of his body hair, sleeping with his wet, laced boots on, standing bunker guard three-on and three-off all night, getting hung up in "wait-a-minute-bushes," "standing to" an hour before dawn and an hour after sunset, getting shot at and blown up regularly.

Best yet, it was the day he got his life back; it was the day he started sleeping in a bed, eating hot food three times a day, seeing animals and plants he could recognize — like puppies and birdies and kitties and crab-grass – wearing underwear, drinking cold beer, strawberry thick shakes, and Puerto Rican rum; taking hot showers, using a bathroom instead of a tree, a hole in the ground or a 55-gallon drum full of diesel fuel and old shit, and acting like a normal twenty-year old; it was the day his mom stopped crying and being afraid to answer the phone and the doorbell, and it was the day before the day he got back into the backseat of his old man's Chevy with Mary Lou.

Dung Lai.   Pronounced DUNG-lie.
Pidgin for "Stop!" "Halt!;" and the opposite of "Lai Day!" ... and you better get the difference straight.
Since a grunt would challenge another grunt in English, this was not something a grunt ever wanted to hear on the bunker line at night. On a good day, "Dung Lai!" was followed by a burst of six ... on a bad day, the burst of six came first.

Duster. The M42, 40mm, self-propelled, anti-aircraft gun, an armored light air-defense gun, owned and operated by an obscure branch of the army called Air-Defense Artillery.

Since the dink air power was negligible – except for very large, black, flying water beetles, called by grunts "Dink Gun Ships" – Dusters were deployed mostly in ground defense security roles.

Dust Off.   This describes removing casualties from the battle field by helicopter (that's the "dust" part); e.g. "The seriously wounded were dusted off first."

Grunts will forever have their helmets off for the guys who rode these slicks with giant red crosses painted on their sides right down into the middle of a fire fight to get some injured grunts out of there. Some rotor-heads, God bless 'em, would even monitor the grunt pushes and, if they heard an evac call in the neighborhood, would just go help out.

Most dust offs were accomplished by slicks because, 1) this was the bird most commonly used by medevac units; 2) slicks were usually proximate — for example, the bird used to bring in ammo and water during contact would be appropriated to take out casualties; and 3) slicks were the most common birds in the air.

Like all forms of army life, slick crews could be divided into the good, the bad and the "fugly." There were some slick crews who didn't want to do anything that might soil their aircraft (I once had a very interesting conversation with a crew chief who was somewhat reluctant to take out some of our wounded because of the "mess" he'd have to clean up before he could get to the NCO club that night).

There were other slick crews who'd do anything they had to do to help out when grunts needed it. These guys would practically clear an LZ with their rotor blades despite heavy ground fire to get to the casualties.

The medevac guys who flew around with the big red-cross RPG aiming points painted on the sides of their birds were the latter type. They would put their birds down on LZs that were no wider than their rotor blades if there was a wounded grunt who needed to be evacuated. They were "flying grunts"!

This may be a good place to tell you the "Tale of the Flying Skull."

Although this was not planned as a dust off, it became one. And, if it weren't for the guys of the good ship "Flying Skull," I'm pretty sure I wouldn't be here telling you this tale ... so guys, if you're out there somewhere reading this, give me a call ... I owe you a couple of brews, at least!

For my first mission as a LRRP team leader, I was given a so-called "cake" mission. I was to sit on top of a hill a few klicks west of a brigade firebase and relay radio traffic for the ranger teams working on lower ground.

The division intelligence boys in the Cave of Winds got the idea that this firebase was going to get hit. So, they deployed a "LRRP screen" across the expected avenue of the enemy approach.

From a grunt point of view, if the S2 thought there were bad guys out there, it was a clear signal that nothing was happening. So, we were at best a bit skeptical going into the mission.

Important Grunt Maxim! Even a tale told by a fool can sometimes be true.

On the mission fly-over, I noticed there was an abandoned village next to my objective and an LZ right on top of it. So, I asked not to be inserted there. I was afraid that if there were bad guys in the neighborhood, they would know where my team was if they saw the slick insert us. And, that village made a good hiding place. My plan was to be inserted into an LZ about a klick or so from the hill and hump in.

Other than that, we were preparing for a four-day vacation; just sit on a hill relaying radio traffic. We even packed a few paperback books to fight the expected boredom.

Of course, things never go quite as planned.

On the day of the mission, the insertions got behind schedule and the mission commander, some brigade staff-weenie, didn't want to be out of commo with the screening teams while my team was humping to its position. So, he directed the insertion bird to insert us right on top of the hill where we were expected to stay. Then, we were told not to move off the hill for the duration of the mission.

Now, it was SOP in the rangers that the team leader in the field was also mission commander with the authority to refuse a directive from control if the team leader believed the directive would unreasonably endanger his team. So, theoretically, if I believed that being inserted directly on my position endangered my team, I could have refused the order to stay put and moved to another location.

But this policy was intended for teams operating independently. I was supporting at least four other ranger teams, who would not be able to communicate if I were not in position. That, and the fact that we didn't believe the intelligence that there were actually bad guys in the area, caused me to decide to stay put on that hill.

That turned out to be not one of my better decisions.

That afternoon turned out fine for us. We got under cover, secured a small area, got the long stick up on the radio, and were soon in communication with all the ranger teams and brigade. At one point, I remember leaning back against my ruck, with the radio handset in my ear, reading a Matt Helm novel.

What we didn't know was that an NVA company, hidden in the abandoned village, had watched the insertion and were maneuvering up the hill toward our location.

Now, things in a combat zone are never as neat as war movies or history books make them seem. Fire fights often are won not by doing the "right thing" but by making the fewest mistakes, especially when the proverbial shit has hit the proverbial fan. This "fog of war" principle was one of the things that saved our butts that night.

The bad guys could not be sure whether there had been an insertion. To confuse the enemy, ranger teams often conducted false insertions; slicks would touch and go on an LZ.

The NVA did know that only one slick came down, so the most grunts there could be on the hill was about six guys. They also under-stood that the number of guys on the ground had nothing to do with the potential fire power that could be brought down on them if they were detected too soon — artillery, mortars, helicopter gunships, fixed wing close air support, and anything else that could be dredged up from the very deep bag of US fire support.

Most importantly, they didn't know exactly where we were on the hill. Four guys practicing good operational security can be very hard to find in the jungle.

So, the NVA were moving up on us very carefully. When they thought they were close, they decided to use a technique called "recon by fire," firing on an expected enemy position hoping they would reveal their position by firing back.

Meanwhile, back at the ranch ...

It was early evening and we were just getting ready for some chow. I remember I was working on a can of peaches with my P38 when I heard a hollow "pop" off in the distance. I and my assistant team leader immediately looked at each other ... we knew what the sound was ... a small mortar firing ... the US and ARVN didn't use 60mm mortars ... the bad guys did. Both of us hit the ground; an HE round impacted some yards behind us. It was a signal; we were immediately under attack by small arms fire.

Immediate contact report:

"Alpha Sierra Two Two; Romeo Two Eight; Contact, over!"

"Romeo Two Eight Go!"

"Two Two; Small arms, automatic fire and mortars on my position; Break; Enemy fire at azimuth two eight eight; break; range, one five zero mikes; break; no visible packs; break; request fire mission, over."

"Two eight; wait one."

The inaccuracy of the fire — the rounds weren't "cracking" around our heads meaning they weren't that close — indicated it was a recon by fire.

The good news—they weren't sure where we were.

The bad news — it was still daylight, so we couldn't bring in an extraction bird and we couldn't move across the open ground behind us. We had to slug it out with them at least until dark.

"Romeo Two Eight; Romeo Two Eight; Alpha Sierra Two Two; Over."

"Two Two; Go!"

"Two Eight; negative fire mission; civilian village danger close; Over."

"Two Six; negative; village not occupied; request fire on coordinates Six Six Niner Seven Eight Zero Three Three; danger close; Over!"

"Two Eight; Wait One."

The Rules of Engagement were just about to screw us. Although the village was abandoned, it still showed on our maps. The artillery would not fire that close to a village.

"Romeo two eight; Alpha Sierra Two Six!"

A Ranger buck sergeant is now talking directly to the Brigade Commander

"Two Six, Go!"

"Two Eight; negative on the fire mission; we're getting some guns in the air."

"Roger that, Two Six."

"Two Eight; are you calling for FPF?"

"Negative! No visible enemy."

"Roger; guns inbound; ETA two zero mikes; hang in there!"

"Good copy, Two Six; we got no place to go."

"Two Six, out!"

We were hunkered down on the ground, foot to foot, three-sixty security. The enemy fire was still all over the place. I crawled over to my number one.

"Get everything back into the rucks; as soon as the guns get here and distract their asses we're moving out in that direction."

I pointed back toward the clearing to our rear away from the apparent enemy fire.

"I'm going back to take a look."

I crawled back along a depression to the edge of the woods. I spotted a place where the clearing was only about fifty meters wide. The sun was just about down. I could detect no enemy movement across the clearing. It was about ten minutes before the guns would be on station. I crawled back to my team's position, and we got our heads together.

"Here's the deal. The guns are inbound. We let them work out on the dinks. As soon as it's fully dark we take off across the LZ. There's a narrow spot. Follow me across. As soon as we're across and into cover, we get off this f'ing hill. We'll go a couple of hundred meters due south then jag east 'til we hit a blue line. It should be wet this time a year, so we'll hear it. We follow the blue line downhill. We need to get at least two klicks from here. We'll find a spot to hold up for the night. Tomorrow we either hump back to brigade, it's about eight klicks, or we find an LZ and hitch a ride. But we put as much distance between us and these dinks as we can. I'll tell you when to move. Stay close! Any questions?"

"Yeah! They're getting closer; I can hear movement down the hill now."

"Okay! Do not return fire! If they see muzzle flashes, we're f'ed. If they get close, toss frags on them; but do not return fire until I do!

"Roger!"

The enemy fire was still erratic, but between bursts the sound of bad guys moving through the brush was unmistakable about twenty-five meters down the hill, moving across our front and getting closer. It was almost full dark.

The monsoon at that time of the year arrived around midnight, and the clouds were already building in the west. That would ground all our aircraft. We were running out of time.

"Romeo Two Eight; Romeo Two Eight; this is Dragon One Six; Over!"

It was a chopper; the voice on the radio sounded like it was coming out of the bottom of a barrel with a garage band tremolo sound to it.

"Dragon One Six; this is Romeo Two Eight; Go!"

"Romeo Two Eight; we are inbound to your location; ETA three mikes; you are in sight!"

"One Six! Welcome to the party!"

"Two Eight! You are lit up like a Christmas tree with green tracer 360; over!"

"Say again, One Six; Green Tracer, three six zero; Over."

"That's affirmative; they're all over you."

"Good copy; One Six."

We could hear the birds now. The first one was into his run; we could see the orange flame spurt from his minigun ...it was going to go right through our position.

"Break off! Break off! That's us! That's us!

"Roger!

The fire ceased and the bird flew about twenty meters over our heads.

"Two Eight! We are taking heavy ground fire from all around your location; can you mark your position?"

"Roger!"

We rustled through our equipment looking for a strobe light we had scored from some Air Force guys down in Pleiku for a case of LRRP rations. The light would mark our position in the dark for the gunships ... and for the NVA. I switched the strobe on and held it as high as I dared.

"One six; marker out; identify!"

"Two Eight; negative!"

Shit! The brush was too thick! The gun couldn't see the strobe. I stood up and lashed the strobe to the top of the radio antenna.

"One six; marker out; identify!"

"Two Eight; strobe light!"

"Affirmative!"

The guns started working out on the bad guys! Now was the time to go, but now we knew the bad guys were across our planned escape route and any bunch of bad guys who were willing to duke it out with gunships were determined to get our asses. But staying where we were was a sure loser.

"Okay! Listen up! The gun says the dinks are around behind us, but we got no place else to go. When the guns break off, I'll blow the claymores. Follow me down the hill. If we run into the dinks, we split up. Get though them any way you can and get the hell away from here. Go due east in the morning. You'll hit Highway 14 in about nine klicks. It's a paved north south redball; you can't miss it. You can pick up a vehicle. Go south to the MP check point at Dragon Mountain outside Pleiku. That's our rendezvous.

The NVA had spotted the strobe and were moving up on our position. They were still out beyond our claymores, so we started pitching some frags down the hill to make them careful.

I had one more thing to do before we tried to di di.

"Redleg Seven Seven; Redleg Seven Seven; this is Romeo Two Eight; Fire Mission; Over!"

"Romeo Two Eight! Redleg Seven Seven; Authenticated Alpha Quebec.

"Negative Seven Seven; too damned busy at the moment; check with Two Six for authentication."

"Roger Two Eight; Go!"

"Enemy in the open; location Bravo Lima X-Ray Lima Quebec Oscar Kilo Delta; Danger Close; on my command! Over."

"Two Eight; Negative; we have that plotted as your location!"

"Affirmative Seven Seven; we won't be here; lay it in and fire when I call, over."

"Roger, Two Eight."

This may not end well for us, but I'm going to take a few of the little bastards with me. Then, I heard,

"Romeo Two Eight; Romeo Two Eight; This is the Flying Skull; over!"

It was a bird! But there is no call sign in any CEOI "Flying Skull"!

"Unknown Station! Unknown Station! Clear the Push! We're too f'ing busy down here!"

"That's a Roge, Two Eight! We are inbound to your location; thought you might need a ride!"

"That's affirmative, Skull; this LZ is hot!

"Figured that one out for myself, Two Eight; I'll be there in about one zero; how about turnin' on the lights."

"Roger!"

Back on the horn to the artillery to get them to hang some illumination on the coordinates I had just given them. When the first flares popped, I realized the monsoon had moved in. There was only about a two-hundred-meter ceiling over the hill.

"Flying Skull! Romeo Two Eight over!"

"This is the Flying Skull; Go ahead Two Eight!"

"The LZ runs east to west, about two five zero meters long and five zero wide at its narrowest. We have no wind and about a two-hundred-meter ceiling; Over."

"Roger! No sweat! Got you in sight ... Whoa ... that's one hell of a party you guys got goin' on down there; my ETA is zero five; get packed up and ready to go!"

I pulled my guys together.

"When you hear the slick coming in, blow the claymores and get down to the LZ; keep moving right onto the bird; I'm going to prep the LZ; somebody grab my ruck; give me the M79."

I grabbed the M79 and a few rounds and belly crawled down to the LZ. The clouds had dropped another fifty meters and the artillery flares were hanging above them. The sky was an illuminated ceiling of amber-pink mother-of=pearl; it was bright enough for me to see the wood line surrounding the clearing.

I could see no enemy movement, but I started working the wood line over with the 40mm grenades. Then I heard the bird above the clouds.

I ran into the clearing to bring the bird in as close to my team's location as I could. If the bad guys were going to get me, this was their chance. I was perfectly visible from the entire wood line. I could hear the bird above the clouds, but not see it.

Then the slick swirled through the clouds right over me surrounded by an illuminated orange and pink mist. I looked up at it and right in the plastic foot bubble under the pilot's feet, a human skull was staring down at me.

The bird no sooner hit the ground when my three guys burst out of the woods running toward the bird. I was following in behind them when my last guy just crumbled. I picked him up on my shoulder, ruck and all, and tossed him into the bird. I dove in behind him. The Flying Skull took the air and was in the clouds in less than a few seconds.

I grabbed my guy. "Where you hit? Where you hit?"

But he had retreated to that magic place where shock takes over a mind, so it doesn't have to acknowledge the damage to the body.

One of my guys grabbed me by the shoulder and pointed, "His leg!"

I ripped open his trousers and found a small round black bottomless hole in the middle of his thigh. Dark blood was oozing from the wound; no major pieces of plumbing hit. I felt around his leg; no exit wound. The crew chief tossed me a first aid kit.

"Got to get him to the medics!" I yelled.

The crew chief gave me a thumbs up! I wrapped a tight bandage around the wound: elevation and pressure.

The Flying Skull landed right in the parking lot of the 4th Division Medical detachment. The medics met us when we landed. Luckily, my guy wasn't that badly hit, no bones broken.

When I got back out to the bird, a warrant officer aircraft commander, "The Flying Skull" himself, gestured me over.

"You guys want to go with us for a couple of beers?"

Oh, Hell Yes!

My career road would have probably been a bit less bumpy had I remembered to call in the extraction instead of going with the Flying Skull and his boys to kill a few brain cells with suds. All that brigade knew was one minute we were on that hill up to our asses in bad guys with a slick coming in ... and then nothing.

The chopper crew, who were from the 4th Division Aviation Company, put us up for the night on the division firebase. The next morning, we hitched a ride with a convoy back to brigade.

When I walked into the TOC, my platoon sergeant didn't know whether to hug me or kick my ass. He had no idea what had happened to us.

So, as punishment, I had to go back out to the bush with a flaming hangover to guide a platoon of grunts around the AO.

Of course, by then the NVA were long gone.

I do remember going back into our team's position. In the daylight, I could see that the bamboo and small trees surrounding our position had been sawn off less than three feet from the ground by the enemy small arms fire.

Maybe they were closer than we thought.

And that, ladies and gentlemen, is a "dust off."

E

Elephant Grass.   The grunt name for a tall, evasive, sharp-edged grass found in the highlands of Vietnam.

Elephant grass was an unmistakable sign that all grunts go to heaven because they've paid for their sins humping through elephant grass.

Humping through elephant grass was hell!

It gave no protection from the sun; was as thick as a brother-in-law; and cut any exposed flesh the shreds. Think of "death by a thousand papercuts," and you begin to approach what elephant grass could do to a guy.

Tactically, a grunt had zero visibility while humping through this stuff. The point man, who had to break trail, was blind ... both by the thickness of the grasses as well as by the rivers of sweat washing down into his eyes.

We actually misplaced a point man while humping across an elephant grass field.

One instant he was there in front of us, thrashing and cursing; the next instant he was gone. For a second, I thought I was in some 1950s horror movie where man-eating aliens, who look like plants, land and begin picking us off one by one for snacks.

Fortunately for us, no aliens; unfortunately, we had stumbled across an old bunker complex, which we couldn't see because of the grasses, and our guy literally dropped into an abandoned foxhole without seeing it. Luckily for him, snakeless.

When we finally got to the other side of the elephant grass, the jungle felt like paradise. It usually took a canteen or two of water to replace the liquids we had sweated out crossing through the grass.

Elephant grass was also a litmus test for slick drivers doing an insertion. None of them would land through the grass. The chopped grass would screw up the blades and get sucked into the engines. And there was no telling what was hidden beneath the grass: logs, rocks, holes, punji stakes, the usual stuff.

The good slick drivers would get low enough to blow the grass aside meaning the bird was hovering about six feet off the ground. The grunts exiting the bird could see what they were jumping onto and weren't doing a fifteen-foot free fall with a full rucksack.

The chicken-shit slick drivers would hover about six feet over the grasses and expect the grunts to disembark. That's about a fifteen-foot drop, fully loaded, onto uncertain terrain.

We were being inserted into a cold LZ on the side of a hill. The terrain was covered with elephant grass with about a good twenty-degree slope. As usual, one of our squaddies was in the door with his feet on the runners ready to go. The bird stopped descending a good distance above the grass; the birds rotors weren't even making ripples in the vegetation.

Our guy in the door didn't move, waiting for the bird to get closer to mother earth. The crew chief gave the hand signal to unass the bird; our guy gave the crew chief the one-finger signal that he wasn't amused.

The crew chief unbuckled his safety harness, reached over, grabbed our guy's ruck sack frame, and pitched him out of the bird. Our guy disappeared into the elephant grass as completely as if he fell into a hundred feet of water.

Now we were committed regardless of what the bird did.

Our squad leader was next in the door. As he jumped, he reached over and grabbed the crew chief's chicken-plate and dragged him out of his seat. The last thing I saw of the guy was the soles of his boots disappearing into the grass.

I was next out the door. I plunged through the grass, hit the ground with my feet, and immediately followed my rucksack over my heels down the slope. The worst that happened to me was getting shredded by the grass and getting the wind knocked out of me.

Since I rolled backward, the next guy out of the bird didn't land on top of me. He rolled backward like I did, and we got into a tangle of arms, legs, and equipment a couple of meters down slope.

We were pretty lucky. Some lost equipment, broken radios, a couple of broken bones. None of our armaments got dislodged, armed themselves and exploded. No injuries from weapons discharges.

Our slick driver was so chickenshit that he didn't even land to get his own crew chief back. So we kept the guy.

The old man was a bit surprised, and vociferously dismayed, by this unexpected addition to his headcount. Regardless of what the rotor-head claimed, our story was we saw nothing! He must have unbuckled his safety harness to pitch our guy out of the bird and fallen out. When the old man heard what the rotor-head did to our guy, he was significantly less simpatico to his plight. War's dangerous; shit happens.

We had to clear an LZ in the grass to get our injured out. When the medivac birds came in, and actually landed on the ground, we sent the rotor-head back with them.

There was of course a bit of a field-grade level blowback over this from lifer-land. But we kept to our story and, since we were out in the boonies, the JAG couldn't get any volunteers to come out and take statements. So, the thing blew over (pun intended).

E-Tool.   This was the army entrenching tool, a small, collapsible shovel and pick combination, and a grunt's own personal shovel for those sunny days at the seashore. Unfortunately, the TOE did not authorize a pail, sand, water, umbrella, or suntan lotion ... so dig with what you got!

Most grunt squads carried a couple of real shovels, a pick and an axe, or two, for its construction work. Digging and filling sandbags was more a part of a grunt's life than shooting (thank God!), eating, and most basic hygiene functions.

Em Yeu Anh.   Pronounced, Em yoo ahn (more or less). This was Vietnamese for "I love you!"

This expression usually marked the early stages of a water point negotiation, "GI! Em yeu anh! Five hundred pi!"

F

Fart Cart. This was the most common mode of Vietnamese civilian mass transit other than feet and truck-tire sandals; they were also called "Lambrettas."

This was a three-wheeled, passenger-carrying vehicle, steered with handle bars, and propelled by what sounded and smelled like a lawn mower engine that ate beans and Nuoc Mam. It was like a motor-scooter SUV and was usually packed with more Vietnamese than drunk undergraduates in the bathroom of a cheap motel room in Ft. Lauderdale during spring break.

These things literally "swarmed" in urban area traffic. Deuce drivers would have to pick them out of their tires during motor stables. Often, they were used as ARVN unarmored personnel carriers when these guys commuted to the war.

FEBA. Pronounced FEE BAH, "Forward Edge of the Battle Area."

The FEBA described the front line, the friendly positions closest to the area of conflict.

The FEBA is the area where the opposing forces are engaged in conflict. In other words, good guys on this side; bad guys on that side. Once the FEBA is crossed, shit happens.

This concept may have been useful in past wars, but in Nam, we didn't have one of these. The bad guys were everywhere, in front, in back, and on a bad day, inside.

The closest thing to a FEBA in Nam was the "Bunker Line." Although the inside of the bunker line wasn't the safest of all places, once the wire was crossed a grunt found himself in "anything can happen land."

Most time, nothing happened.

Either the dinks weren't there or they decided they didn't want to play today. But, when they decided they wanted to ruin our day for us, it was nasty.

One of their favorite ploys was to ambush a small patrol, pin them down, and hold them in place. They knew we'd be coming to get our guys out of there. So, they'd set up an ambush across the most like avenues of approach, wait, and ambush the relief force. If their plan worked, they caused a lot of casualties in the relief force, finished off the patrol, and withdrew.

Very bad for morale.

One of our patrols got pinned down in the mountains near the village of Duc Lap. We went out to get them. The old man anticipated the ambush, detected it, and attacked through it. We took our lumps in the kill zone, but we were able to get to our guys before the dinks finished them off.

Not a good day, but it could have been a hell of a lot worse.

May God hold our brothers who fell that day in the palms of his hands, never forgotten by us who survived.

Fire and Maneuver. This was the essential principle of any offensive action.

One element of the advancing force fires suppressing fires on the objective — essentially getting the bad guys' heads down and disrupting their defensive fires.

The other element maneuvers onto the objective.

If either of these two elements was missing, or not executed effectively, many body bags would be needed to clean up the resulting mess.

Due to the terrain and enemy tactics, the nature of combat in Nam was mostly meeting engagement, ambush, and deliberate attack-defense. Many firefights were like the climactic scene in a Western— both sides shooting at each other until one side loses or gives up (which neither the US nor the NVA would do).

This "stand-off" tactic was preferred by grunts because of the superiority of US fire power — hold the bad guys in place and pour in artillery, gunships, and fixed-wing air support. So, grunts were happy to hunker down while calling down fire and iron from the sky on the bad guys until the little buggers bugged.

Sometimes the bad guys were dug in tight and didn't have any intention of leaving, in which case grunts had to employ both fire and maneuver.

The least desired maneuver was a frontal assault, or as grunts called it, a "John Wayne," or "High Diddle Diddle, Right Up the Middle."

This maneuver required overwhelming force on the part of the attacker, an advantage of at least three to one in firepower. Even with this, the attacker is going to take punishment, and one well-sited machine gun in the defense was usually enough to ruin the attacker's day.

Usually, this tactic was reserved for a platoon or more to roll very quickly over a squad or less in a meeting engagement or close ambush.

The more desired form of maneuver, besides asking your date if she had plans for breakfast after a few martinis, was to maneuver around the defender's flank and into his rear.

The maneuvering element would take advantage of whatever cover and concealment the terrain could provide, while the firing element pounded the defenders with everything they had to get them to keep their heads down. Once the maneuver element got around, behind or among the bad guys, suppressing fire was shifted and it became a fist fight.

The NVA had a bad habit of digging bunkers and tunneling — they even hollowed out mountains and built concrete reinforced bunkers and tunnels, à la Iwo Jima, overlooking Highway 14 in the Central Highlands to inhibit or prevent logistics and movement between Kontum, Pleiku and Ban Me Thuot.

All an Arc Light could do is give them a slight headache and spill their martinis. In this situation "maneuver" required many grunts, shovels, tunnel rats, flashlights, C4, and a lot a *cojones*.

Fire Base.   A fire base or fire support base was a military installation designed to provide indirect fire, artillery and motor support, to infantry operating in the proximate area of operations.

A battalion-level fire base usually hosted a battery of artillery, usually 105mm or 155mm, and a section or two of mortars.

A company-sized fire base would normally host its own section of 81mm mortars.

Battalion fire bases also housed the TOC, which tended to make grunts a bit nervous for two reasons: too much brass around — the Battalion Commander, the Battalion Sergeant Major, and a Major or two — and the cluster of antennas surrounding the TOC were prime sapper and rocket magnets.

The good news though, the battalion mess hall followed the TOC around, so the eating was usually good.

Fire bases were also logistics centers for their AO and had a landing pad to accommodate slicks and shithooks.

Grunts typically didn't want the shithooks getting too close to their hootches because their ponchos would be blown into the next AO or sucked into the chopper blades and shredded.

"The Tale of the 2X4 Purple Heart."

My company had just arrived to secure what was to become a "model" battalion firebase which was under construction. There were engineers and construction material on site; the cooks were using immersion heaters to heat C-Rats; a staff-weanie met us on the LZ and directed us where to pitch our hootches.

We were amazed and impressed.

We had just spread out our ponchos to build a hootch when a shithook came down right next to where we were setting up. We scrambled to secure our stuff before it got sucked up into the chopper's rotors.

Next thing I knew, I was laid out across a poncho, and my squad leader was asking me if I was alright.

A piece of construction material, a 2x4 board, became airborne in the shithook's propwash, and this projectile had found the back of my head. Cold-conked, I fell across our ponchos and equipment.

Since I had suffered a concussion a couple of weeks earlier in a firefight where my helmet was killed, our company medic decided my injury was more than aspirin and GI gin could handle. Battalion wanted no part of me, so I was airlifted to brigade, who immediately send me back to division.

So, by evening, I had had a hot meal, a hot shower, issued a set of clean, blue PJs, and assigned to a real bed with clean sheets and a mattress. In other words, except for a headache, a couple of stiches, and a dramatic bandage around my head, I was in grunt heaven.

The next morning, one of the grand and august division staff-weanies, a bird colonel, made a walk-thru inspection of my ward. We were actually instructed to sit up straight, our sheets were forded four inches over the blanket, and we were told that, except for responding to any direct question his lordship might ask, just smile and nod.

Finally, the grand and glorious poohbah made his appearance.

Of course he was leading a parade. To his right, the nurse in charge of the ward with a clipboard introducing each patient. Behind him, pretty much in this order, the hospital commander, an assistant division staff-weanie, an NCO staff weanie with a cardboard box, and a member of the hospital staff with another clipboard.

As his colonelship progressed down the aisle of the ward, he'd stop at each bed and ask a stupidly innocuous question, like, "Where you from in the states, son?" or, "Are you getting enough to eat?" or, "You getting your mail on time?"

We had all been in the army long enough to know that the answer to question one was the name of a state, whether you were really from there or not. For the other two questions, just say, "Yes, sir!"

Then I noticed that, after the "where you from in the states" ritual, the colonel held out his hand to the staff-weanie with the cardboard box, who put something in the colonel's hand. The colonel then pinned a Purple Heart medal to the four-inch collar of sheet, said something like, "Thank you for your service," then moved on.

I wondered briefly how this was going to work out for me. A concussion from shithook-propelled 2X4 was not considered injury from hostile action.

Finally, it was my turn.

"Where you from in the states?" his highness asked.

"New York, sir!" I responded with adequate gusto for a field-grade weanie.

The hand went out; the medal was plopped in; the medal got pinned to my sheet; and "Thank you for your, service!"

And on the next bed.

When the full bird was gone, the guy at the end of the procession, a SP4 with the clipboard, asked, "Name, rank, service number and unit for the orders."

"What orders?" I said low enough not to disturb the colonel's parade. "I don't deserve this! I was hit in the head by a shithook-propelled 2X4."

The SP4 looked at me, "Do you want to tell the Assistant Division Commander he's made a mistake?"

I had been in the army long enough to know the correct answer. "Not me!"

"Me neither," the clerk said. "Name, rank, service number and unit."

When I was discharged from the hospital, I was given the medal in a presentation box and a set of orders. Since I had a week of light duty, I took these over to our company orderly room on basecamp, and asked my First Sergeant what I should do about it.

Top was sure *he* wasn't the guy to tell an O6 he had screwed up, and he was equally sure the company commander out in the field had better thinks to worry about. So Top's opinion was for me to keep the damn medal; if I hadn't earned this time, I had more than enough time left in my tour for Nam to equal things out.

Sure enough, a couple of months later, I was involved in a convoy ambush and got hit by some small pieces of shrapnel in a place I'd rather not mention ... let's just call it my "lower back." Doc removed the dink tin with a pair of plyers and painted my "lower back" with mercurochrome, which hurt a hell of a lot worse than the damn shrapnel. Then he sent me on my way, saying, "You may not want to sit down for a couple a days."

So, in my mind, that pretty much squared the 2X4 Purple Heart

Now, back to the main narrative.

Fire bases would typically be secured by one or two companies of infantry, who manned a bunker line surrounding the TOC, artillery, and mortars, a duty called "palace guard."

This gave birth to the grunt FDR principle, "Firebase Diminishing Returns." Initially pulling palace guard on a fire base was good news for grunts (as long as the grunts didn't have to build the damned thing) — no humping, sleeping in nice, dry hootches, and the bad guys had to come and dig you out for a change.

But, as fire bases became secure, lifers would show up to get their "field time" and qualify themselves for a CIB. So, soon what was once a mini stand down, became a hell of stringing redundant rows of concertina wire, filling sandbags, digging trenches, and burning shit.

When someone made a point about boots being un- shined or some derogatory remark about a haircut or boonie hat, it was time to didi where the lifers wouldn't follow ... any place outside the wire.

Fire bases were typically named either after "the girls you left behind you" like "Jackie," "Mary Lou" or "Nancy;" or they had macho names, like "Eagle," "Steadfast," "Loyal" and crap like that.

Firefight.   Proof that Sherman only had it half right. War is hell, but firefights are a mother f'er.

A firefight is trading small arms fire, not-too-small arms fire, kitchen sinks, and anything else you can get your hands on with the bad guys.

This is the ultimate occupational hazard of being a grunt.

Flak Jacket.   A flak jacket, or flak vest, was a form of protective clothing designed to provide protection from shrapnel and other indirect low velocity projectiles.

Unfortunately, flak jackets did neither, and there weren't many "indirect low velocity projectiles" flying around the boonies except rocks, large flying water bugs, and insults, against most of which flak jackets were quite effective.

But, flak jackets did weigh a lot, and no grunt would hump so much seemingly useless weight. So flak jackets suffered a high incidence of "combat loss" in Nam ... in fact, archeologists will still be digging them up out in the Vietnamese boonies five hundred years from now.

On palace guard, flak jackets often served as tools of harassment by lifers. Grunts would wake up one morning to find a new policy that helmets and flak jackets were to be worn at all times while on the fire base.

When this happened, grunts countered by decorating the flak jackets with various anti-lifer bons mots and irreverent caricatures.

One of my favorites — and this must have taken the artist quite some time to do — was a picture of Snoopy, as the WWI flying ace, flying his bullet-riddled dog house in his leather flying cap with his arm (paw?) extended and his index finger up. Underneath was a greeting to the artist's favorite lifer.

If I tried to reproduce this here, I'd be in more copyright shit than even I could imagine.

FNG.   An abbreviation for "F'ing New Guy;" in other words, a rookie, a "cherry," a grunt-hopeful should he live beyond his three-minute life expectancy.

Some guys did not even want to find out an FNGs name or where he was from. When I was a grunt squad leader with about nine months in-country, we got a chatty cherry who seemed to think it was important that we all knew where he was from, what he wanted to be when he grew up, and the names of everybody in his family.

It was like some war-movie cliché where, right before the big battle, some guy pulls a creased, folded picture of his girlfriend out of his wallet, and starts talking about their plans for when he gets back from the war. Well, you know he's screwed. (I carried a picture of my girlfriend in my ruck. Believe me, it never saw the light of day as long as I was in the field. I didn't believe in "movie fate" but why tempt the gods?)

I remember being a bit grunt-sergeant-grumpy with that young man:

> "Look, Cherry! No one around here gives a shit about you, your girlfriend, or any of this shit. Maybe you haven't noticed, but no one has even taken the time to learn your f'ing name. If you're still around in a month, then we'll think about taking warm showers together. Until then, shut your f'ing mouth, keep your f'ing weapon clean, your feet dry, and keep your f'ing eyes on me and the rest of the guys. If I drop; you drop! If I fire; you fire! If I run, you follow me wherever I go, even if it doesn't make sense, just stay close and shut your f'ing mouth."

That's pretty much the initial lecture in Grunt 101.

One of the major FNG liabilities was this.

Maybe, when you were in high school biology, you learned that, when faced with danger, an animal will do one of two things: fight or flee. If that were true, we'd all be grunts by nature.

The problem is, when faced with danger, an animal is most likely neither to fight nor flee. It will freeze. And that's what produces casualties in a firefight.

To stay alive, a grunt must learn instinctually to return fire and seek cover and concealment simultaneously ... shoot and duck! Even a few seconds hesitation could be fatal.

After the war, I was training infantry recruits in the States. During training, we would run them through what the army called ARTEP exercises, Army Training and Evaluation Program, essentially simulated combat.

We'd run a squad, about ten newbies, down a lane through the woods about a klick long and about 250 meters wide. In the lane, we'd conceal an assistant instructor with a weapon and a few magazines of blanks.

When the trainees came up to the instructor's position, he'd cut loose, "rock 'n' roll," with the blanks. And there were ten trainees just standing there looking around trying to figure out where the fire had come from ... no return of fire ... no one under cover ... ten guys just standing in the middle of the woods rubbernecking, thinking, "Gee! That's interesting. Wonder what's going on?"

You're being killed, you idiots!

Hell! When that guy cut loose with a few bursts, especially when we found an AK47 to play with, I'd start chewing dirt ... almost ten years out of Nam, knowing it was coming, and even knowing he was shooting blanks!

Maybe you've seen this.

There's a scene in the movie *Heartbreak Ridge* where the Clint Eastwood character, "Gunny Highway," cuts loose on his platoon with a loaded AK while they're out running. You see his guys duck a bit, then gape at him with that shocked "What-the-F" look.

That's the last living expression of an FNG in combat. A natural human reaction to unexpected danger and exactly what will get a grunt killed.

(Just so you know, unlike movie Marines, the army, or the real Marines, wouldn't let anyone use live rounds in training. That in itself would be a career-ender. And, if anyone got hurt, ten years in Leavenworth. Good scene, though!)

Here's an old, grunt anecdote, entitled "How to Tell a Grunt from an FNG."

There was a rifle platoon in Nam with twenty-five guys, twenty-four grunts and an FNG. The platoon leader calls them together and says,

"Men, we got a hell of a mission. We're going up against a dink bunker complex. The dinks are dug in; they have machine guns, mortars, RPGs, everything. I wouldn't be surprised if twenty-four of you didn't come back."

After that, there were twenty-four grunts wondering how the hell to get out of the mission, and one FNG thinking, "Gee! I'm really going to miss you guys!"

FO. This is an abbreviation for "Forward Observer,"

This was usually an artillery officer or NCO, who had so thoroughly pissed someone off that he was sentenced to do penance by serving in an infantry unit instead of enjoying the good life with an artillery battery.

The FO's job was to coordinate fire support and call in artillery fire missions in support of grunts.

Sometimes, the FO was an artillery officer who was out in the bush with the grunts because he wanted to do as much as he could to help.

In the summer of 1968, we had such an artillery lieutenant with our battalion. He was a great guy, very proficient but not at all pretentious, and a hell of a poker player.

He made an interesting contrast with our platoon leader, who was one of those officers who considered any questioning of his decisions an attack on his authority. His idea of a "discussion" was to stick his chest out, raise his voice, and remind everyone that he was the lieutenant and the rest of us were there to do his bidding. Unfortunately, he didn't know much, only having been on the line a month or so and didn't seem very willing to listen to his NCOs.

One day, we were coming back to the firebase from a patrol. It was an interesting experience in a number of ways.

First, our platoon leader was technically lost from the time he got outside the wire. So, we just wandered around the woods for a couple of hours looking for stuff he couldn't find.

Let me explain how the army teaches soldiers basic land navigation in those wonderful days before the invention of the GPS.

The basic land nav technique was the straight line and pace method. The azimuth, the direction of travel, and the distance to the objective were calculated from a map in degrees and meters. The azimuth then had to be converted from "map north," a line drawn on a map theoretically intersecting the north pole, to "magnetic north," the direction to the magnetic pole toward which magnetic compasses were likely to point, more or less.

(The compass might be pointing to a steel rifle barrel or some other piece of equipment if these things got too close to the compass when shooting the azimuth. This meant walking in circles — literally - until someone figured out what's wrong ... believe me... it happened).

The azimuth was then "shot" on the ground with the compass pointed in the desired direction toward some easily recognizable land-mark. Then one walked along the azimuth in a straight line for the calculated distance.

The distance was calculated by a "pace man" who measured the distance traveled based on how many of his paces were in a hundred meters. (For me, a hundred meters were 125 paces ... walking across terrain as flat as a lawn with no mud, no jungle and no equipment ... beginning to see the potential flaw in this theory?)

Okay that's the theory. And, it probably would have worked if grunts were navigating across a golf course. But, the mountainous jungle ter-rain of the highlands, through which grunts were typically humping, added some additional challenges.

The first reaction of most grunts when they got into the jungle was mild panic ... not only was it the place where bad guys lurk ... but it was claustrophobic ... a grunt was enclosed by the trees and brush, and he could literally see no more than about twenty meters around himself.

Even after a grunt got over this brief bout of claustrophobic disori-entation, it was obvious that navigating by the "azimuth-straight line—distance" method was impractical in that terrain ... "impractical" here is a euphemism here for "lost."

First, a grunt couldn't get a good landmark in the jungle to stay on azimuth. All he could see were trees and bush, and trees and bush all looked alike in the jungle — especially to a city boy.

Second, no one could walk a straight line through the bush. Even if a grunt wasn't going around trees, bushes, swamps and large reptiles, no one really walks in a straight line. Right-handed people tend to veer left and vice versa.

Finally, distance couldn't be measured by pacing. Pace length varies with terrain and obstacles, which is the essential definition of "boonies."

So, anyone attempting to navigate more than a couple of hundred meters in the bush using the "azimuth-straight line—distance" method was officially and potentially irrevocably "lost," which was ironically pretty close to the basic grunt definition of an FNG Infantry lieutenant.

Before I continue my tale, let me share with you how grunts did navigate in the bush. It was a combination of map and compass with a technique called "navigating by terrain," which I learned in Ranger school and perfected while roaming around the hills and dales of Vietnam with the LRRPs.

The first rule was never go more than about five hundred meters without identifying a definite land mark — something seen on the ground which can be identified with something on a map. These terrain features themselves came in two varieties: point and linear.

A "point" feature was something specific on the map, for example, a hilltop, a lake, a bridge, a building, a crossroad. These features, when found on the map, indicated exactly where a grunt was located. But these features were difficult to find, especially in the bush, and therefore difficult to navigate by.

In the bush, a grunt could be within ten meters of a two-story Cape Cod with an Olympic-sized swimming pool and not see it.

So, when navigating, linear terrain features were more helpful. These were roads, trails, blue lines (steams & rivers), ridge lines, valleys; something that was both obvious and really hard to miss when a grunt was wandering through the bush.

When trying to navigate to a specific point on the map — which was essentially the whole point of the exercise — a linear feature was used to get close to a point feature, a specific location, and the direction of travel was then corrected to find it.

Let me give an example.

I'm a ranger team leader and I've just been inserted into an LZ. I want to get to a hill top, a "point" feature, about a klick east of the LZ. The hilltop should be an obvious terrain feature on the map, but it can't be seen from the LZ.

On the map, I see there's a trail running north/south about 500 meters to the east of the LZ, which should be difficult to miss even for a 2nd lieutenant.

The first leg of my course is to move east as well as I can until I make contact with the trail. Based on how I went around obstacles and the fact that, as a right hander I naturally drift left,

I know I'm on the trail but probably a bit north of my planned intersection. According to the map, the trail crosses a blue line which runs down and along the south side of my hill. This intersection is another point feature.

So, I parallel the trail south until I get to the stream. Now I know that I'm on specific location on the map, the intersection of the trail and stream, which I mark and report in case I need fire support in a hurry; in fact, I have the artillery plot it as a target so I can adjust fire from that point.

I then follow the stream east in an uphill direction until I see my hill to the north (that would be rising ground to my left) and climb the hill. The top is where I see low ground in all directions.

I can verify my position if I can see recognizable terrain features from the hilltop, using a map and compass technique with back azimuths and intersection. Again, I have a specific point on the map, the hilltop, which I plot and report.

Simple, huh? Even a city boy can do it!

One summer, I was up in Fort Drum with a New York army National Guard unit.

An infantry squad had a night mission to do a recon of an "enemy" location. In order to accomplish its mission, the squad had to navigate from their assembly area about two klicks through the woods, find the objective, observe it, and get back to report.

The assembly area and the objective were located on parallel north/south roads about two klicks apart. To the south was a two-lane paved county road; to the north, boonies, swamps and indescribable monsters in the dark.

The macho way of accomplishing the mission would have been along a northern route. There was a ridgeline running due west from the assembly area through the swampy area almost to the objective. If the squad could find and stay on the ridgeline, they would hit a dirt road which would lead them south to the objective. They'd get their feet wet, but that was the most tactically sound approach the objective.

The trick for these city kids was finding the ridgeline and staying on it in the dark.

But, these were mostly weekend warriors, and city kids at that. So, had I been asked, I would have recommended they just parallel their dirt road south (Go that way!) until they hit the highway; parallel the county road west (that would be a right turn at the paved road) until it intersected with the dirt road leading to their objective; then parallel that road north (a right up the dirt road) until they hit the objective.

Not all that tactically sound, but hard to screw up ... even for city kids in the boonies at night.

So, at full dark, the squad took off into the night led by a young buck sergeant. I trailed along at the end of the column.

Initially, I was pretty impressed! They seemed to be taking the northern route and actually found the ridgeline. We bumped around in the dark for about an hour — a little "stop-start" as the leader tried to navigate his way through the bush.

Then the column stopped and stayed stopped; not a good sign because, according to my reckoning, they were at least a klick away from the objective.

After a while, I worked my way up the column and found the patrol leader and a couple of other guys under a poncho with a map, compass and flashlight ... a very bad sign.

They had wandered off the ridgeline, so we were surrounded by water, mud, frogs and snakes ... a very, very bad sign. So, I stuck my head under the poncho and asked, "Do you guys know where you are?"

Now there's nothing like boonies, swamps and darkness to transform a tough city kid into a helpless baby.

"I don't know, sir!" the patrol leader whinged.

I could almost see his lower lip quivering; he had pretty much convinced himself he was going to die in that swamp and never see Broadway again.

"Okay!" I said, "No reason to panic! Look at your map! You have roads on three sides and the redline to the south is really easy to find. Watch this!"

I had them put out the flashlight, come out from under the poncho and we stood in the dark listening. In less than a minute we heard a car running along on the county road to the south.

"That's south!" I said, "Just go in that direction until you hit the paved road! If you get lost, just stop until you hear another car and keep going in that direction. When you hit the road, turn right and keep going until you hit a dirt road ... it's about a klick. Turn right again, you'll find the objective about 500 meters up."

My plan was to let them go on their way through the swamp. I knew the squad had a quagmire between themselves and the county road and nighttime swamp swimming wasn't part of my plans for the evening. I intended to stay nice and dry and get back to the starting point by going back along the ridgeline.

But the squad leader was pretty sure he didn't want to move around in the scary, dark woods, so I wound up leading the squad through the swamp ... a nice pool of northern New York State winter melt water about four feet deep ... down to the county road.

But that, my dear children, is how land navigation was done before the GPS was invented. So, let's get back to my platoon leader's wandering around the bush in Nam.

As I said, the platoon leader was an "azimuth—straight line—distance" guy. And, of course, he didn't find a damned thing he was supposed to. He of course blamed it on the maps being out of date ... someone obviously moved the hill he was looking for and neglected to tell the USGS ... clever devils, those NVA.

On the way back ... at least we thought it was the way back ... his azimuth took us through the biggest concentration of wait-a-minute bushes I had ever seen. I looked back at him and signaled we should go around them. He just looked down at his compass and pointed me straight through them.

I didn't get more than three feet into the thicket before I was hung up like a fly on a spider web. That's when he decided to take the detour but left me dangling in the thorns until some guys from my squad helped me cut myself out.

Since our return leg was taking about three times longer than our outbound leg, we were starting to get a bit fretful.

At one point we stopped. The platoon leader, the platoon sergeant and the artillery FO were huddling around a map when we heard a "pop" in the distance.

"That's our mortars!" announced our fearless platoon leader. "We got about a klick to go in that direction."

Then he and the platoon sergeant walked away.

The FO, who was holding about half my pay from our last poker game, called me over with a rather enigmatic smile on his face. He pointed to a spot on his map that was right next to our firebase.

"We're right here!" he said, "That pop wasn't a mortar; it's a peanut butter frag going off in the garbage sump. So, be careful. You're about to hit our bunker line."

Sure enough, I went about a hundred meters through some brush and was staring at our bunker line, which was staring right back with a bit of a surprised look and an M16 pointed right at me ... not a desired reaction from a nervous, keyed-up grunt on bunker guard.

We lost the FO and one of our riflemen a couple of days later to a "friendly fire" incident. I was off the firebase on a night LP at the time.

What we think happened was one of our mortar rounds hit a radio antenna over the TOC and exploded above the firebase ... an airburst.

Being out on patrol probably saved my life; my hootch was destroyed by shrapnel. But the FO was hit while he slept in his hootch. He was conscious when they dusted him off, but he didn't make it back to the aid station.

Bobby Ross was a good man and a friend ... a good grunt despite being a "cannon cocker."

A quick word about "friendly fire" casualties.

First of all, there is no "friendly fire" in a combat zone.

Once a weapon is fired, it isn't friendly, has no allegiance to any side, and will do what it is designed to do to anyone who is unfortunate enough to get in its way.

Nor does a "friendly fire" incident necessarily mean that someone screwed up.

Combat zones are by their nature dangerous places, and anyone who wants to witness the workings of "Murphy's Law," "chaos theory," and the grunt concept of "Wrong Place Wrong Time," ought to observe a firefight.

Once the first shot is fired, it's confusion and mayhem with thousands of deadly projectiles flying around. If a grunt runs into his own covering fire, he's just as dead as if he were hit by hostile fire. But he died doing his duty; in army-speak, in the "Line of Duty" (LOD).

Anyone killed while doing his or her job in combat died LOD. That's what the army tells, and should tell, the soldier's family.

In fact, I know of instances where a soldier was killed shirking duty, and the army still reported his death LOD to spare those who loved him the added heartbreak of having to know he died in such a manner.

Anyone — whether in the "pursuit of truth," or to discredit the military, or to create dissatisfaction with some mission the military is conducting, or to gain some advantage in an election, or to pursue some ideological goal, or to sell newspapers and advertising space — who exacerbates the tragedy of a soldier's LOD death by making a point of its having been caused by "friendly fire," is a REMF ... with emphasis on the "F."

Until our next poker game, Bobby! It's my turn to deal!

1LT Robert Leslie Ross
B BATTERY, 2ND BN, 9TH ARTILLERY, 4TH INF DIV,
USARV
Peabody, Massachusetts
May 17, 1947 to August 22, 1968

SP4 Fredfor Edwards
A COMPANY, 2ND BN, 35TH INFANTRY, 4TH INF DIV,
USARV
Effingham, South Carolina
October 07, 1947 to August 22, 1968

Foo Gas.   This was home-made, bootleg napalm used for "booby- traps" in a static defense.

Recipe: put some gasoline, "Mo Gas," in an old ammo can; mix it with flour to thicken; liberally add old ammo and other metallic odds and ends; place the ammo can out in the wire; bury and camouflage, and at the appropriate moment — optimally while a bad guy is standing over it — ignite it with a trip flare or a claymore.

Four Deuce.   A grunt term for the M2 4.2 Inch (120-mm) mortar.

The four deuce guys were pretty much on top of the 11 Charley, "mortar grunt," food chain. These babies were "battalion-level" assets and could fire a 120 mm high explosive or Willy-Pete round out almost three klicks. It was great to know these guys had your six.

Since the four deuce was a battalion-level asset and fired a round, which was too big to hump without a deuce or a couple of shithooks, grunts didn't have to hump their luggage.

Considering the amount of scunion a four-deuce section could bring when a grunt needed it, grunts loved 'em.

FPF.   This is an abbreviation for "Final Protective Fires."

FPF were used defending a position when the bad guys were in the wire and coming hard. If FPF fail, it's a fistfight.

Any unit calling "FPF" had priority for fire support in its AO — close air, naval gunfire, artillery, mortars, machine guns, small arms, short arms, kitchen sinks, bed pans, P38s, and church keys.

This was the ultimate "danger-close—deep-shit" situation for a grunt. The "final" in final protective fires is about as final as it gets this side of the River Styx.

FPF are called when a well-planned and executed deliberate attack slugs it out head-to-head with a well-planned and executed deliberate defense. In other words, irresistible force meets the immovable object with determination, firepower and balls.

The NVA typically tended to avoid direct assault because of the devastating effect of US fire power on any enemy troop concentrations; they favored ambush, infiltration, meeting engagement, siege, defense and catch us if you can.

But anytime the NVA did make a direct assault on a US position, they believed they had the overwhelming numerical superiority to be successful, a minimum of five to one, because the US army wouldn't break, had no place to run, and would light them up and smoke them like a cheap cigar.

Bottom line, if you had the NVA in the wire, you knew you had a lot of determined, motivated and well-trained bad guys closing in on your ass, and they wouldn't go away until they had it or you convinced them it wasn't worth their while.

In planning a defense, every weapon in the unit is given a "sector of fire" which is usually diagonally across the front of the defensive positions adjacent to the position of the weapon assigned. So, basically a grunt is covering his neighbor's front without having to expose himself to hostile fire to his front. This takes a little getting used to because a grunt has to trust that the guys on either side of his position are doing their job, or he is going to meet some interesting and deadly people ... quite suddenly...

Optimally, the platoon's M60 machine guns are positioned on the platoon's flanks and have interlocking fire across the entire platoon front. When FPF are called, the M60s traversing and elevation mechanism is locked into the pre-determined FPF position, and the gunner fires a burst which ends when one or more of the following conditions apply: no more standing bad guys in front of the friendly positions and cease fire is called; the machine gun is destroyed; the machine gun crew is down and no one can get to the gun; the barrel, the spare barrel and the spare, spare barrel have melted.

One of the most amazing and strangely comforting things for a grunt during FPF is when the mortar section drops HE rounds right in front of the friendly positions. In FPF. the mortars typically fire from directly behind the defensive positions with their tubes at maximum elevation — almost straight up. The tiny charge used to propel the round sounds like a party favor when it comes out of the tube, up over the bunker line, and down on the bad guys in about FIVE seconds flash to bang.

The other typical mission for the mortars during a night attack —and they almost all were because the NVA didn't work the dayshift very often — was to hang flares over the battle area. These were white parachute flares that popped, whistled, and hung in the sky like bizarre Christmas decorations. The smoke in the battle area seemed to glow and everything in the kill zone cast long distorted shadows ... oops! ... went Coleridge on you for a second.

FPF are about as scary as things could get in a very scary place. The closest thing FPF could be related to is an action movie when the special effects guys blow everything up, except:

- There are no huge, red clouds of flame. That's a gasoline explosion used in movies. HE rounds actually explode black and brown with very little flash depending on the color of the soil, vegetation, and the flesh consumed by the blast. The only noticeable colors in the battle area are the red star clusters signaling the FPF, the smoke grenades obscuring the kill zone, the dirty OD and tan of the NVA uniforms, the red wet clouds of armaments hitting flesh, and the green star clusters signaling cease fire (if a grunt is still around to see it).

- There are an incalculable number of small arms rounds in a very restricted area in a very short time — the whole point of FPF. These are actually visible as gray-black, fast-moving blurry lines that shred any flesh they encounter.
- The taste the cordite is mixed with the smell of fear, sweat, shit, smoke, piss, blood and meat.
- The sounds are of explosions, bugles, whistles, curses, screams, sobbing, and 7.62 shorts breaking the sound barrier with an explosive whip-crack as they tear past your head (hopefully).

A couple of years ago, a friend of mine took me to see *Saving Private Ryan*. After the movie, she asked me if that was what combat was like.

She seemed shocked when I told her no, combat's a hell of a lot worse.

"How can it be worse than that?", she asked.

"Simple," I said, "You know you're getting out of the theater alive, and you can't smell anything!"

Other than that, *Ryan* is about as real as it gets without ending up in a body bag.

Frag.   This is slang for a fragmentation grenade, also called a "hand grenade" because it was deployed by hand i.e., thrown, i.e. Duh!

On exploding, the frag released shrapnel, sharp pieces of the casing and serrated wire "fragments," hence the term "frag." Casualties were caused by concussion and shrapnel.

There were two types of fragmentation grenades used in Nam, the regular "pineapple" shaped frag and a round "baseball" frag, under the theory that grunts could throw baseballs more accurately than pine-apples. Typically, they could, except the guys from Hawaii who could put a pineapple ... never mind ... I wasn't there ... I just heard stories.

For those of you who depend on Hollywood for an understanding of combat, frags were smooth, not lumpy, and when they exploded they didn't destroy entire buildings in huge red flames — that's a Hollywood, special-effects, gasoline explosion.

The maximum effective range of a frag was as far as you could throw it with a fifteen-meter blast radius ... in theory ... but since most theories didn't work in combat, and in the jungle a grunt couldn't see more than a few meters, five to ten meters was usually the best you got.

For those of you who have never read The Anarchist's Cookbook, here's how these things worked.

A detonator mechanism sat on top of the frag.

A thin metal handle called the "spoon," held the detonator down and in turn was held in place by a cotter pin with a large, round metal ring through it.

A grunt placed the frag in his throwing hand with his thumb over the spoon (all frags were "right-handed," so a south paw had to hold the frag upside down in order to get his thumb across the spoon).

A grunt placed the "pointer" finger (that's the one used to point at things, not the one used to salute lifers) of his other hand through the ring attached to the cotter pin and pulled the cotter pin out.

When he removed his thumb from the spoon, or just threw the grenade, the spoon was flung aside by a spring which allowed a spring-loaded triggering device to strike the head of the timed fuse, igniting it.

The fuse would ignite the main charge in five seconds and blow all sorts of nasty stuff at the bad guys.

The five seconds delay was according to the government contractor who got the contract by being the least cost alternative. In other words, grunts didn't count to four before throwing the damn things but didn't throw it too soon either because the bad guys had a real nasty habit of picking up unexploded grenades and throwing them back.

You might have noticed that nowhere in this description did I mention or suggest that the pin be pulled out with the teeth, like all the movie heroes do. There's a good reason for that ... your teeth would pop out and the pin would stay in the grenade.

Grunts carried a bunch of frags, at least four strapped to ammo pouches and a few more attached in various places to their web gear, jock straps, and underwear.

Grunts would bend the cotter pins and strap or tape the spoon down so it could not be pulled out by accident. This may sound counter-intuitive because a grunt would have to un-strap, un-tape' and un-bend the pin before pulling it. But the next-to-last-thing a grunt wanted to have happen while humping through some thick bush with a bunch of frags strapped to his body is to hear the "pop" of the fuse igniting. This could really ruin his day unless he could drop his ruck and all his equipment and run ten yards through the bush in less than four seconds.

This could be done ... believe me!

But the last thing a grunt wanted to have happen with frags is to get into a nighttime firefight and hear the guy next to him pop a frag, hear a "thump" in the dark, and then his buddy says, "Oh, Shit!" That would clear a bunker faster than a Ham & Lima Bean fart.

Grunts also used the term "frag" as a verb meaning to engage a target with a frag, e.g. "Frag his ass!"; or to assassinate a superior, e.g. "His men fragged him."

I'm going to take some time here to speak to this last meaning because much has been made of it, especially in movies, rumors, claims, slanted journalism, ideologically biased academic research, and urban legends of combat in Nam.

First, let's take a look at the tone and purpose of what has been published about "fragging."

A university researcher at Texas A & M University claimed the army knew that at least six-hundred officers had been murdered by fragging in Nam. The argument claimed further that the army also knew that 1,400 others had "died mysteriously." "Consequently," the report concludes, "By early 1970, the army [was] at war not with the enemy but with itself."

I was still a grunt in Nam in the early 1970s and the army I was in was not "at war with itself," but was still "doing the impossible for the ungrateful" against a determined and well- trained enemy. So, I suspect that both the statistics and the claims in this argument are somewhat overstated to make some point.

The US army Center for History mentions "fragging" in its chapter on "The U.S. army in Vietnam:"

> As American forces were withdrawn by a government eager to escape the war, the lack of a clear military objective contributed to a weakened sense of mission and a slackening of discipline. The short-timer syndrome, the reluctance to take risks in combat toward the end of a soldier's one-year tour, was compounded by the "last-casualty" syndrome. Knowing that all U.S. troops would soon leave Vietnam, no soldier wanted to be the last to die. Meanwhile, in the United States harsh criticism of the war, the military, and traditional military values had become widespread. Heightened individualism, growing permissiveness, and a weakening of traditional bonds of authority pervaded American society and affected the army's rank and file. The army grappled with problems of drug abuse, racial tensions, weakened discipline, and lapses of leadership. While outright refusals to fight were few in number, incidents of "fragging"— murderous attacks on officers and noncoms—occurred frequently enough to compel commands to institute a host of new security measures within their cantonments. All these problems were symptoms of larger social and political forces and underlined a growing disenchantment with the war among soldiers in the field. (US army Center of Military History.
>
> (American Military History. Army Historical Series. Chapter 28, "The U.S. army in Vietnam." 4 February 2009: http://www.history.army.mil/books/amh/AMH-28.htm)

This argument presents "fragging" as if it were part of a general decline in army discipline reflecting a general decline in social mores of the country as a whole. Further, it suggests that "fragging" was a phenomenon that existed in the context of the army's expected withdrawal from Vietnam in the early 1970s as if "fragging" were only part of "last casualty" and "short timer" anxiety.

I suggest that this argument may "understate" the issue.

Now that I have the "bracketed" issue in "academic" and "popular" writing, let me share some "anecdotal" evidence based on my experience. I'm going to share three stories with you: "the fragging that never was"; "the lifer's black spot"; and an actual fragging that occurred in a division base camp in 1970.

"The Fragging That Never Was"

I was with an infantry unit in 1969, which got a new company commander, and within a month the grunts in the command despised the guy. This captain was a "glory hound" with little regard for the safety and welfare of his men. For example, we were operating in the highlands west of Highway 14 on a sweep of suspected enemy locations. While climbing toward an objective, it became obvious to the point element that we were directly approaching an NVA bunker complex of unknown size. Experienced NCOs recommended that the commander slow his approach and send some scouting elements forward to check out what was out there before the entire company stumbled right into a well-fortified NVA defensive position. Our fearless leader, however, rejected this advice because he was afraid that it would give the bad guys an opportunity to "get away" ... most of us were afraid they didn't want to get away. Unfortunately, the point guys were right. There was a major NVA bunker complex right in our axis of advance. The good news was that the bad guys had already left. "Captain Courageous" was pushing us forward so hard from behind the forward elements that I almost tripped over one of the bunkers, they were so well camouflaged. We did find a nice little weapons cache and our brave commander made sure he got his picture in Stars and Stripes holding his new-found toys.

Another one of this moron's pernicious little tricks was sneaking up on his own defensive positions at night to see if he could catch someone sleeping. Now sleeping on guard was a major "no-no" and, if caught by a grunt NCO, the heavy-eyed wrongdoer would get his ass soundly kicked. But no one in their right mind would sneak up on a grunt at night, even from the "friendly" side ... that's exactly what an NVA sapper would try. And we were never sure what our fearless captain's motivation was: to improve security or to build up his Article 15 statistics to show battalion what a strac unit he was running.

My personal experience with this moron was not positive.

I was getting ready to go before the battalion promotion board for my sergeant stripes and without telling me … I found out from the battalion Sergeant Major while waiting for my turn to be boarded … the captain took me off the promotion list. He claimed "he didn't know me that well" despite the fact that I had been an "acting jack, a sergeant E4, for the las four months and the former CO, for whom I had worked six months, and the company First Sergeant recommended my promotion. Our merry moron had been assigned to the company less than a month! Luckily for me, the First Sergeant fixed it. I passed the board and got my stripes.

Then, when after ten months on the line, I extended my tour for six months to go to the rangers and by Reg was supposed to be released to my new unit, he refused … even after the S1 directed him to release me.

The only thing I could figure is 1) the guy didn't like me (feeling absolutely mutual) and 2) I was in charge of his "personal security squad" (I never claimed that the guy was smart). He had actually detailed a rifle squad to do nothing else but protect his ass … act as his bodyguard … and he put me in charge of it! I was never sure who I was supposed to protect him from … the bad guys or us.

The unit was humping along Highway 14 south of Kontum at the time. We had no sooner pulled into our night laager when the Battalion Commander and the Battalion Sergeant Major showed up at our location in a quarter ton (jeep). Ten months on the line in Nam and I had never seen anything like this before! You usually didn't put that much brass in one jeep driving around the countryside. The Sergeant Major ordered me to "collect my shit and get into the jeep," while the Battalion Commander had an unpleasantly private "conversation" with our fearless leader.

Here's the point of the story.

In all my time in Nam, I never saw a field infantry leader who was so universally despised by his unit. Every grunt knew that the guy had no regard for his men; they were just a means of furthering his career. And most grunts were convinced that, sooner or later, this moron was going to get somebody, or a bunch of somebodies, fed up. But no one even considered raising a hand against him.

Ironically, the way he used to sneak up on grunts at night, someone could have easily blown him away or dropped a frag on his ass and said, "I thought he was a dink!" and no one would have thought twice about it ... except "stupid is as stupid does."

But no one did.

It simply was not what a well-disciplined unit of grunts did. We wouldn't have shed tear one if the bad guys got him, but we were damned if we were going to do their dirty work for them.

In well-led infantry units, guys like this are detected fast and moved out. The Battalion Commander eventually relieved him "without prejudice," thanked him for his service and assigned him to some staff-weenie position where he couldn't do much damage.

"Fragging" was never considered when the "system worked" — it's called leadership!

"The Lifer's Black Spot."

You may remember in Robert Louis Stevenson's novel, *Treasure Island*, when pirates had doomed one of their own to death, they sent him a "black spot" as a warning. Pretty ineffective too, as I remember. Long John Silver got his black spot in the first half of the book but was still able to stump off over the horizon (row off, more accurately) at the end of the story ... but maybe that was the point ... don't kill someone when you can make him just go away.

In late 1968, there was a lifer who took up residence in a battalion combat trains area near Ban Me Thuot. Although this guy was technically assigned to a line company that was out humping the boonies, for whatever mysterious army lifer-lore, he never joined his company ... could be he wasn't physically able (humping the bush is a young man's game), or the commander didn't want him out there (he might disrupt a good leadership team), or he was just scared shitless like the rest of us but had enough pull to avoid being sent to the field.

In the trains, he declared himself the "field first sergeant" and started screwing around with all the enlisted guys he considered "lax and sloppy," which was just about all of them.

Now, in this trains area there were a bunch of grunt NCOs whose job was "re-supply" — an army euphemism for pushing needed supply through the chain and scrounging whatever their units in the field needed through the informal army logistics process called "re-allocation."

These guys had been sent back out of the field for various reasons — recovering from wounds or disease, one firefight too close to the edge — whatever — but they all were aggressive, dedicated, and shrewd enough to work the ash and trash to their unit's benefit. These guys were responsible directly to their own company commanders but pretty much "played the game" in the rear area and helped each other out.

These were the guys this lifer decided to really focus on. He started with the regular lifer crap ... boots, haircuts, formations, shaves, police calls ... then that escalated to restrictions from going into town ... and the grunts, although they recognized that this guy was himself a shirker, pretty much ignored the chicken shit they could and absorbed the chicken shit they couldn't ignore.

Then the lifer started on the babysahns.

A bunch of babysahns hung out with the grunts on the air-strip where the slicks came in. Initially, they went there to sell cokes, trash, and trinkets to the GIs, but after a while the re- supply grunts "adopted" them.

This was pretty typical when grunts mixed with kids. The grunts missed their families and being Americans, were naturally protective of children.

After a while, the babysahns and the grunts just hung out with each other ... kind of a grunt "nuclear family" and combat day-care center. The grunts even had pet names for the kids: "VC," "Dragon Lady,"

"Hobbit;" and the kids called the grunts by their *noms de guerre* ... "Short Round," "Hippy."

The kids even called one of the grunts "Ho Chi Minh." It happened like this:

>"Hey Babysahn! You VC"
>
>"No way, GI! Me VC, you Ho Chi Minh!"
>
>*Et Voilà!*

One day this lifer began to focus his toxic attentions on the kids. His "official" reason was that they were a "security" threat. Duh! Why did he think the grunts called one of the kids "VC"?

But it became apparent to the grunts that his real reason was some combination of despising Vietnamese, hating kids, and loathing the fact that being with the kids softened some of the homesickness for the grunts.

At first, the grunts complied somewhat maliciously with his demands; they even hid the kids when he came around. But, after a while, even lifers get it.

So, one day he came out to the strip with his M16 and threatened to kill the kids! Although the grunts would not allow him to do that, he scared the shit out of a bunch of little girls ... not an easy thing to do with children who had grown up in the midst of a very messy war. He destroyed their merchandise — the cokes and trinkets — which was their livelihood and beat one of the kids up pretty badly when she tried to protect her stuff.

That was it for the grunts!

The inherent frustration of not being able to do anything to protect these kids was bad enough, but the grunts wouldn't stand by watching another GI abuse them.

So, a meeting was held that night over a few beers to discuss what was to be done about this guy. Quite frankly, fragging his ass was mentioned, but immediately rejected; again, grunts were unwilling to harm their own, even "lifers." But it was decided to send this lifer the "black spot."

Here's how it was done.

A frag was obtained, not much of a trick in a place where Class Five (army term for ammo) was stockpiled. The fuse was removed, popped and replaced. The frag was then placed in the lifer's hootch.

To the casual observer — and believe me if you were to run across a frag with the hammer down, your relationship with it better be "casual" — it appeared that the only reason the grenade didn't explode was because it was a dud.

Message sent, over! Message received, out!

The XO got the lifer out of the trains, never to be seen again.

The point here should be fairly obvious. The concept of "fragging" was familiar enough that it could be considered, and the use of the seemingly inert frag could invoke it. The obvious message was, "the only reason you're alive is because you were fragged with a dud", or "this is a warning of what could happen to you unless you change your evil ways." Also, grunts only resorted to the threat of fragging when the lifer began harming the children; what he did to the grunts themselves was ignored. Finally, at whatever point that grunts might seriously consider fragging a superior, this wasn't it.

In fact, it illustrates the American soldiers' resistance to committing such an extreme act. Scare the shit out of a shamming and shirking lifer who richly deserves it ... no problem ... kill the SOB ... not likely.

Finally, good leadership prevents the perceived necessity of extreme actions. The XO finally got it and realized the lifer was the problem for that unit ... the "black spot" only served to dramatize it!

"Short Timer Base Camp Blues"

Finally, let me tell you the story of an actual fragging of which I was almost the unintended victim.

I left country in early 1970. Before heading down to Binh Hoa to catch the "Freedom Bird," I had to "out process" on a division firebase near Pleiku.

On my last night in country, a buddy of mine, a mess sergeant for my original infantry battalions, let me sleep in his hootch because he had to run the mess hall that night.

Man! I was in grunt heaven. I was a little buzzed from the beer guys had bought me as a farewell, and I was sleeping under a roof with my boots off, on a nice fat air mattress, wrapped in my poncho liner.

I just didn't realize how close to grunt heaven I almost came.

During the night I was blown out of my cot by an explosion right next to the building. I thought it was incoming and ran out of the building bare-foot and dove into the nearest bunker.

But we weren't taking incoming; there were no more explosions. So, I left the bunker. Outside, I found a KIA lying next to the building where I had been sleeping – in fact, right underneath the window of my room. He had been killed by some sort of explosion; it wasn't pretty.

Here's what had happened.

The mess sergeant, whose hootch I was sleeping in, was having a lot of trouble with one of his cooks. This guy wasn't a cook by training but was a grunt reject.

This may sound strange to civilians considering the nature of grunt work, but an infantry unit in Nam wasn't a dumping ground for all the army's and society's misfits and rejects. In fact, if grunts were convinced that some guy couldn't be relied on, they got rid of him.

Now, in Nam you can't get fired or quit ... or many of us would have tendered our resignation on the spot ... but when some guy was tossed off the line, the army found him some other "useful" work for him to do in Nam.

The mess hall was a common solution. So, this guy found himself assigned as a "cook." Since he wasn't trained to cook but was a natural-born screwup with a piss-poor attitude, and a drunk, the mess sergeant was always down on him to get any work out of him.

So, on the night in question, this psycho disguised as a cook got himself completely fed up on some handy hallucinogen. In the midst of his walking delirium, he decided to wreak his revenge on the mess sergeant, who had been making his life a misery by insisting he work, by fragging him in his hootch while he slept.

There were a couple things wrong with the plan.

First, his intended victim wasn't sleeping in his hootch — I was.

Second, there were screens on the windows, so a frag couldn't be thrown in from the outside.

Third, the moron was much too fed up to be playing with frags.

But there are few things in the world as persistent as a psychopath.

Our hero got himself a frag, armed it, and tried to throw it through the mess sergeant's window. Fortunately for me, he missed; unfortunately for him, he hit the side of the building and the frag bounced right back on him ... so he fragged himself.

They say God loves drunks and Irishmen and I was hitting on all pistons that night ... my last night in Nam.

So, if someone wrote an article claiming that in Nam a drunken psycho attempted to frag an NCO, I'd have to agree. But in almost two-years of line combat experience in Nam, I neither saw a grunt attempt an act of fragging nor met one who claimed to have actually fragged a friendly.

Did guys, after a few beers, talk about a guy, who knew a guy, who said he knew a guy, who fragged someone? Yep!

Did these things happen? I didn't witness any, but I imagine it's possible.

But, I also imagine there were "fraggings" in Korea and World War II when grunts believed some bozo (my apologies to the clown), who couldn't find his ass with both hands in a phone booth, was about to get them all killed by ordering them to do something even the FNG knew was suicidally stupid, and the leadership system, that was supposed to prevent these guys from being in a position for which they had no technical, emotional, or psychological qualifications, had broken down.

Remember! We're talking a "high stakes game" here; you can't recover from being killed!

But you don't see "fraggings" in WWII movies! Hollywood reserves that scene solely for Vietnam grunts. I believe such a selective use of this convention is more the antiwar "Vietnam grunts were psychos and druggies" obsession than an accurate depiction of anything that happened there.

That's my story, and I'm sticking to it!

Besides, I don't remember meeting any university researchers or army historians out in the boonies ... so as far as I'm concerned, their stories are more anecdotal than mine — I was actually there at least.

Free Fire Zone.   A Vietnam-war urban legend.

It was reputedly a specifically designated area into which any weapon system may fire without additional coordination with the authority that established the Rules of Engagement.

This was a mythical place in the combat zone where all Vietnamese were considered "bad guys" and could be engaged with deadly force without positively identifying them as "hostile."

The "free fire zone," like the civilian concept, "the real world," was often mentioned but never experienced. The use of deadly force, contrary to the rules of engagement, was always a court martial offense for US personnel.

Even in the bad old days of the early stages of the Tet '68 counter offensive, while grunts were trying to dig the NVA out of their hidey-holes in Dak To and Kontum and to push them back across Highway 14 in the highlands, and grunts knew there were no friendlies in the neighborhood, there were no "free fire zones."

One time, a grunt point man was going down a trail in an area where the army knew there were no "friendlies." Suddenly, he had a "meeting engagement" with a Vietnamese woman wearing nothing but fatigue trousers, sandals, a headband, and a brassiere, humping a large rucksack and carrying an AK.

The grunt froze: Woman = Non-Combatant = No Shoot; AK = Enemy Equipment = Shoot; No Formal Uniform = Civilian = No Shoot; Woman in Bra = Hot to a Nineteen-year-old = WOW!

Too many conflicting signals mobbing a teenaged boy-brain made him freeze.

The woman didn't; she raised her AK to fire!

Luckily for this kid, his lieutenant, who was a couple of meters behind him, didn't freeze. He lit up that female NVA ammo-mule just as she was about to light up the kid.

An American soldier's most decent instincts almost screwed him — women are not readily perceived as combatants, even in a combat zone carrying an AK47!

And the ROE required that, when in doubt, hostile intent must be overt before the use of deadly force was authorized.

Respecting those ideals almost cost a nineteen-year-old American soldier his life.

The use of deadly force without compelling reasons in populated areas was a one-way ticket to Leavenworth. But one of the essential perceptual conflicts between grunts and uninformed civilian onlookers (especially those with some ideological axe to grind) is what constituted a "civilian" in the combat zone of an insurgency and how the enemy deployed in Nam.

Consider first the following statement by a former US Senator, failed presidential candidate, and Secretary of State:

> These were not isolated incidents but crimes committed on a day-to-day basis with the full awareness of officers at all levels of command...(These veterans) told stories that at times they had personally raped, cut off ears, cut off heads, taped wires from portable telephones to human genitals and turned up the power, cut off limbs, blown up bodies, randomly shot at civilians, razed villages in fashion reminiscent of Genghis Khan, shot cattle and dogs for fun, poisoned food stocks, and generally ravaged the countryside of South Vietnam...(Speech before the Senate Foreign Relations Committee on 23 April 1971).

Things must have been pretty squirrelly in the brown water Navy! Or perhaps Mr. Secretary was dissembling for some ideological or political reason.

There was no formal appointment to a guerrilla movement and, despite the popular myth of "VC freedom fighters in black pajamas," guerilla fighters tend not to wear recognizable uniforms.

In fact, based on Chairman Mao's "Little Red Book," the whole point of guerilla warfare is to destabilize and overcome a superior force by "swimming in the sea of the people" and attacking it unexpectedly from "concealment."

In other words, the guerilla, or "terrorist" as we call it today, was typically camouflaged as a civilian among civilians so the intended victims ... usually some poor, unsuspecting grunts who were very obvious in uniforms ... never saw it coming.

Firing on a target while hiding among a group of civilians provided excellent cover for the VC, especially since US soldiers would in fact hesitate in returning fire at perceived civilian targets even at the risk of their own lives.

Further, having been told not to fire at civilians under the rules of engagement, grunts avoided harming civilians, even "civilians" obviously trying to harm them.

So, ironically, the enemy was able to deploy a successful insurgent strategy and inflict casualties on US Troops, by taking advantage of the compassionate tendencies in grunts and their compliance to the ROE, while the soldiers' fellow countrymen condemned them for violating these very ideals.

This reminds me of a precept of the great philosopher, Boris Badinov, "I drop safe on Moose and Squirrel ... who gets squished? Me!"

In other words, a grunt does the right thing and still gets screwed.

"NO! NO! NO!" you say! Grunts massacred entire villages and murdered civilians! Look at LT Calley at My Lai, the mass murder of 347 unarmed citizens! Are you denying that?

No, I'm not!

My Lai happened, and it was an atrocity.

But I will point out that if this example is being used to claim general and continual atrocities against civilians by grunts, at best the assertion demonstrates the fallacy of "false composition" — even if a member of a group possesses a certain characteristic or property, it does not necessarily follow that the all members of the group possesses the same characteristic or property.

In other words, simply because Calley was a homicidal psychopath, it does not follow that grunts in general necessarily shared such attributes.

It has long been my practice that once the fallacious nature of an assertion has been demonstrated, there is no need to present facts to refute it. But this issue has been used to batter the reputation of Vietnam veterans too long!

Enough of the pedantic professor crap and back to the grunt-speak.

I was involved in the sweeps of dozens of Vietnamese and Hmong villages in which not a single civilian, piece of livestock, building or crops were harmed, destroyed or stolen. People were inconvenienced and frightened, but they were not harmed in any material way!

Let me share what those soi-disant "heroic freedom fighters" of North Vietnam did to civilians who did not cooperate with them.

I was on a squad-sized recon patrol in the central highlands west of Ban Me Thuot in 1968. We were moving up on a Hmong village that we were going to check for enemy activity.

As we got close, we noticed something strange ... there were no "village noises." You can usually hear human voices, barking dogs and the snorting of the pigs within five hundred meters of an inhabited village.

In fact, as we got within about two hundred meters of the place, we heard nothing — no birds, no insects—nothing. It was starting to get pretty "twilight zone" out there.

We decided to enter the village.

Everybody and everything was dead — men, women, children, babies, dogs, pigs, chickens, birds, insects — everything was dead, bloated and rotting.

There was no sign of panic or a fire fight. It was as if the people had been simultaneously "struck down" by some invisible force. Hardened grunts were struck dumb by the sight.

We reported what we saw but were never given an explanation for it.

However, our training indicated what might have caused it. A biological agent would not have worked fast enough — we saw no sign of panic or attempts to escape; people seemed to have literally been struck dead where they stood.

A chemical agent like nerve gas — some V-series agent or sarin — could have produced what we saw. It must have been a non-persistent form or we would have been affected too.

Who had a motive to do such a thing?

The Hmong were generally hostile to the Vietnamese and friendly to Americans. There were no ARVN elements in the AO. The only Vietnamese in the area were the NVA.

The Hmong were also perceived to be US allies. They typically co-operated with the US forces. They did not provide safe havens for NVA units, and they did not cache enemy supplies.

So, who would have a motive to harm them?

The NVA had access to chemical weapons, including nerve agents, through their Soviet sponsors.

Had this village been punished for not cooperating with the North Vietnamese?

Had a message been sent to the other villages in the area? "Cooperate with us or this will happen to you!"

So, the NVA had motive, means and opportunity to destroy this village.

We were never told. Nothing of this ever appeared in a UPI story or on the network news.

But Calley was prime time for months! He was tried and convicted for his crimes. He violated the "rules of war," "rules of engagement," as well as the ethics and the mores of the vast majority of grunts.

What Calley did in My Lai on 16 March, 1968 does not represent what tens of thousands of grunts and other American soldiers did over almost ten years in Nam or of their treatment of civilians.

That unfortunately would not have made a good headline ... it's merely the truth!

Freedom Bird.　　　A grunt's ride back to the world when his tour was over.

These were government contract flights provided by a number of bargain-basement contractors such as Overseas National Airways, Seaboard World Airlines, Flying Tiger Line, Saturn, World Airways, and also a few well-known domestic airlines such as United, Northwest Orient, Continental, and Pan Am (remember them?).

Flights from Nam operated out of Da Nang, Cam Ranh Bay, Tan Son Nhut, Bien Hoa, and Phu Cat landing mostly at Travis and McChord AFB in the States. There was usually a stop-over in Alaska, Japan, the Philippines, Guam, or Honolulu to refuel and stock up on beer and booze.

If the flight into Nam had all the ambiance of a funeral, the flight back to the world was a rollicking party at thirty-six thousand feet. There was booze, cold beer, air conditioning, reclining seats, flight attendants (called stewardesses back in those nasty un-woke days), and the knowledge that you had survived, unless the pilot screwed up.

Guys tended to get a bit boisterous and flirty with the ladies. (I think I proposed to the entire cabin crew ... not sure ... wrapped in a beer-fog). The ladies took it all with good humor as long as the grunts observed the Rules of Engagement: no touching; no attempts at a sloppy kisses; keep the clothes on; and keep all the parts in the clothes.

If things did get out of hand, word was sent up to the front of the cabin where the officers and senior enlisted sat. A senior grunt sergeant would be dispatched and would quickly restore order while some officer stayed in his seat supervising the operation and his martini.

Most guys would calm right down, but every now and then a hard-head was encountered who thought his army career was over as soon as the bird landed and he was mustered out, so he didn't have to pay attention to any more army bullshit.

For these unfortunates, their immediate future was clearly explained to them.

　　　"Son ... you got two choices here ... you can behave yourself and enjoy the rest of the ride, or I will assist you in going to

eep ... as far as you're getting out of the army, this will happen
1 one of three ways. First, you land, get processed out, and
o home. Second, you land, get out of the hospital, finish your
hysical therapy, and go home. Third, you land, do your time
1 Leavenworth, get released, meet with your parole officer, and
o home. Personally, I don't give a shit which one you choose,
ut I'd like to avoid all the f'ing army paperwork explaining
your non-LOD accident if I can avoid it ... so which one's it
gonna be?"

Passing the hat at the end of the flight was customary. The flight
crew was not allowed to accept tips, but if a hat full of money got "acci-
dently" left on a seat ... and since a lot of guys were carrying their separation bonuses in greenbacks, had long ago forgotten how to function in
a cash-based society, and were all madly in love with the stewardesses ...
and did I mention the cold beer and booze ... the hat was usually filled
to overflowing with tens and twenties (a lot of money back then).

To the ladies who worked in the cabin, thank you for your tolerance
and sense of humor! We still love you!

To the cockpit crew, thanks for not crashing ... that would have been
a grunt's last irony!

FTA.   This is an abbreviation for "F#%k the army."
Reputedly, this was the motto of the army re-enlistment program
aimed at grunts in 1968. If not, it should have been. It was written on
every latrine wall and drawn on every steel pot (usually under a peace
sign) in Nam.

You can't get free publicity like that anywhere!

FUBAR.   Pronounced, FOO-bar.
An acronym for "F'ed Up Beyond All Recognition."
This was the primary principle for army operational and support
planning, hence, the status quo. All army activities are evaluated according to this principle, in other words according to the degree of FUBAR
achieved.

There's an inherent oxymoron: the more fed up things got th..
likely a grunt was to recognize them. "Oh! I've seen this before ... a
10 of 10 on the FUBAR scale!"

F#%K You Bird. This has nothing to do with lifers and fing
gestures. Seriously! In fact, it has nothing to do with birds.

Confused? Good!

The F#%k You Bird was actually a giant nocturnal tree lizard in the
Central Highlands (now you really think I smoked too much Agent
Orange) whose call sounded like, "F#%K You F#%K You F#%K You!"

When one of these critters got up close to a grunt at night before it
let loose, it usually precipitated an underwear changing event (if grunts
wore underwear).

The F#%k You Bird was a rite of passage for FNGs, especially those
who had watched too many war movies back in the world where the
cunning Japanese infiltrator taunts the rugged but exhausted Marine in
the dark, "Hey, Maline! F#$k Babe Luth!"

Just put an FNG on the bunker line without telling them about the
F#%K You Bird and take bets about what he'll do:

1. Crap in his pants thinking some sapper was out their f'ing
   with him
2. Scream "f#%K you" back at the lizard
3. Ignore the damn thing
4. Open up on the lizard
5. Call in mortars on the lizard
6. Pop a few flares

Odds were pretty even, but the ones who did #3 or #6 were the
keepers; #2, #4 & #5 went into the LRRPS, and #1 got him thrown out
of the hootch.

G

GI Gin.   A generally prescribed and generously supplied medication for various ailments. Reputedly, a concoction of alcohol, terpin hydrate, codeine, alcohol, orange flavoring, and alcohol.

While I was in the infantry NCO academy on Ft. McClellan, I went on sick call with "flu-like symptoms." I must have been sick enough to scare our training cadre because they let me go.

The doc on duty took my temperature and issued me a bottle of an orange, translucent liquid, with the instructions "Take a swig and lay down."

The instructions were backward. I should have lied down and taken a swig. The stuff tasted pretty good, once my eyes stopped watering.

Don't know if it cured me, but I didn't give a crap!

Greased.   v. trans., to kill.

Greased was a common expression among grunts to describe killing or being killed, e.g., "I greased the SOB!", and "He was greased on Mile High."

This was never a pleasant subject for grunts, at least those who were able to keep a grip, albeit tenuous, on their humanity. When addressed to the bad guys, the NVA or Viet Cong, there may be undertones of triumph and satisfaction. However, when addressed to one of our own, it was a simple statement of fact followed by a quick change of subject.

Psychologically, the term enabled grunts to distance themselves from the results of their actions and their own mortality. "There but for the grace of God go I."

LTC Dave Grossman, in his excellent examination of the psychology of killing, *On Killing,* talks about the "Flight-Fight-Freeze" instincts of human beings facing danger. I'd like to break down the "fight" reaction necessary for a grunt to be effective and to have any hope of survival.

The "fight" instinct is probably 80% percent instinct/muscle-memory conditioning and 20% thought. It's a bit like the baseball movie where the veteran catcher tells the rookie pitcher, "Don't think; just throw, meat!"

I remember when I was an FNG and all hell broke out, my mind was in compete chaos while the veterans seemed to react immediately, knowing where the threat was and countering it. It's a miracle I survived those days.

When coming under fire, grunts needed simultaneously to return fire and seek cover. No thought, just reaction. Failure to do so could get a grunt greased. It's only after initial contact that the thought processes engage ... size and location of the enemy force, fire and maneuver, withdrawal, fire support. Initial contact is all muscle-memory ... return fire, find cover.

When in the initial "Condition Red," grunts do not think about killing ... in fact, they're not thinking of being killed ... they're thinking about functioning as infantrymen. Return fire in the direction of the threat, find cover, suppress the threat, follow your leaders. There's no room for fear or thought in Condition Red. The reptile brain is in charge and the neo-cortex is on hold.

Condition Red is the state and condition for "greasing." Grunts didn't intend to kill anyone, just do their job and keep from getting greased. If enemy soldiers are KIA, they were greased, not killed.

I always felt waves of fear and often got the shakes *after* a firefight! Adrenalin drain was part of it, but mostly it was my rational brain taking control, assessing what I just went through, and letting me know I was damn near greased.

Green Tabber.   An expression designating a soldier in a leadership position.

In the "old, black-boot" army, a soldier assigned to a "leadership position," such as squad leader, platoon sergeant, platoon leader, company commander, was authorized to wear a green tab on the epaulette of a uniform that had epaulettes, such as Class-A Greens, Class-B Khakis, or the army field jacket.

Jungle fatigues did not have epaulettes, and no grunt in his right mind ... let me rephrase that ... any grunt who did not have a death wish would wear anything in the boonies to mark himself as a choice target. So, green tabs were never seen in the field.

Rumor had it that, once an officer made full colonel, 06, he was issued a set of Class-A, silk pajamas with epaulettes so he could wear his insignia of rank and green tabs to bed. This enabled a colonel to be still impressive in the sack.

Grid Coordinates. This was a way to designate a grunt's address in the boonies.

They were a four, six or eight-digit sequence of numbers designating a location on a military map.

Locations on a military map were identified by grid coordinates. The map was divided into numbered vertical and horizontal lines whose intersection created one square klick areas (for the geometry-challenged and artillery guys, this is a square, one kilometer on each side).

Grid coordinates were expressed by numbered groups of four, six and eight calculated "right up." In other words, the first set of numbers were calculated from the left side of the map (west if you're holding it correctly) to the "right" of the most proximate vertical grid line; the second group was calculated up from the bottom of the map (south, more or less) up past the significant horizontal grid line.

Four-digit grid coordinates, since they identified a square kilometer of terrain, were useless for finding things or hitting targets unless there was a wing of B52's overhead.

Eight-digit grid coordinates, which the artillery insisted on, were delusional, since no one on the ground in a mountainous jungle could be that precise about a location (about a ten-meter accuracy; remember there were no GPS's in Nam; grunts were doing this with maps, compasses, terrain features, prayer, spit and dead reckoning).

Six-digit grid coordinates, which gave a about 100 meters of wiggle room, were just about right for grunt work.

For fire support, all a grunt had to do was put a 105mm smoke round within a hundred meters of the bad guys; they duck, then the grunt adjusts the fire.

Et voilà ... "Fire for Effect" ... *c'est une belle chose.*

Grunt. This is the sound made by a human being trying to hump seventy pounds of equipment up a mud-slick mountain during a monsoon, hence an infantryman.

The opposite of "grunt" is REMF, lifer, civilian, anyone with a future.

The grunt is the basic and standard of army "combat arms," ... take the ground, hold the ground! The standard against which all soldiers are evaluated, be you airborne, be you ranger, be you NCO, officer or warrant, you were essentially a grunt with a few extra badges.

The infantry along with the artillery, cavalry and armor were the "primary" combat arms ... the tip of the spear. All other army functions existed solely to support them in achieving their mission.

The support elements that humped alongside us ... medics, artillery FOs, dog handlers, etc. ... were adopted into the brotherhood as grunts.

Grunt Rant. This was a little ditty or *bon mot* expressing a grunt's delight and joy at his condition and his appreciation to all those who made it possible, e.g.

"Yea verily though I walk through the valley of the shadow of the darkness of death I fear no evil ... because I'm the baddest mother f'er in the valley."

"We, the unwilling, led by the unknowing, do the impossible for the ungrateful. We have done so much, for so long, with so little, we can do anything with nothing."

"When I die, bury me face down so the whole world can kiss my ass."

"When I die, I'll go to heaven, because I've spent my time in hell."

Gua Ca Chua. Pronounced, GA-chew-ah ... Bless you! Vietnamese for "tomato" and pidgin for "Ah Shit!"

Gunship. This referred to a helicopter gunship, or attack helicopter, a chopper equipped with weapons, missiles, and chain guns used for close air support.

The original gunships were slicks on testosterone ... the crews and the birds. Initially, the birds used the door-gunners' two M60s. Later, the army began to equip slicks with chain guns and rockets.

In late 1967, the army began to deploy the AH-1G Cobra which with a chain gun mounted in its nose looked like a fire- breathing shark.

Cobras (the helicopters, not the snakes) were much beloved by grunts. Unlike close air support by fixed wing aircraft, the Cobras hung around and took their time working over a target.

Being part of a gunship crew assured free drinks in any grunt bar ... offer's still good today.

H

Hand and Arm Signals. This was a method of silent, non-verbal communications in order to maintain OPSEC (Operational Security). These were used when in proximity to the bad guys in order not to reveal the presence of the good guys.

Once the shit hits the fan, shout all you like!

I love watching these war or police SWAT team movies where the stealthy special ops guys start waving their hands around to coordinate a maneuver that would challenge Busby Berkeley. Hand and arm signals were used on a very limited basis because no one could remember them or keep up with the flapping hands, arms, and fingers.

Basic Universal Point-Man hand and arm signals.

1. FREEZE – Fist held straight up
2. LOOK or I SEE – Two fingers pointing to eyes
3. MOE – Two fingers jammed into eyes
4. DIRECTION – Bladed hand indicating a direction
5. COVER ME, I'M SCREWED – Bladed hand resting on top of extended middle finger.
6. NO! I'M NOT DOING THAT – Fist moving back and forth in front of crotch ... usually pointed in direction of the LT
7. BRING ME ONE FROM THE BAR – Hand held up at mouth level, fingers clenched, thumb extended toward mouth mimicking pouring motion.
8. AMF – Just wave.

Most standard hand and arm signals were established by unit TSOP.

Hawk Eye.   This has nothing to do with James Fennimore Cooper's *The Last of the Mohicans*; this was an insane LRRP.

In theory, this was a ranger team that conducted sniper missions, snatches, and other PSYOPs. In practice, three guys with really bad attitudes but without the sense not to tongue kiss a cobra (the snake, not the helicopter).

Whereas LRRPs would find the bad guys, report, and leave quickly, Hawk Eyes would find the bad guys, hang out a large banner saying "Ho Chi Minh Wears Women's Underwear" in Vietnamese, English, French, Russian and Chinese, moon an entire NVA regiment, then hang around to see what was going to happen next.

Reputedly, one Hawk Eye team in the Central Highlands so thoroughly pissed off an NVA regiment that they chased them twenty klicks out of their line of march, got themselves thoroughly lost, Chieu Hoi'd in mass, and now run a chain of dry cleaners, bordellos, and heroin outlets in Southern California on the proceeds from the Chieu Hoi program.

Heads and Juicers.   A way of classifying grunts according to their hallucinogen of choice: heads, pot; juicers, booze.

According to the army culture of the day, if a grunt didn't drink and smoke, there was something intrinsically wrong with him. However, pot was illegal, evil, and only authorized for hippies and jazz musicians.

All of this was frowned upon in the field, not only by the lifers but by the grunts themselves. No one wanted a drunk or tripper out on patrol or pulling guard on the bunker line.

However, many grunt units had a "Beer and Soda" fund. Everybody pitched in a buck or so ... beer was ten cents a can at a Class VI store ... and the last supply bird of the day flew in cases of beer and soda. In the little socialist state of an army LZ, these were divvied up equally among the grunts ... two cans each was the average dole.

However, the serious juicers would trade their soda for beer. I was always a mark for one of my squaddies, a guy we called "Blinky"; it took me a while to get used to 80-degree PBR in a can.

In fact, I would invest in "Blinky Futures." He owned a deli in Manhattan, and his wife would send him care packages packed with NYC deli goodies. So, a couple cans of hot PBR today meant a whole peperoni tomorrow.

No such luck for the heads in the field. The best they could hope for was when we burned fields of fire. Since pot seemed to grow everywhere in Nam, the smoke lit up the entire LZ. Almost made us want to eat C-Rats ... almost.

I tried to find Blinky after I got back to the world. I knew his deli was somewhere along Second Avenue, and I would canvass a few blocks of Manhattan trying to find his place.

I didn't know that Blinky never recovered his health and passed away a couple of years after getting back from Nam.

I knew he didn't have the stamina that most of us possessed; we used to carry his ruck and sometimes him when we were humping hard in the mountains. I wrote it off to his being an "old guy" ... he had to have been at least in his mid-twenties.

When I finally hooked up with my old platoon a couple of years ago, we agreed that Blinky had no business being in Nam health-wise.

As far as I'm concerned, though his name will never be put on the wall, Nam killed Blinky as sure as if he were hit with a 7.62 short.

So, when you get a chance, raise a can of warm PBR to the memory of SP4 Joe Dremmel of New York, New York.

Headspace Problem. Literally, this describes an operating problem with the 50 Cal machine gun.

Metaphorically, it describes anyone who isn't hitting on all pistons, not making much sense ... therefore "stupid;" for instance, "That new officer has a real headspace problem."

The metaphor is based on setting the M2 Browning 50 Cal Machine Gun "headspace," the distance between the end of the neck of a round seated in the chamber and the face of the bolt, and the "timing." Both have to be measured and adjusted before the gun is ready to fire.

A "head space" problem causes the gun to misfire just as a head-space problem causes an individual to "misfire;" that is, miss the point, misunderstand, miscommunicate, etc.

Headspace can be easily adjusted on the 50 Cal with a headspace and timing gauge.

With people it is more difficult, short of using a baseball bat, and this phenomenon is not restricted to the army ... look around yourself some time.

Hearts and Minds.   What the civil affairs officer was trying to win.

This is a somewhat tongue-in-cheek expression for a PSYOP effort ... army jargon for a mind screw ... to win over the indigenous population to democracy, capitalism, baseball, Rock 'n' Roll, and Disney movies.

The S5, "Civil Affairs Officer," would go into villages, distribute food, facilitate medical treatment, give candy to kids, cigarettes, and even cash in an effort to get the population to like us. The essential fault with the approach was that the Vietnamese up in the hills didn't give a shit about ideologies; they just wanted to stay alive, but they were willing to accept gifts and cash.

So, during the day, they smiled and bowed at us, took whatever we were doling out, and told us what they knew about enemy activity in the area ... essentially *nada*.

At night, they smiled and bowed to the NVA and VC, paid their taxes with the money we just gave them, and told the dinks what they knew about us.

"Dey ovah dere ... barbed wire and sandbag ... no can miss dem ... you go get 'em, comrade!"

Civil affairs guys kind of creeped grunts out. They seemed to be cut from the "Mr. Rogers" mold but with a flack vest and helmet instead of a cardigan. we never knew what they were on, but we wanted some.

It's a beautiful day in the neighborhood
A beautiful day for a neighbor
Would you be mine?

Could you be mine?

Would you be my neighbor.

"No sweat, GI! You give me cigarette. No Kent, Salem menthol!"

Grunts were not really in the "hearts and minds" business. Our job in this program was usually reduced to cleaning up the mess after the civil affairs guys left the area.

Hippy.   pl. hippies

These were the social heroes of the left during the late sixties — large groups of young people who rejected the bourgeois values of conventional society to live a life of free expression, drugs, sex – and let's not forget the rock 'n' roll, babies – while collecting social benefits and living off their parents. Hippies were commonly found disguised as college students or faculty.

In Nam, this was a common grunt nickname to describe someone whose weirdness was pronounced enough to be noticed by other grunts.

Although the phenomenon has never been studied, the condition was probably caused by the stress resulting from the conflict between seven years of undergraduate work in the humanities at Berkeley and exposure to the mayhem of a combat zone.

"Hippy" was a stock character in any rifle squad along with a "Short Round," the "Point Guy," the "Fixer," the "Cowboy," the "Loner," the "Card Shark," the "Scrounge," who was always bumming smokes and warm beers, and the guy no one ever talked to because he was just too damned scary.

The squad "hippy" could usually be identified by piles of Montagnard beads around his neck, square-lens purple sunglasses, images of flowers drawn on his camo cover, and a tendency to address everyone as "man."

Peace! Love! Rock 'n' Roll, man!

Ho Chi Minh.   As far as grunts were concerned, the second most unpopular celebrity of the war, right after Jane Fonda. At least Uncle Ho was sincere.

Ho Chi Minh was President of the Democratic Republic of Vietnam; Chairman and First Secretary of the Workers' Party of Vietnam. In emulation of his mentor and hero, Lenin, his embalmed body is currently on display in a mausoleum in Ba Dinh Square in Hanoi, while his spirit looks up at all he created from that special place that all commies go.

I all fairness, the polls are somewhat indeterminate; some clearly show Donald Sutherland tied with Uncle Ho for second place on the grunt shit-list.

I guess this screws my chances of book sales in Vietnam ... and Hollywood.

Ho Chi Minh Sandals.   These were "shower shoes" made from vehicle tires. The soles were made from the tire treads, and the straps to hold them on from inner tubes.

Reputedly, these were the footwear of choice of the Viet Cong. There weren't many VC up in the highlands, and the NVA wore combat boots just like us ... in fact, they seemed to acquire their footwear from us! The quartermaster had to do something with the Size 5 Narrows.

These were "Class C" combat trophies, after weapons, especially Czech-made AK's and Chicom 9-mil pistols (Class A), and pith helmets, belt buckles and collar insignia, (Class B).

What depreciated these as trophies was the fact that most well-stocked coke girls had them in stock ... 500 pi after some energetic bargaining.

That doesn't mean that, back in the rear, a grunt wouldn't tell a REMF that he scored a pair of waterpoint sandals after an horrific firefight with a dink regiment in order to trade for a fifth of Suntory Japanese Whiskey, Yamazaki 12.

Since most REMFs didn't penetrate the Vietnamese commercial market any further than the PX, they had no clue what the waterpoint ladies had in stock.

Ho Chi Minh Trail.   A network of roads and trails that ran from North Vietnam to South Vietnam through North Vietnam, South Vietnam, Laos and Cambodia. The system provided logistical support to the VC and the NVA, during the war.

After the Tet Offensive of 1968, the US was effectively interdicting most traffic down Highway Ho. By September / October 1968, the NVA units south of I CORPS, who survived the Tet debacle and were dependent on Highway Ho for logistics, were starving for supply and replacements. A bad day for us was when the dinks threw all three of their 82 rounds at us ... and usually missed.

Then Richard Nixon got elected.

"Tricky Dick" made a deal with the North Vietnamese. "You sit down with us in Paris for peace talks and we'll stop bombing the shit out of you."

This of course was a godsend for the dinks ... sorry, Commies are atheists ... "comrade-send" ... because, as any married person knows, talking and understanding are not the same as agreeing. Just grin, nod your head, and don't say a thing until the noise stops.

So, while North Vietnamese diplomats grin f'ed US diplomats in the conference room of some swank hotel in Paris, the bombing of the Ho Chi Minh trail stopped, the dinks reopened their resupply routes to the south, and resupplied their units in South Vietnam, which they swore were not there.

By the middle of 1969, it was business as usual for grunts in Nam.

"Today's weather report calls for heavy monsoon rains and a chance of rocket attacks west of Highway 14."

US ground troops, of course, were not allowed to cross the border or fire into Laos and Cambodia.

Thank God our maps were based on wildly inaccurate, decades-old French surveys, and the fact that, unlike cartoons, there was no dotted line drawn across the mountainous jungles of the highlands with the words "Vietnam" printed on one side and "Cambodia" on the other. Sometimes, "mistakes were made," and US artillery landed on a North Vietnamese supple convoy in the forbidden zone.

"Bad FDC! Bad! No beer for a week! Ignore the case of champagne mixed in with your c-rats."

In September 1969, I was in the highlands with K/75 Rangers, aka, the LRRPS. We had a platoon sergeant named Alvin Floyd, who was quite a character.

Despite Floyd's many idiosyncrasies, we all perceived him as a grunts' grunt, the whole package. And it was considered the highest compliment for Floyd to invite one of us to go out with him on one of his "special missions." Few were called and fewer were chosen, to paraphrase the Book.

One day, Floyd tapped me to go up in the mountains with him and play. Just the two of us. There was no mission briefing in the TOC. The only thing he told me was to pack for four to six days and be ready to hump ... and I was carrying the CEOI, the PRC-25, a long-stick, a small reel of commo wire, and two extra batteries.

The next morning I met Floyd on the landing pad; our slick was already there. Curiously, our slick was a *tabula rasa* ... army green with no markings. Before we climbed in, Floyd handed me a map and said only, "Our AO."

The slick took us west; I thought we flew for almost an hour. I had no idea where we were going. My operations map wasn't connected to anything I recognized.

The bird finally put us down in a jungle clearing; it was back in the air and headed east before we even got to cover. It flew away low, almost nap of the earth.

I was able to establish comms with the long stick. The Network Control Station was not the one we rangers usually used on missions. But it was there, clear, and seemed to know who we were and what we were doing, which was more than I could say for myself.

Before we moved out, Floyd showed me on my map where we were and said we were moving out on an azimuth of 280 degrees, due west.

Then he said no sitreps. "We call when we have to ... if they need us, they'll call us."

Then he told me all our locations were coded; we report our status by the code. I asked Floyd about pre-planned artillery targets. Floyd gave me a funny grin, "Ain't any," he said.

We moved out at a good pace almost due west, and hump we did. Up the hills, down the hills. Floyd seemed to have a destination in mind; I was being dragged along for the ride ... someone had to hump the radio.

Sometime in the late afternoon, we cut a trail. Let me correct myself, we hit a dirt road about two-trucks wide straight as an arrow north to south. The trees arched over it creating cover from above. We didn't actually venture out onto it, but from the lack of vegetation and visible tire tracks along the roadbed, I assumed it was well travelled.

Floyd just gave me his inscrutable grin and said, "We have arrived," then indicated where we were on my map. There was no redline on my map, no road.

Floyd told me to transmit a code, "ROS ... Romeo Oscar Sierra" to control and get an ACK, acknowledgement. I assumed that was the "we're here" message.

This time, establishing commo was tricky. We had high ground, a ridge, to our east beyond which I assumed our control station was located, and I had no idea how far away we were from the friendlies.

I climbed the ridge and managed to rig a wire antenna in a tree with what I assumed was line of site to our control. I ran the wire back down to where we had established our observation post overlooking the road. When I hooked my Rube Goldberg antenna up to the PRC-25 it worked, more or less. I got a fuzzy acknowledgement of our code from network control.

I remember thinking that at least some of the stuff in the Ranger Handbook worked.

Since it was still daylight, we moved east back over the ridge, me dragging the radio and the tail end of my wire antenna with me, and we found a sheltered, well concealed area on the east face of the ridge.

Floyd said, "Nothing to do till sunset ... we go one-on-one-off till we move out." Before I could nod, Floyd was flat out, back against his rucksack, breathing regularly, eyes closed.

We moved back over the ridge after sundown, during nautical twilight while it was still light enough to see. We found a concealed position from which we could overlook the road.

I connected the wire end of the antenna to the PRC-25. We both pulled down the sleeves of our camouflaged fatigues; buttoned our jackets to the neck, collars up around the ears; slathered our faces, ears and the backs of our hands with a combination of loam commo stick and bug juice; flopped our boonie hats down over our heads, and draped our camouflaged poncho liners over our head and shoulders to break up our outline.

Floyd: "We just observe ... write shit down best you can in the dark ... who, what, when, where, how shit ... don't unpack anything ... if we gotta move quick, take your rifle and as much of your shit you can run with."

"Run with!" I thought.

There wasn't much moonlight that night. I may have dozed a bit but, as soon as I heard the truck engines, I was fully awake. Sounded like army deuces moving down on the road.

We counted about twenty driving past our location headed south. Headlights on but painted down to blackout slits; brake lights fully illuminated. We had no idea what they were carrying but, from the engine sounds, they seemed loaded. No apparent security for the convoy, and it was much too dark to make out any markings on the trucks. I checked my handy-dandy Captain Midnight Ranger watch and noted 2320 hrs.

We counted four convoys headed south that night, about twenty trucks each. Nothing headed north.

When we detected the morning light beginning to break over the ridgeline behind us, we checked our location for any litter, fluffed up the foliage in our little lair, and headed back over the ridge, me dragging my poncho liner, radio and antenna wire.

When we crossed the ridge, we found another nice place to hide. We compared notes to ensure we both saw the same things and transposed the scratchings we made in the dark into something that was readable in the light.

When I finally looked up from editing my notes, Floyd was in dreamland.

We repeated this routine for the next three nights with the same results, heavily laden truck convoys moving south along the road almost as if on a schedule.

On the fourth night, we got a surprise.

The 2300 Dink Redball Express had already rolled through, and we were waiting for the Midnight Special. Then, I heard the unmistakable sound of infantry walking down the road ... the clink and squeak of loose equipment, the thud and stumble of feet, the mumble of whispered conversation, and the smell of cigarette smoke.

For a few brief seconds, I expected to see a line of grunts humping down the road. Then I noticed this smoke had the acrid tang of commie tobacco, and I saw flashlights! As unstealthily as US infantry moved around in Nam, they never used flashlights to maneuver around in the dark; only the dinks did that!

A column of NVA infantry was marching south down the road. I could make out the shape of their pith helmets and saw them carrying AK's, SKS carbines, and even RPG's at sling arms. About fifty of them just strolling down the road below us, every other one using a flashlight to illumine the route.

I felt my neck trying to turtle down into my jacket; I didn't dare breathe. "Please don't take a break here ... please don't shine those damned flashlights in my direction!

The infantry passed us down the road. In the dark, I heard Floyd breathe out, almost sigh ... this had gotten even his attention!

We remained in place the rest of that night and noted the rest of the now regularly scheduled commie-convoys. As soon as it was light enough, we went back east over the ridge. Floyd gave me a code to transmit which I did over the long stick. I collected my antenna and rolled up the wire; no trace of our having been there.

Then we started humping east. After a couple hours, Floyd found a clearing large enough for a slick. I transmitted another three-letter code and in less than half an hour an unmarked slick flew low into our clearing and landed without marking smoke. We jumped in and flew back to LZ Oasis.

When we landed, my two football buddies, Skip and Scooter, the CIA guys who weren't there, along with Captain Mysterious, the brigade S2, the Intel Officer, were waiting for us. Floyd asked me for my notebook, map, and CEOI. Then, he told me to go back to our compound and wait for him; he had to attend a de-brief.

About an hour later, when Floyd got back to the compound, he handed me back my notebook. I noticed all the pages from our recent excursion had been ripped out.

All Floyd said to me was, "You did good!" Coming from Floyd, that was better than a Bronze Star.

Alvin Winslow Floyd
Sergeant First Class
K Co, 75TH INFANTRY, 4TH INF DIV, USARV
F CO, 75TH INFANTRY, 25TH INF DIV, USARV
Army of the United States
Augusta, Georgia
February 09, 1942 to April 02, 1970
Tay Ninh Province, South Vietnam

Hook.   In Nam, this didn't refer to the captain of a pirate ship, but a large ... very large ... and scary helicopter, the Sikorsky CH-54 Tarhe, commonly called the "Flying Crane."

This bird looked like a humped-back praying mantis with a 155 mm howitzer, a deuce, and a pallet of artillery shells dangling between its legs as it flew.

Grunts didn't want to be anywhere near this thing when it got close to the ground. If the propellants in its prop-wash — boulders, 2X4's, unwary Vietnamese, small water buffalos — didn't kill them, the static electricity it discharged when it got close to a ground would.

I was watching a supply guy trying to hook a water trailer to one of these jobs during the rainy season ... when the air is nice and humid. When the hook got within about ten feet of the guy, a blue-white bolt of lightning shot out from it and blew the poor SOB off the trailer and ten meters across the perimeter.

We gave it a 9.5; even the French judge loved it.

Hootch.   This was the name of any abode of a soldier in Nam.

In gruntdom, a hootch was a shelter constructed from ponchos. It had various manifestations:

1. the one-man hootch was a poncho thrown over a branch;
2. the two-man hootch was two ponchos snapped together and thrown over a branch;
3. the deluxe, duplex, three-man hootch was the two-man hootch with a third poncho draped across one of the open ends.

I imagine if grunts stayed in Nam long enough, the multi-unit, high-rise hootch made totally from sticks, ponchos, and strings would have graced the central highlands ... but thank God no one stayed that long!

Hot A's.   This was a grunt term for real food, as in regular, hot, cooked food, the stuff civilians eat every day: mashed potatoes, string beans, white bread, roast beef, butter, etc.

In formal army terminology, these were called "A Rations."

A's were rare but always welcomed by grunts unless they arrived accompanied by a chaplain, in which case grunts were being fattened up for the kill.

The bacon sandwich on toast with black coffee served on the bunker line during stand-to was the start of a good day for a grunt.

For this to happen, grunts had to be on palace guard on a battalion fire base with a mess unit. Grunts would pick up the smell of the bacon while on morning stand to. One of the guys would go back to the mess tent and bring some sandwiches and coffee up to the guys on the bunker line.

Talk about Pavlov's dog; I still salivate when I smell bacon at Oh Dark Thirty ... smells like ... Palace Guard!

Hump. This word had three distinct meanings.

The first was used to describe any SOB, "The XO's a real hump!"

The second described grunts moving over difficult terrain with heavy loads; e.g. "Hump the boonies." It's essentially the shape of a human body trying to move sixty pounds of equipment in a ruck sack up a muddy mountain during a monsoon. In other words, what a grunt commonly does and what he looks like while doing it ... a mud-splattered, OD snail.

Finally and psychologically, humping described bearing an impossible burden for a bunch of indifferent-at-best-but-commonly-hostile civilians and self-serving-and-deceitful politicians (see M1A1).

I

Immediate Action Drills.   This describes a set of standard unit and individual actions taken upon suddenly finding oneself in deep shit.

"Strac" units (in the grunt sense of the term) developed and practiced "immediate action drills" for various common combat situations.

Like a good football team practices its plays, units practiced these drills, so all members of the unit, when encountering a specific situation, would immediately perform the correct action without thinking much about it ... because if a grunt has to take the time to think through these things when they actually happen, his thinking days would be suddenly abbreviated.

Common immediate action drills include "meeting engagement," "close ambush," "far ambush," "sniper," "incoming artillery," or "virgin at the water point," e.g.

Immediate Action Drill: Close Ambush

Situation: the unit receives high volume of fire along its entire flank and/or flank and front; opposing force (OPFOR) is within 100 meters of the unit.

Immediate Action:

1. All individuals in the "kill zone" immediately return fire and attack OPFOR.
2. Signal smoke when OPFOR engaged.
3. Individuals outside the kill zone engage OPFOR with high volume of cover fire for attacking element.

On signal smoke shift fire to visible fleeing OPFOR; if OPFOR not visible, shift fire to flank of attacking element.

Immediate Action Drill: Close Nuclear Strike

Situation: OPFOR deploys a nuclear device less than a klick from the unit's position.
Immediate Action:

1. Spread your feet shoulder distance apart.
2. Place your right hand on your right knee.
3. Place your left hand on your left knee.
4. Place your head between your knees.
5. Kiss your ass goodbye.

J

Jane Fonda.   Grrrrrrr!

Two words which most immediately – and most surely – evoke a violently negative reaction from a grunt are "Jane Fonda," a.k.a. "Hanoi Jane."

She was an actress and an activist against the war, who most infamously visited Hanoi in April 1970 and was photographed sitting in an anti-aircraft battery wearing an NVA helmet.

Also, while touring the infamous POW prison, the "Hanoi Hilton," Miss Fonda reputedly turned over notes, given to her by the POWs, to prison officials causing the prisoners to be severely beaten as punishment.

Fonda, Fred Gardner, and Donald Sutherland formed the "FTA (Free the army) tour," a play on the grunt expression "F' The Army", as an anti-war road show designed as a perverse parody of Bob Hope's USO tour. I wonder who they used as Joey Heatherton?

Most grunts hearing her name, after they had stopped grinding their teeth and regained the use of any form of articulate language, might characterize her career as an example of the use of a shallow political ideology to enhance an equally shallow acting talent.

However, she did apologize in 1988:

> "I would like to say something, not just to Vietnam veterans in New England, but to men who were in Vietnam, who I hurt, or whose pain I caused to deepen because of things that I said or did. I was trying to help end the killing and the war, but there were times when I was thoughtless and careless about it and I'm very sorry that I hurt them. And I want to apologize to them and their families [...] I will go to my grave regretting the photograph of me in an anti-aircraft gun, which looks like I was

trying to shoot at American planes. It hurt so many soldiers. It galvanized such hostility. It was the most horrible thing I could possibly have done. It was just thoughtless..."

Ms. Fonda, I accept your apology and thank you both for your honesty and remorse. I don't know how other Vietnam vets have reacted to this statement, but I think this damn war has lasted too long, and I actually feel better not despising you anymore. For what it's worth, grunts also hated that damned war, the destruction it caused, and the injury it did to us, our friends, families, and the Vietnamese. We actually agree with you on that. I just wish you hadn't waited almost fifteen years to make up. We could have patched this thing up long ago.

A piece of advice from an old grunt. The primary purpose of an actor is to be entertaining ... not politically profound, not socially moralizing, not an ideologue ... just entertaining.

Once an actor ceases to be entertaining but continues to harangue the public from the platform of the actor's notoriety for acting about issues tiny, little, actor brains cannot possibly encompass, that actor becomes a noisome, pernicious, annoying pain-in-the-ass.

So, memorize your script, deliver your lines, stay on your mark, and take direction. Otherwise, keep your uninformed, destructive, and hurtful hate-speech to yourself.

By the way, only a grunt can say "FTA" to another grunt; if a civilian says it, it's a fistfight.

Loved your work in *Cat Ballou, On Golden Pond,* and *Monster In-Law*!

Love! Peace! Rock n Roll, Janey!

Jody. A (not-so) mythical creature who preys on the girl friends of grunts and other soldiers while they're away serving their county.

Also, "Jody Calls," is a term used to describe marching songs used to keep cadence in which "Jody" plays a major role; e.g.:

> Ain't no use in goin' home
> Jody got yo' girl 'n' gone
> Am I right or wrong?

You're Right!
Am I goin' strong?
You're right!
Sound off!
One! Two!
Sound off!
Three! Four!
Bring it on down!
One, Two, Three, Four,
One, Two ... THREE, FOUR!"

Just another way in which the army made grunts feel good about themselves and their recent choice not to emigrate to Canada.

John Wayne.   An American actor known for his macho roles in cowboy and war flicks.

Also, a term used by grunts to describe any action or attitude characterized by lots of macho, panache, and little brain; in other words, foolhardiness.

> "He pulled a real John Wayne on that machine gun, poor bastard."

Finally, the term describes an ill-advised tactical maneuver also known by grunts as "High Diddle Diddle! Right Up The Middle!"

These concepts were named for this macho and rather hawkish actor, who made a zillion westerns and war movies but is often criticized for never having served in any branch of the service during WWII, Korea, and Nam (except the Green Berets, I guess).

But, like Bob Hope, the Duke always had our six and never stopped supporting the grunts in Nam.

Love ya, Duke, wherever you are!

Jungle Boots.   The footwear of choice for style-conscious grunts to hump the boonies.

Jungle boots were a type of combat boot designed for use in hot, wet and humid environments (i.e., Vietnam). They were light, with a rubber sole, black leather toe and heel (which lifers wanted shined), OD nylon uppers, removable ventilating insoles made of a plastic screen, vent holes in the instep, and a sump pump for the rainy season, rice paddies, and water-walking.

In the boonies, grunts always slept in their boots because it was not advisable to get yourself killed looking for your boots in the dark, or lighting something to look for your boots in the dark, or trying to lace them up in the dark, or tripping over the laces you didn't lace up in the dark.

There were times when the dark was your friend and you didn't want to interrupt it.

After a few months of this treatment, a grunt's feet, which were two of his most essential assets, were hosting some strange and wonderful forms of alien life and growing webs between the toes.

One of the common and ongoing grunt fantasies about the world was being able to sleep without boots (ours, not hers).

So, if one were to ask a grunt to list in order what he was going to do when he got back to the world,

> Number one had something to do with a woman;
> Number two had something to do with booze; and
> Number three had to do with sleeping without his boots on
(unless he decided to sober up and repeat number 1).

Jungle Fatigues.   Grunt line units wore OD (Olive Drab) "jungle fatigues." These were jackets and trousers made of a light "rip resistant" material.

"Rip resistant" meant that some low-cost government contractor tested these garments be letting a bunch of toothless toddlers gnaw on them for a couple of weeks. If the babies couldn't tear or chew through the fabric, they were classified "rip resistant" as specified in the government contract.

When they got to where they were designed to be used, in the boonies, they surrendered to every "wait-a-minute" bush in the AO.

When a grunt shipped to Nam, he was issued three sets of jungle fatigues in the Repl Depl. When he got to his unit, he turned two sets into supply, because extra sets of fatigues were something he didn't want to hump.

The principle for changes of clothes in the field was based on a bad joke:

This grunt unit had been humping the bush for a month up in the highlands during the rainy season. One night, when they pulled into a night laager, the platoon sergeant called them together and said,

>"Men! I got good news for you! We got a change of underwear tonight!"
>
>"Yea!" said the grunts.
>
>"Johnson! You change with Jones! Peters! You change with Gleason ..."

The story is obviously apocryphal because, as I've already told you, grunts didn't wear underwear.

Periodically, the army would ship big red mailbags full of "clean" fatigues out to the grunts in the field.

Now "clean" was an interesting concept in Nam. It didn't mean that your Aunt Tilly would let you sit on her parlor sofa wearing this stuff. When applied to jungle fatigues, clean usually meant that months of accumulated dirt, filth, and sweat, through some secret and mysterious process, had been sublimated into the fabric and sealed there by some steamy and mysterious Vietnamese process only known to mamasahns.

On that special day when the "clean" stuff arrived, the grunts would strip off their dirty fatigues and replace them with "clean" ones. Then the dirty fatigues would be shipped back in the mailbags to mamasahn's laundry services somewhere in the rear.

Unlike REMFs, lifers, and other denizens of the rear areas, grunts never wore any identifying patches in the boonies; no unit patches, name tags, CIBs, and especially no indication of rank ... nothing that would help some NVA sniper or rifleman to select a target ... if a grunt didn't know who the good guys and the bosses were in the field, something was seriously wrong.

One of the eternal debates among grunts was whether it was better to have button-fly or zipper-fly trousers.

Pro button grunts claimed buttons didn't rot in the rain so you could always close your fly. The counter argument said who cared if your fly was open.

Pro Zipper: it closed and didn't let any crucial bits dangle or let any undesirable critters in.

Pro Button: they couldn't rust shut, so you never had to pee in your pants.

Personally, I didn't care until one night I had some unwanted guests whose arrival was unrestricted by my button fly.

I was out on an LP with my squad leader and two other guys in the mountains west of Pleiku. We were in concealment along a stream ("blue line" in grunt-speak) and I was asleep on a nice comfortable flat rock when two carnivorous Vietnamese red tree ants infiltrated past my button fly and began to make a meal out of a body part that I was carefully guarding between my legs for future use when I got back to the world. Without fully waking, I jumped up and was just about to scream when I remembered where I was. In the dark, I dropped trou, plucked the offending insects from my anatomy, re-trou'd, and went back to sleep. The grunt on guard said it was one of the most amazing acts he had ever witnessed in a combat tour fraught with amazement.

After that, I was a confirmed zipper man.

Let me clear the air on this underwear thing.

Grunts didn't wear it ... T-shirts, yes, but nothing else.

Why? No matter what a grunt wore — shorts, briefs, loin cloth or thong — these things got into a knot and bunched up in uncomfortable places when a grunt was humping and, because a grunt was hauling a fifty-pound ruck on his back, he couldn't reach around to his ass to make the needed adjustment. So, no underwear.

Probably more than you wanted to know.

K

Khe Sanh, Battle of.   An indecisive yet bloody battle fought between the US army, Marines, ARVN, and Laotian troops against the NVA from approximately January to July, 1968.

The combat base at Khe Sanh was originally established as a base for operations against the Ho Chi Minh trail in Laos. Eventually, it evolved into the western anchor of Marine defenses along the DMZ in northern I Corps.

NVA strategy in this battle seemed to suffer from Dien-Bien-Phu-envy, an attempt to repeat the Viet Minh's victory against the French by surrounding a major military installation and forcing its surrender. Unfortunately, NVA planners mistook US Marines and army Air Cav troops for French colonial forces.

The Battle of Khe Sanh did highlight the tactical weaknesses of both sides of the conflict.

NVA seemed to have problems adhering to a "George Washington Strategy" – we don't have to defeat them; we just have to prevent them from defeating us. Each time, NVA massed against US targets – Khe Sanh, Tet '68, the 1972 Offensive – US firepower devastated them.

The US tactics seemed to be an ongoing series of "build up an enemy body count by seizing the terrain, holding the terrain, abandoning the terrain, repeat as necessary." And true to form, Khe Sanh was dismantled in July 1968 after the siege was lifted.

Both sides claimed Khe Sanh a victory.

NVA claimed they forced a US withdrawal; the US claimed it didn't need to maintain the position any longer.

Some historians claim the battle was a feint to distract the US from the Tet Offensive; the US claimed a couple of US regiments tied down tens of thousands of NVA and VC troops who were not available to participate in Tet.

The historical question is sometimes referred to as "riddle of Khe Sanh."

> Either the Tet Offensive was a diversion intended to facilitate PAVN/VC preparations for a war-winning battle at Khe Sanh, or Khe Sanh was a diversion to mesmerize Westmoreland in the days before Tet." (John Prados and Ray Stubbe. *Valley of Decision: The Siege of Khe Sanh*. Annapolis, Maryland: Naval Institute Press, 1991).

From the point of view of the grunts who fought the battle, who gives a shit what the eggheads think. Khe Sanh was a dirty, brutal struggle lasting months.

Estimated US and allied casualties

> Khe Sanh: 274 killed 2,541 wounded
> Operation Scotland I and Operation Pegasus: 730 killed, 2,642 wounded, 7 missing
> Operation Scotland II: 485 killed, 2,396 wounded
> Operation Charlie: 11 killed, wounded unknown
> ARVN losses: 229 killed, 436 wounded
> Laotian losses are unknown

From this, estimate the number of parents who lost children, the number of wives who lost husbands, the number of children who lost fathers, and the magnitude of the tragedy begins to take shape.

Ironic postscript.

During Operation Desert Shield, I was assigned to the 85th Division on Ft. Sheridan, IL. This post was a bit of an army anomaly since it sat on land on the north shore of Lake Michigan just north of Chicago worth zillions to real estate developers. When a grunt walked out though the gate, he could hardly afford the air he was breathing.

After work, my team and I liked to go to a VFW bar outside the gate for a few beers. It was safe and affordable. One night, we came in and there was an old guy (probably younger then than I am now) nursing a beer at the end of the bar.

He looked at my CIB and combat patch and asked, "Vietnam?"

When I said yes, he said, "That wasn't a real war."

I did not offer to buy him one. He should have known better!

The Vietnam-Veteran-Syndrome in a nutshell. Always the unwanted stepchild ... even in the VFW!

KIA. An abbreviation for "Killed In Action", something a grunt never wanted said about himself or someone he knew.

Unfortunately, it was a common occupational hazard for grunts in Nam.

The term was commonly used as a euphemism when talking about someone a grunt knew when he wanted to avoid using the word "dead," e.g. "Where's Smith?" "KIA, Sarge."

Other classifications for casualties were WIA — "Wounded in Action" and MIA — "Missing in Action."

The real perverse thing about this concept is when a guy was killed, a grunt had three simultaneous reactions: loss, relief and guilt. Loss for a friend, relief that it wasn't him, and guilt that it was someone else.

"Why him and not me?" Syndrome.

One of a grunt's way of dealing with the latter was to adopt the WTWP principle, "Wrong Time Wrong Place."

I know I'm not sounding very sensitive here, but it's a grunt-thing.

This is how grunts protected themselves and stayed functional. A grunt couldn't wander around a combat zone mourning and musing even for someone who was as close to him as a brother; that would have been suicidal.

When the shit hit the fan, a grunt had to have his mind on business or he would become a statistic, classified KIA.

The tricky part was when a grunt got back to the world; what did he do with this trauma, these memories ... these feelings ...

In the eighties, the "traveling" Vietnam Memorial Wall was on display in Chicago. I took one of my daughters to see it — she was about six at the time.

I had never paid much attention to the memorial. Part of my general "get on with life and stay functional" policy was to lock all that messy Vietnam crap away. So, I didn't know that the wall was organized chronologically, by time of the soldiers' deaths.

My daughter and I were strolling along the wall looking at the names of people we never knew. Then I came to the panel for 27 September 1968 and saw a cluster of names "Joseph G. Ambrosio ... Mark A. Barnes ... Derris Brown ... David K. Chahoc ... Richard L. Jones Jr. ... Robert E. Knoll ... Roger A. Rickert ... Bradford D. Wright."

I was instantly back on a firebase near the village of Duc Lap.

The day before, my platoon had sent out a patrol – what we called a LRLP, "Long-Range Listening Post" – four guys from my squad and a new lieutenant.

The next morning, I was in the Battalion Combat Trains, waiting for a ride back to our firebase.

Our patrol radioed in; they had hit the shit and couldn't get out. The NVA were all over them.

The rest of the company saddled up to get them out.

I managed to hijack a seat in a supply slick and rode out with the Class V, Ammo. By the time I got out there, the third herd was going through the wire, so I tailed along one of their squads, Bobby Knoll's squad.

A typical NVA tactic was to attack a small unit and set up an ambush to hit the relief force when it came to get their buddies out.

We knew that, but we didn't really give a shit ... we couldn't ... our brothers needed us.

Almost as soon as we heard the small arms fire, we attacked through the NVA ambush. We did nothing clever ... we were too pissed off ... we just smashed through it to get to our guys.

We lost nine guys that day from our company, a few of them from my squad. We had almost as many wounded.

That was the fight where my helmet got killed. A round from an RPM hit the back of my helmet and knocked me flat. I had a concussion and needed a few stiches. The guys in front of me weren't as lucky.

I knew them all; they were my brothers.

In fact, just the night before I was sitting on the helicopter pad with Doc Ambrosio trying to get back out to the company. He was talking about his family in Ohio ... how much he missed them ... 27 September was his mom's birthday.

The last bird out that evening had room for one pack. A medic with needed medical supplies had a higher priority than a grunt. So, Doc got the seat, and I stayed behind.

My daughter was pulling on my arm.

"Daddy! Daddy! Are you alright? Are you sick, Daddy?"

My heart was racing; I was hyperventilating.

"I'm okay, sweetie! Daddy's just breathing heavy. Let's go get some ice cream! Okay?"

When I hear "KIA," even after all these years, I see the faces... I wonder why them, not me ...

I don't want to stay here anymore ... I have to go "get some ice cream."

IN MEMORIAM
Alpha Company, 2nd Battalion, 35th Infantry
"Cacti Blue"
27 September 1968

JOSEPH G. AMBROSIO, SP4, Age 20, Elyria, OH
MARK A. BARNES, PFC, Age 21, Wyandanch, NY
DERRIS BROWN, SGT, Age 28, Bladenboro, NC
DAVID K. CHAHOC, 1LT, Age 21, Lakewood, OH
RICHARD L. JONES, CPL, Age 21, Wichita, KS
ROBERT E. KNOLL, SSG, Age 20, Holland, MI
ROGER A. RICKERT, CPL, Age 20, Bowler, WI
GERALD S. STOZEK, SP4, Age 21, Fond Du Lac, WI
BRADFORD D. WRIGHT, SGT, Age 19, Duluth, MN

"Farewell!

Farewell!

Comrades true, born anew, peace to you!

Your souls shall be where heroes are,

And your memory shine like the morning star.
Brave and dear,
Shield us here.
Farewell!"

"Rouge Bouquet", Joyce Kilmer

Kill Zone.   Either

1. The part of an ambush into which the target enters so the attacking force can bring its most effective firepower against them; in other words, it's the grunt version of the Hotel California ... you check in anytime you like but you may never leave,
Or
2. The conference room in the offices of your ex-wife's divorce lawyer.

Klick.   A kilometer, or for those who are not French, "almost a mile."

This is a measurement of distance and humping:

"How hilly was it?!"

"We humped twenty klicks up and down and two klicks in a straight line!"

L

Lai Day.   Pidgin for "Come here!" or "Get your ass over here!" It's the opposite of Di Di Mau.

This was used only when talking to Vietnamese. If you said this to another grunt, you'd need some dental work ... which could get you back to base camp for a at least a week if you milked it right.

LAW (M72).   Pronounced, "LAW."

This is an acronym for "Light Anti-Tank Weapon," a portable, collapsible, one-shot, 66 mm anti-tank weapon designed to bounce off the armor of most post-WWII Soviet tanks, give away a grunt's position, and really piss off a commie tank crew.

The weapon had little or no resistance to moisture, so it had little or no use in Nam.

But it did demonstrate that the army had RPG envy.

It's prime function was harassing FNGs.

> "Here, you carry the LAW, the shovel, a few extra M79 rounds, a few belts of M60 ammo, a couple of those 81 rounds, the five- gallon can of water and the old man's recliner."

LBJ.   This had two immediate meanings in the late 1960's

First, it was the initials of the US President who got us into this mess, Lyndon Baynes Johnson.

Second, it was an abbreviation for "Long Binh Jail," an in-country place of military incarceration named after the afore-mentioned and beloved president, who got us into this mess.

Ironically, the possibility of three hots a day, a bed, a roof over your head, no guard duty, no stand to, no one shooting at you was at times quite appealing to grunts.

Lifer.   Any soldier with a bad attitude, no sense of reality or proportion, and a bad case of "minutia myopia," a mental condition in which petty and irrelevant bullshit is made to seem critical.

Also, it describes the bad attitude itself, e.g. "Don't go lifer on me!"

This was the primary source of chicken shit.

Lifers are not to be mistaken for career soldiers, because, unlike career soldiers, lifer's had little common or any other forms of sense and liked to concentrate on the minutiae of army life — formations, shining shoes, haircuts, police calls, etc.

Lifers were rarely found in the boonies when there was a reason to be in the boonies, e.g. NVA crowd-control. When this happened, they usually found some excuse to get back to a base camp, or at least to the combat trains, for medical or dental appointments (can you believe it; come all the way to Nam to get your teeth fixed), private fittings for their web gear, 201 file audits, lobotomies ... anything that would get them out of harm's way. And most grunts were happy to see them go. "When the going gets tough, the lifers get going."

When things got really quiet in the field, they would reappear, assume some pompous title like "Field First Sergeant," and start seeing cigarette butts around every bunker.

Let me be absolutely clear on one point. Although the term "lifer" was commonly applied to senior "regular army" NCOs, the concept referred to a state of mind and not to the career duration or rank of a soldier.

My platoon sergeant in LRRPs was a Regular Army Sergeant First Class, named Alvin Floyd, and every Ranger in the platoon loved this guy.

Floyd was pure "grunt." When I met him, he was going through his second or third incarnation as a senior non-commissioned officer. If Floyd spent too much time in a rear area, he had a really bad habit of telling the absolutely wrong people something they absolutely did not want to hear — even if they absolutely needed to hear it. So, occasionally Floyd would get his ass busted down to buck private.

But the army soon realized what a superb infantry leader he was, promoted him and sent him somewhere where his skills were needed, and he couldn't piss anyone off ... like out in the boonies with a bunch of rangers.

What we really loved about Floyd was that he was one of us while never losing — or worrying about losing — his authority. He was simply the best there was and a grunt could do a hell of a lot worse, and probably no better, by having Floyd as a role model.

Floyd would never ask us to do anything he wasn't doing himself; he lived in the same holes as we did; he ate the same chow; he pulled the same missions; and he took the same risks. He taught us how to do our jobs well and stay alive, and he made sure we had what we needed.

One of Floyd's ironclad rules was, if someone wanted to ball out one of his guys, that person had better talk to Floyd first. Not that Floyd would let any of us skate, but he knew what messages had to be delivered and how to deliver them to a grunt so he understood what he was being told and why it was important to pay attention.

If Floyd got on a grunt's case, everybody understood — especially the object of Floyd's attention — that there was a valid and important issue that had to be addressed.

But, if someone wanted to commend one of his guys, Floyd would be happy to point the guy out and step aside.

In short, grunts trusted the guy. They trusted his competence; they trusted his ability to help them get the job done; and they trusted his ability to watch their six.

Although Floyd was a "regular army" E7, he was not a "lifer." Floyd was a competent grunt, a role-model, leader, and a comrade.

It was a dark day for me when I found out that SFC Alvin Winslow Floyd was killed in action in Tay Ninh province on 2 April 1970.

God bless you and keep you, Sarge, until we meet again!

Line of Duty.   This is like a report of survey except, instead of investigating the damage, loss, or destruction of government property, the army is assessing the damage, loss, or destruction of some poor grunt.

When a grunt becomes sick or injured to the point that he is unable to perform his regular duties, the commander would initially conduct an informal investigation into the circumstances. If the commander concluded the condition "in the line of duty," the investigation is terminated.

If, however, the commander determined that the grunt's condition was due to negligence or misconduct, a formal investigation is conducted.

There were three possible outcomes:

1. **LD – "In Line of Duty"**: The grunt was acting properly and not with intentional misconduct or willful negligence and is therefore qualified for all government benefits.
2. **NLD-NDOM – "Not in Line of Duty, Not Due to Own Misconduct"**: The grunt was absent without leave (AWOL) and not of unsound mind and died, or became sick, or was injured, and therefore the grunt was not qualified for benefits and subject to military discipline;
3. **NLD-DOM – "Not in the Line of Duty: Due to Own Misconduct"**: The grunt's condition was the result of intentional misconduct or willful negligence. He was not entitled to benefits but is subject to disciplinary action.

There was a consistent rumor in the army that getting sunburned, and going on sick call, which would render a grunt unfit for duty, was a disciplinary action event, "Not in the Line of Duty: Due to Own Misconduct."

"The Fabulous Tale of the OCS Candidate Who Set His Face On Fire."
(Names have been omitted to protect the guilty)
Once upon a time, a long time ago, in a magical kingdom nestled among the peach orchids, there was an Infantry OCS candidate, who

had finally made it to the final phase of his officer training and was no longer being treated like whale shit.

So, to celebrate his elevation, our hero attended a drunken brawl with a few of his compatriots.

Now our hero was renowned for a magical trick called "The Human Flame Thrower."

The way this trick worked was, our hero would put some lighter fluid in his mouth, hold out his hand away from his face, light a cigarette lighter, hold the flame up to his mouth, spray the lighter fluid over the flame, and fill the room with a brilliant, blue flame.

Did I mention that this guy was in *Infantry* OCS?

Well ... back to the story ... at this drunken brawl, our hero had imbibed of the magic potions and witch's brews a bit too much. His friends, knowing that he was in fact "The Human Frame Thrower" encouraged him to thrill and amaze them with his feat of daring do.

Finally, our hero agreed.

Unfortunately, while preparing for his trick, he dribbled some lighter fluid on his chin and spilled some on the hand holding the lighter.

This caused his hand to catch fire,

Which caused a sudden intake of breath,

Which caused the flame to move towards his mouth,

Which caused his face to catch fire.

So, our hero stood in the midst of his admirers, face and hand aflame, to the wonder, amazement, and applause of all his fellow drunken OCS candidates (Did I mention it was INFANTRY OCS?).

Fortunately, our hero's wife, who had seen "The Human Flame Thrower" before, realized that a flaming face and hand were not part of the act.

So, she quickly put our hero out.

Unfortunately, not before he suffered burns to his lower face and hand.

For most people, this would have been bad enough. A trip to the emergency room, slave, bandages and a couple of weeks of pain and derision.

But our hero had to report back to OCS at zero-dark-thirty Monday morning!

If he went on sick call and missed training, he would be found "Not in the Line of Duty: Due to Own Misconduct," which was the usual judgment for setting one won's face on fire.

This would have resulted in his being kicked out of OCS, given an Article 15, and shipped off to NAM where his demonstrated judgment and performance as a human frame thrower indicated clearly he should be remanded.

So, despite his injuries, our hero bandaged his face, endured his pain, and carried on.

When asked what had happened, his response was, "I cut myself shaving!"

Everyone in this magical kingdom nestled among the peach orchids pretended to buy this story (Infantry, remember?) but by this time everyone knew the true story of the last performance of "The Human Flame Thrower."

LOACH. An acronym for Light Observation and Control Helicopter.

The LOACH was the Hughes' OH-6 Cayuse Helicopter; a single-engine light craft with a four-bladed main rotor used for personnel transport, escort and attack missions, and observation.

The LOACH was often used as a command-and-control helicopter by lifers to encourage grunts on the ground to kill more bad guys ... "Go, Team!"

How do you define crazy? Try this!

The helicopter guys used to go out on a perverse little search and destroy mission by pulling a "high low" trick. A LOACH would come in low, right at tree-top level, while a flock of gunships would circle high above it.

The LOACH would try to draw hostile fire, even blowing the canopy aside if there was a suspected target. If the bad guys were dumb enough to shoot at the loach, or just hang around gaping at it, the pilot dropped a red smoke on them and didi'd, while the guns swooped down and ruined the bad guy's day.

These guys were really good at finding targets.

I was on a LRRP on a ridgeline above the Ia Drang valley when a LOACH flew over my position, turned around, hovered over me, then descended through the canopy until the observer and I were practically eye-to-eye.

I gave the guy a big smile through my camo paint, waved, and tried to make my eyes as round as I could.

He dropped a red smoke on my ass!

A rotorhead's idea of a joke, I guess.

I still hold the world outdoor record for running a klick through the jungle while screaming and cursing.

LP. For grunts in the late 1960's, this had two possible meanings.

A large, black, vinal 33rpm record containing multiple recordings on each side, what one of my darlin' daughters referred to as, "Your big black CDs, dad!"

An abbreviation for "listening post,"

A listening post was a couple of grunts deployed at night forward of the fighting positions to provide an early warning of approaching bad guys.

During the daylight, LP's became OP's, Observation Posts, because in the daylight grunts could "see;" get it?

In case a grunt could actually convince himself that the crap couldn't get any worse, someone would stick him on LP.

LP's were usually two or three grunts, who had pissed off the platoon sergeant, so he kicked them out of the perimeter for the night, equipped with a radio, and placed out on the wrong side of the wire ... out beyond the trip flares and claymores ... in the dark, where bad guys lurked.

Although the principle of the LP was to give an early warning of enemy approach, it was never too clear exactly what a grunt was supposed to do if the bad guys really did show up since movement or talking on the radio would most likely be fatal.

Oh yeah! Then there's the problem of getting back into the perimeter through the claymore mines, flares, and wire, in the dark, while there's a bunch of nervous, keyed up, armed-to-the teeth grunts on the bunker line.

Did I mention the dark?

Returning for a second to other the possible meaning of LP, "Big Black CDs".

When I used to pick my daughters up at their mother's house for our weekends, we fell into a routine.

My older daughter, who in my darker moments I referred to as "My Mother's Revenge" – as in, "I hope someday you have one just like yourself ... then you'll know" – immediately appropriated the front seat, so she could control the sound system.

Her younger sister was permanently consigned to the back seat, which seemed to work for her. She spread out her stuffed animals and her blankie for the trip, and I didn't have to listen to ... "Daaaad! She's looking at me!" and "Daaaad! She's touching my stuff!" and "Daaaad! She's breathing my air!"

Anyway, back to the front seat.

I once referred to Revenge's music as "mother-mind-dog teenager music." For her, this meant "game on."

So, every time she got into the car, she'd announce, "I got a new one for you, daddy! You'll love this one! They're called the Slime Buckets from Hell!"

She would then slam the Slime Bucket CD into the player and crank up the sound for the trip to my place. I swear, by the time we got home, my eyes, nose, and ears were bleeding!

One day, with each daughter in her accustomed spot, Revenge announced, "I got a new one for you, daddy! You'll love this one! They're called the Rolling Stones!"

I paused for a second, not believing what I had just heard. Then I asked, "Did you say the Rolling Stones?"

"Oh yeah, Daddy! They're REALLY REALLY good,"
Revenge snickered twisting up the volume knob.

"Is their lead singer a guy named Mick Jagger?" I asked.

Silence and confusion from Revenge ... how could an old square know this?

"Uhhh ... yeaahh ..." Revenge answered warily, sensing a trap.

"Oh Sweetie, the Rolling Stones have been around forever!" I told her. "*I* listened to them in high school!"

Sacrilege, Revenge thought! No uncool, boomer, parent-type from the time of Peter, Paul and Mary, rotary-dial phones, and black-and-white, antenna TVs with only five channels could possibly be allowed to appropriate cool, 90's-teenager sounds.

So, all the way to my place, we argued about the vintage and the provenance of the Rolling Stones.

Meanwhile, the younger sister blissfully enjoyed the company of her stuffed animals and her blankie in the back seat.

When we got to my place, I dragged my "big black CDs" of the Rolling Stones from the time before the invention of teenaged-cool ... 1964.

The first thing I heard from Revenge as she sorted through my albums was, "Jagger! He looks so young!"

Then, "Daddy! Do you have a CD player for these things?"

LRRP.   Pronounced, LURP.

Never say this in a crowded restaurant; people around you will dive for cover.

This is an acronym for "Long Range Reconnaissance Patrol." It refers both to a type of mission and to the grunts who did it.

This was a unique and insidious concept of army special ops with assistance and financing of the CIA, who didn't exist and were never there, in which a team of four rangers, or volunteer grunts (now there's an oxymoron), who have grown tired of the relative safety and comfort of a chest—deep, shoulder-wide holes in the ground, swept through four square klicks of impossibly mountainous, thick, jungle terrain trying to find out who was there and what they were doing.

The fundamental problem with the concept was large concentrations of bad guys who were very protective about their turf.

The term also described the personnel who do such things — not God's sanest creatures, but much saner than Hawk Eyes, e.g.

"Dad, this is my new boyfriend, Lurch. He was a LRRP in Vietnam, but he's OK now. He has his papers from the VA — or was that the vet?"

The bad guys really hated LRRPS, Hawk Eyes, and Rangers in general. According to a CIA friend of mine, who wasn't there, a bounty of $500 green backs was placed on the head of every one of them by the NVA.

That's a form of praise grunts appreciate.

LRRP Rations.   Again, don't say this is a crowded restaurant.

These were freeze-dried, vacuum-packed, individual rations.

The "entrées" included: Beef Hash, Chili con Carne, Spaghetti with Meat Sauce, Beef with Rice, Chicken Stew, Pork with Scalloped Potatoes, Beef Stew, and Chicken with Rice. The desserts included two chocolate-coated candy discs or a "corn flake" bar.

What the hell's a "corn flake" bar you might ask?

Just imagine pulverized corn flakes pressed together with orangey, lemony-flavored grease into the shape a rectangular bar. Yummy!

You can actually develop a taste for these things. That, and a taste for tropical chocolate, were the classical signs that you had been in Nam too long.

The army theory behind LRRP rations was to issue them to rangers and special ops guys as a less weighty alternative to C Rats — move fast, stay mobile sort of stuff.

The practical problem was that a freeze-dried ration required about half a canteen of water to reconstitute it. So, any weight offset by the rations was replaced by having to carry extra water.

Do the math:

If little Johnny were going on a four-day LRRP mission, and was carrying enough LRRP rations for three meals a day, and each meal required .5 pints of water to reconstitute, how many pounds of water would little Johnny have to carry?

1. Enough to give him a hernia
2. Enough to require a spare mule
3. Silly! Water doesn't come by the pound
4. All of the above answer.

As any high school kid knows, "D" is always the right answer.

The concept of "reconstituting" these mummified meals was also a bit optimistic. With enough water, most of the meals could be rendered into a reasonable Beef-Hash, Chicken-with-Rice, Pork-with-Scalloped-Potatoes tasting paste.

But "Chili Con Bullets" resisted all attempts at being re-converted into anything resembling edible material — at least the beans did. No process – chemical, physical or metaphysical – could convert the beans into anything chewable. Their only practical use was to pile them up in front of a claymore as extra shrapnel.

LZ.   This is an abbreviation for "Landing Zone," a place where choppers, grunts, airborne, and rangers initially touch the earth … hopefully to rise again.

LZs came in two conditions: cold and hot.

A "cold" LZ was one where no one was waiting for the grunts to arrive.

A "hot" LZ had a reception committee.

M

M1A1.   This was an expression used to describe anything basic, fundamental and unadorned, e.g. "It was an M1A1 cluster f'ck."

M16.   The basic tool of grunts.

The M16 is a lightweight, 5.56 mm, air-cooled, gas-operated, magazine-fed rifle known affectionately (or not) by grunts as the "Tinker Toy."

The M16 was an object of both love and loathing for grunts. It was not especially known for its stopping power, accuracy or reliability ... other than that, it was great to have around.

When a grunt was issued an M16 in Nam, the first thing he looked at was the bolt ... silver bolts (stainless steel) were bad news ... blued bolts (no ... not blue ... "blued" ... in other words, the same color as the rifle barrel) were good news. Weapons with silver bolts were notorious for reliability problems, i.e. going "click" instead of "bang" at the worst possible moment.

The secret to keeping this little monster happy was getting rid of dented and funky ammo, keeping the chamber dry and clean, and keeping the bolt clean and operational.

Grunts typically taped the barrels shut to keep the chamber and bolt clean. So, the first thing down range during a fire fight were bits of flaming duct tape.

There was a pervasive "urban legend" about the high velocity, unstable round launched by the M16. The round would either bounce off its intended victim, or enter one part of the anatomy, take about three right-angle turns and exit on a totally different spatial plane ... like entering the right arm and exiting from the big toe of the left foot.

M16s were useless for stopping pissed-off, charging water buffalos ... trust me on this one ... use the M79 to stun the beast and run like hell.

M60. The M60, affectionally called "The Hog," is an air-cooled and gas-operated machine gun firing the 7.62mm NATO round from an open bolt.

It was SOP for every fifth round in a belt of machine gun ammo to be a tracer. The good news was that the tracers were a hell of a show at night, helped aim the gun, and identified the gunner as a friendly (we used orange tracers and the bad guys used green, unless they were using our ammo sold to them at the local ARVN thrift store).

The other news was that tracers gave away the gun's position and hence the squad's position. So, gunners were known to pull the tracers out of the ammo belts.

A machine gunner was at the top of the grunt food-chain. The M60 was given to the most-experienced big guy in the platoon because this was most of a platoon's fire power and humping this monster, with all its ammo, its tripod, its traverse and search mechanism, and its extra barrel would strain "Hoss" Cartwright.

Gunners were known to develop very close, and somewhat unnatural, attachments to their machine guns (hell, we all slept with our weapons). They'd give them pet names, build little beds for them, give them presents on their birthdays and special occasions ... after all this time I still don't like to think about this.

Suffice it to say that all grunts knew there were two things in Nam you kept your hands off ... Montagnard women and some other grunt's machine gun.

M79. A single-shot, shoulder-fired, break-open grenade launcher firing a variety of 40mm rounds: HE (High Explosive), smoke, buckshot (never worked well), slug (deer shot) and "lume" (illumination).

The M79 was much beloved by grunts and a definite status symbol in the grunt food chain. Only really trusted guys got the M79; this was one step below machine gunner in the grunt food-chain.

The M79 was very, very reliable (except the buckshot round) and easy to maintain with only five or so moving parts. So, of course, the army tried to replace it with the M203, a combination M16 / Grenade Launcher dingus, which was an operational, maintenance, and tactical nightmare—unless a grunt liked to hear his weapon go "click" in the middle of a firefight.

The only problems with the M79 was the weight of the ammo and what the hell does a grunt do to protect himself when the bad guys are right on top of him (remember the 40 mm shotgun round wasn't worth crap and the 40mm HE took 20 meters to arm).

Grenadiers carried 45s when they could steal ... Oops! I meant "acquire" ... them from officers or any local REMFs — or even an additional M16 — or just clubbed the little bastards with the M79's wooden stock (not recommended, but effective).

A grunt could usually get a grenadier's pound cake and peaches if he carried a few of his 40 mm rounds or just stuck close in a fire fight.

MACV. Pronounced MACK-vee; this was an acronym for "Military Assistance Command—Vietnam."

This designated the United States' unified command structure for all of its military forces in South Vietnam during the Vietnam War for those who believe there was a meaningful organizational structure above battalion level. MACV-types were sometimes found in air-conditioned trailers in Saigon and various in-country R&R centers.

Yes! Yes! We were jealous! Very, very jealous!

Malaria. This was the normal condition of a grunt who didn't have dengue.

Malaria was the result of grunts feeding the non-dengue-bearing mosquitoes with their own blood.

Malaria was carried by the anopheles mosquito, which according to the army Medical Corps could be easily detected since it only fed in the early evening or early morning and bit at a 45-degree angle unlike all the rest of the bugs and lifers in Nam who sucked a grunt dry at different angles any time of the day.

Typical symptoms of malaria include fever, shivering, joint pain, and vomiting with cyclical occurrences of sudden chills followed by rigor and then fever and sweating, which were identical with the symptoms resulting from eating a can of Ham & Lima Beans.

The consequences of severe malaria include coma and death. Even army aspirin and GI Gin couldn't beat it. So, even grunt medics would send a grunt with malaria out of the field.

There were two flavors of malaria in the highlands: regular, or M1A1 malaria, and "brain" malaria.

Regular malaria got you sick enough to get out of the field, packed in ice, cleaned up, and sleeping between sheets until the fever went down.

Brain malaria killed you or left you an idiot, in which case you re-enlisted, extended your tour, and got promoted. I had brain malaria and did all three ... and I'm still not legally responsible for anything I do ... so buy my books and stay on my good side!

Malaria Pill.   A pill a grunt took to prevent malaria, so he could fully enjoy his dengue.

In the highlands, there were two malaria pills, an orange- colored horse pill taken every Monday for "regular" malaria and a small white pill taken daily for "brain" malaria.

Being handed the orange pill by the medic every Monday was the only way a grunt could tell what day of the week it was ... if he cared. Some grunts didn't take the orange pills; they thought a dose of malaria was better than being shot at. A lifestyle choice, I guess.

So, the army used to administer surprise piss tests which were pretty easy to beat as long as you didn't use the urine of a pregnant coke-girl (the Vietnamese took our malaria pills religiously).

Everybody took the white pill daily — brain malaria was just too scary — a fried brain could cause you to do mad and impulsive things, like re-enlist and turn into a lifer.

Mamasahn. Pronounced, MA-ma-san.

In general, this referred to any older Vietnamese woman.

"Older" was a difficult concept to apply in Nam; it usually applied to women who were over thirty and whose teeth were stained brown by betel nut.

It also applied to a madam, procuress, or water-point queen, whose associates were referred to as "babysahns."

The women living in the rural areas in Vietnam had a short youth. The work in the fields and rice paddies alone was backbreaking. But trying to survive and protect a family in the middle of a war of insurgency matured them long before their time. This was a land that tolerated no lingering youth—in mamasahns and grunts.

Marmite Can. The M-1944 Insulated Food "Marmite" Cans were used to keep chow hot.

Marmite Cans have a rubber gasket and locking lid to keep the contents either hot or cold, thereby one of the best beer coolers ever made if a grunt could figure out the beer and ice part.

The appearance of marmites on an LZ was usually good news because they meant hot chow.

They were sometimes bad news when a grunt found out what the army wanted in return for giving him hot chow.

Marmite cans accompanied by a cook were good news; marmite cans accompanied by a chaplain were not.

MARS Station. GI ... Phone home!

The Military Auxiliary Radio System is a United States Department of Defense sponsored program, managed and operated program by the Army and the Air Force. During the Vietnam War, MARS was most known for enabling in-country servicemen to contact their families at home.

I actually used this service from Camp Enari, near Pleiku; I damn near killed my mother!

Can you imagine having to deal with having a child in Vietnam then receiving a phone call in the middle of the night from Vietnam?

My end of the call was mostly ... I'm fine, over ... Getting enough to eat, over ... Be home soon, over ...

While on my mom's end ... Sob, over ... Sob, over ... Sob, over ...

If I go to hell, it won't be for anything I did in Nam; it will be for what I did to my mom by going to Nam.

Max Nix.   Pronounced MAHCKS-Nicks.

This was pidgin for "I don't care!" "I don't give a shit!"

Reputedly, this expression was derived from the German expression, *mich nicht*. Typically, it was used by grunts who had done a tour in Germany to express their indifference to the concerns of lifers, REMFs and anything that didn't get you killed, "It's max nix to me!"

Meeting Engagement.   This was a blind date, grunt-style.

It's an army euphemism used to describe what happens when two moving and well-armed opposing forces essentially collide unexpectedly.

This was also known as a "cluster f*#k".

"Meeting Engagement" describes most forms of combat in Vietnam, because if the bad guys knew where the grunts were, they tended not to be there.

The most famous meeting engagement in American history was when General Custer and the 7th Cavalry unexpectedly met Sitting Bull, Crazy Horse, and a few thousand pissed-off, well-armed Sioux and Cheyenne at the Little Big Horn.

These things rarely worked out well for anyone involved.

Remember: If the point man runs by you in the opposite direction screaming, follow... quickly!

MIA.   This is an abbreviation for "Missing In Action;" the casualty status assigned to any member of the armed services who can't be accounted for after combat. The individual so designated may have actually been killed, wounded, or captured, but unless the individual could be positively accounted for, and in the case of KIA be positively identified, the individual would be designated MIA.

Essentially, the army doesn't want to tell someone's wife, children, or parents they've been killed, then have to go back and say "Oops! We're sorry. We made a mistake." So positive identification is required for reporting a KIA and, until it's accomplished, the individual remains MIA.

At the Repl Depl, soldiers coming in-country were asked for what degree of injury did they want their families notified. Most declared nothing short of being killed or severely injured. Spare the home front!

For example, I was believed to be KIA after a firefight—luckily for me only my helmet was killed. But there was no notification until my status could be confirmed. They finally found me at the medevac unit frolicking with the nurses and, since my injuries were hardly "life threatening," no one at home was told.

Following the Paris Peace Accords of 1973, the US listed about 1,350 Americans as prisoners of war or missing in action and roughly 1,200 Americans reported killed in action and bodies not recovered, most of whom remain unaccounted for to this day.

War's a messy business, especially with the nasty weapons used in Nam and the terrain over which the war was fought. The US is still bringing home soldiers from the Pacific jungles where WWII was fought! Accounting for guys who were lost in tens of thousands of square miles of jungle and mountains is not an easy or an exact science.

The chances of large numbers of US soldiers being found alive in secret camps is unlikely. Nor is it likely that the government is keeping the whereabouts of MIA's secret to cover up some nefarious agreement made with the North Vietnamese or the Russians in 1973.

Those who claim such things without compelling evidence in order to sensationalize some tired and tragic story, should become MIA themselves. Par example:

> It is not conspiracy theory, not a paranoid myth, not Rambo fantasy. It is only hard evidence of a national disgrace: American prisoners were left behind at the end of the Vietnam War. They

were abandoned because six presidents and official Washington could not admit their guilty secret. They were forgotten because the press and most Americans turned away from all things that reminded them of Vietnam." (*Penthouse*. September 1994).

Basta! Let our dead comrades rest and their families find some peace! We will never forget them!

The rest of you just shut the hell up!

Military Time. This is enough to make an existentialist weep, but there is a reality in the universal space-time continuum known as "military time." Just walk through the door, go down about three blocks, turn left at the deli, and enter the Twilight Zone.

The military operates off a twenty-four-hour clock, beginning at midnight, which is 0000 hours (zero zero zero zero hours) and ending at 11:59 PM, which is 2359 hours (two three five niner hours).

To make matters just a bit more convoluted, since the military must be able to tell time all over the world, military time calibrates on Greenwich, England — Greenwich Mean Time (GMT), which the Military refers to as "Z" or "Zulu Time," and to which it attaches the "Zulu" (Z) suffix, to ensure the time-zone referred to is clear.

For example a military message might state, "Your unit will cross the Lima Oscar Delta at 1300 Zulu."

That means you've got to get your ass across the line of departure at 1 PM in Greenwich, England ... which is less than helpful if you're in Kontum, South Viet Nam:

> "Now when the little hand's on three you subtract the square root of ... wait a minute ... is there Daylight Savings Time in Nam?"

For any civilians who are still with me on this, here's the basic run down:

Civilian Time	Military Time
12 AM	0000 Hrs
1 AM	0100 Hrs

2 AM	0200 Hrs
3 AM	0300 Hrs
4 AM	0400 Hrs
5 AM	0500 Hrs
6 AM	0600 Hrs
7 AM	0700 Hrs
8 AM	0800 Hrs
9 AM	0900 Hrs
10 AM	1000 Hrs
11 AM	1100 Hrs
12 PM	1200 Hrs
1 PM	1300 Hrs
2 PM	1400 Hrs
3 PM	1500 Hrs
4 PM	1600 Hrs
5 PM	1700 Hrs
6 PM	1800 Hrs
7 PM	1900 Hrs
8 PM	2000 Hrs
9 PM	2100 Hrs
10 PM	2200 Hrs
11 PM	2300 Hrs

Always calculate military time by adding minutes to the hour, e.g., 7:45 PM is 1945 hrs., not a quarter to 2000. You can use this to confuse your kids, family members and co-workers ... unless you're in the army or the European Union and still have to take it seriously.

"Does anybody really know what time it is? / Does any-body really care?" — Chicago

Montagnard.   (also, "Yard")
Grunt term for the Indigenous, mountain people of the central highlands of Vietnam. Montagnard was a name given to the various tribal peoples of the highlands by the French.

These were basically "good guys" as long as you remembered one immutable rule ... stay away from the women! They were known for generosity, hospitality, home-made rice wine that could remove the bluing from an M16, and very, very, very sharp knives (remember rule one despite how good the rice wine makes you feel).

The Montagnards also displayed a very problematic, but generally grunt-approved, interpretation of the rules of engagement. They never differentiated between "good" and "bad" Vietnamese; they just wanted to shoot them all and let Buddha sort them out.

This attitude seems to stem from the historic relationship between the Montagnards and the Vietnamese, which is curiously similar to that between Native Americans and the Europeans who came to "settle" the US.

The Montagnards believed that they were the original inhabitants of what is now known as Vietnam. When the Vietnamese migrated south from China, they pushed the Montagnards off the fertile lowlands and into the mountains. So, the Montagnards were happy to try to get theirs back from the Vietnamese ... any brand of Vietnamese ... if the US would be so kind as to arm them.

When encountering Montagnards in the bush, communication was always a problem ... conversational Montagnard was not taught in the army language schools ... until grunts found out that many Montagnards understood French.

Having had a French-speaking grandfather and having reinforced that experience with four years of French in high school and college, I often served as an interpreter when we entered a Montagnard village (hence, my nom de guerre "Frenchy," despite my being an Irish kid).

Although we thought we had a common language, the semantics were at times interesting. To illustrate:

GLOSSARY
What One Guy Said
What He Meant
What The Other Guy Understood

ACTUAL CONVERSATION

Bonjour!

Hey!

We French are finally back!

> *Soyez bienvenus à mon village!*
>
> It's about time you guys showed up!
>
> They're not going to start a firefight.

Qui est la chef du village?

Who's running the show here?

Who commands the local French militia?

> *C'est moi! Sergent Vung!*
>
> Sergeant Vung at your service!
>
> Why do they call the village chief "sergeant"?

Nous sommes Américains. Nous voudrions entrer dans votre village pour chercher des armes ennemies et des munitions.

We're Americans. We'd like to come in and search for enemy arms and ammunition.

AH! Our French friends want to see how well we have maintained the equipment they gave us to fight *les sales et maudits Vietnamiens.* What the hell kind of Frenchman is an <<American>>?

> *Bien sûr! Pas de problème! C'est á vous de toute façon. Nous allons*
> *vous montrer comment nous avons maintenu tout votre équipement en*
> *bon état.*
>
> Of course ... not a problem ... it's yours anyway ... it's all in good
> shape ... we're ready to get back into the fight and wipe out these
> damned Vietnamese who stole our country!
>
> How did the contraband become ours? I guess they're willing to
> give it up.

Montagnards commonly served with army Ranger and Special Forces units. Here's a piece of advice—if you ever plan to go out on a four-day LRRP with a bunch of Montagnards and they tell you not to weigh yourself down with rations and water because they have to "move fast" and Montagnards can "live off the land," don't believe it, unless you're okay with eating bugs, worms and freeze-dried fish heads for four days. Don't ask me how I know this! It's classified!

Political correctness these days dictates that these people now be referred to as "Hmong." Since the war, many have migrated here and colonized unwanted and underutilized parts of the country like Wisconsin, where they are fervently praying for global warming.

I don't want to toss my hat into the immigration debate, but the Montagnards were one of our most faithful allies in Vietnam. Because of that, and their historical troubles with the Vietnamese, I think we owe them. So, if they want Wisconsin, I can live with that as long as they keep producing cheese, brats, and beer.

Personally, I remember one of the Montagnard grunts who worked with our Ranger teams — a guy everybody called "Jack' Son" — who spoke what I would characterize as fluent "jive-grunt English."

Jack's Son thought certain words, very common in grunt speech but would get a bar of soap in the mouth back in the world, were socially acceptable speech. He and I did a lot of quality time together up near the Cambodian border (I won't say which side of the border) ... and I forgive him for the "bugs, worms and freeze -dried fish heads" thing he pulled on me.

I hope he and his family got out and are enjoying life up in Green Bay.

In return for the fish-head joke he pulled on me in Nam, I give him the following advice, "Don't bother packing warm clothes. Wisconsin never gets cold in the winter. The balmy waters of Lake Michigan keep it warm all winter."

MOS.   An abbreviation for "Military Occupation Specialty."

MOS is army-speak for "your job," or if your MOS were "11B," "Eleven Bravo", a grunt, "your uncertain and uninsurable future."

Personnel (army-speak for "humans," "individuals" or "people") were classified by their MOS.

"What's his MOS?

"11B!"

"Poor bastard!"

Common grunt-related Vietnam-era MOS were 11B-Light Infantry (aka Grunt, Ground Pounder); 11C-Mortars; 11F-Light Infantry Recon (LRRPS and Hawk Eyes); 11H-Heavy Weapons Infantry; 11M-Mechanized Infantry (an apparent oxymoron); and 61B Medic (Doc).

Other MOS a grunt might run into in the bush were Artillery (13X), Armored Cav & Armor (19X), Helicopter Crews (15X), Engineers (12X) and occasionally Cooks (92X) and Signal Corps (10X).

"89 X-Ray" indicated Explosive Ordinance Disposal, the only people on the battle field crazier than a grunt (with the possible exception of a combat engineer with a Bangalore torpedo). EOD guys rushed in where even grunts feared to tread.

The disposal of explosive ordinance always made sense to me, as long as it wasn't me doing the disposing.

A "71 Lima" was a "clerk/typist."

Since these guys had complete access to and mastery over a grunt's 201 File and came equipped with typewriters, paper, carbon paper, and white-out, they were treated with awe and dread. Only they knew the secret army administrative codes that could either damn or bless a grunt's existence.

MP.   Abbreviation for Military Police, Pronounced Em Pee

The Military Police Corps is the law enforcement branch of the US army.

In Nam, the army deployed MP's as their "fun police."

MP's were the nemesis of gruntdom. They ruled the basecamps and any civilian town big enough and safe enough for a grunt to relax and have fun in. When MP's weren't too busy policing up grunts who were "off limits," they had time to worry about shined shoes, haircuts, and saluting.

Pleiku City was the closest town to the 4th Division base camp, Camp Enari, and was off limits to 4th Division personnel. I imagine the explicit reason was the danger of terrorist acts against US personnel by the National Liberation Front. Why the VC would single out guys wearing the 4th ID patch was beyond me. GI's from the other bases around the town, and even Air Force guys from the airbase, had access to Pleiku and, as long as they weren't stupid, seemed not to have too much of a problem. Made sense. Their money was providing a steady revenue stream for the VC.

We grunts suspected that the little old ladies who ran the 4th Division were afraid that with all the bars and bargirls downtown, that a grunt might actually relax for an afternoon and ... dare I say it ... have fun.

So, the fun police were deployed into Pleiku City.

There were two flavors of MP's in Pleiku; both wore the standard black brassard on the left arm with MP in white lettering. The 4th Division cops wore the division patch; the other guys were the "Double Hatchet" MP's, so identified by their shoulder patch for the 18th MP Brigade.

The 4th Division cops were reasonable. As long as you didn't force them to act, they left you alone. So, when 4th Division guys went into Pleiku, they didn't wear the division patch, didn't get into fights, didn't throw up on the streets, didn't get up the cops' faces. At the end of the day, they threw each other onto the back of a deuce and went back to Enari. No harm, no foul.

The Double Hatchets seemed to be working on a quota system. If a grunt as much as made eye contact, he was up against a wall with his pockets turned inside out.

While I was with LRRPS, we had kind of a running war with the Double Hatchets. The 75th Infantry was a provisional unit with company-sized detachments assigned to various commands in Nam.

My company, K, was LOGCOM to the 4th ID, in other words, they fed, clothed and housed us. Our OPCOM status, army-speak for who told us what to do, was fuzzy.

The CIA guys who weren't there, acted like they owned us, but so did the S2 section of the 4th ID brigade whose firebase we sat on, LZ Oasis. The only way we had a clue who we were working for at any instant was who did the mission brief, either Skip and Scooter, or the brigade S2.

So, no one was too clear about who actually owned us.

The Double Hatchets assumed we were 4th ID and harassed us accordingly. To make matters worse for me, since I was technically on my second tour, I wore a 4th ID patch on my right shoulder as a combat patch. And no few of the Double Hatchet cops were obviously dyslexic, so I'd get hassled based on my combat patch regularly. "Okay ... we'll go over this one more time ... right shoulder, where I've been ... left shoulder, where I am ..."

MPC. This was an abbreviation for "Military Pay Certificate," the ersatz currency used to pay soldiers in Nam; also known as "monopoly money" "play money" and "funny money."

The use of MPC in Nam was supposed to prevent real money, "green backs," from getting in the hands of the Vietnamese black market, who would gladly trade with you for MPC or "piasters" at a disadvantageous rate of exchange only equaled in modern times by credit card companies.

The cash "hierarchy" in Nam was greenbacks, MPC and "piasters" or "Dong" (Vietnamese currency). The going exchange rate at most water points was $5 MPC = 500 Pi = 10 Cans of Carling Black Label = *mot boom boom*. Periodically, the army would change the MPC, at which time the exchange rate became a bushel basket of MPC in Vietnamese hands = 500 Pi in grunt hands = all the CBL you could drink (which actually wasn't that much if you had working taste buds and a functioning lower abdominal tract) = boocoo boom boom.

N

Napalm. The name of a somewhat infamous armament consisting of flaming, jellied gasoline composed primarily of benzene and polystyrene and delivered principally by aircraft in close air support roles ("delivered" of course is another one of those military euphemisms to make napalm sound benign, like this stuff came by a uniformed courier; "Knock! Knock! Flaming gasoline for Mr. Victor Charlie ... would you sign here, sir?").

Napalm could also be delivered by flame thrower but, despite the movie Deer Hunter, this was rarely, if ever, done in Nam due to the complete lack of grunts crazy enough to run around in a fire fight with a tank of flammable jelly strapped to their backs.

If the antiwar movement or the media wanted to illustrate US cruelty to the poor, defenseless freedom fighters of the NVA, putting stock footage of a napalm strike (even if the film was from Okinawa in WWII) always did the trick.

What the media never showed were the US casualties caused by trying to dig those little fers out of their caves and bunkers to make them stop pumping RPGs into military convoys and civilian vehicles on Highway 14.

Number Ten. Pidgin meaning "the worst," e.g. "You numbah ten, GI; you rifer!"

The opposite of "Number 10" was "Number One," the way you felt about the 71L who handed you your DEROS orders. But don't kiss him!

Nuoc Mam.　　　Pronounced NOOK-mom.

This is the national fish sauce of Vietnam, the vilest looking, evilest-smelling substance on the planet ... maybe the entire universe.

Recipe: take all the parts of a fish that a Vietnamese peasant won't eat ... guts, entrails, droppings, eye balls, other balls, fins, bones and scales; place in a press; leave for a few months in tropical heat; open spigot ... *et voilà* ... Nuoc Mam.

This was the one thing grunts would not use to kill the taste of C Rats.

The bad guys used this stuff as cologne!

Point man advice: if you're walking point in the middle of the boonies and get a whiff of rotten fish ... stop or you're screwed ... really, really screwed.

NVA.　　　This was an abbreviation for the North Vietnamese Army, also known as the Peoples' Army of Vietnam (PAVN).

These were bad guys on testosterone.

The NVA were typically well-trained, well-equipped, and motivated, unlike the Viet Cong whose training and sub-standard weapons were as much a danger to themselves as they were to any grunts they might encounter.

The NVA could be recognized by their pith helmets, tan or OD uniforms, red collar tabs (if you got that close, you were about to have a bad day) shiny, clean, Czech-made AK's, and bad attitudes.

Grunts' attitude toward the NVA was a combination of hate, fear and respect.

The "hate" and "fear" part is obvious— their job was to kill us and they were damn good at it.

The "respect" is harder to explain.

First, like us they were "good grunts" — they were trained, tough and determined.

Second, these guys were sharing our experience — putting up with the same crap, living in the dirt amidst the bugs and reptiles, losing friends, missing home — and putting up with their own version of lifer

— the political cadre (I'm sure more than one of these blokes wound up with a frag in his blankets).

Ironically, the NVA were the closest thing to us we had in Nam.

Thomas Hardy had it right, I think:

> Had he and I but met
> By some old ancient inn,
> We should have sat us down to wet
> Right many a nipperkin!
>
> But ranged as infantry,
> And staring face to face,
> I shot at him and he at me,
> And killed him in his place.
>
> I shot him dead because –
> Because he was my foe,
> Just so – my foe of course he was;
> That's clear enough; although
>
> He thought he'd 'list perhaps,
> Off-hand like – just as I –
> Was out of work – had sold his traps –
> No other reason why.
>
> Yes; quaint and curious war is!
> You shoot a fellow down
> You'd treat if met where any bar is,
> Or help to half-a-crown.

One thing we had that the NVA didn't have was a bunch of civilians thousands of miles away, enjoying all the comforts that a peaceful and free society could offer, and exercising their right to free speech by lionizing the "heroic insurgents" in Vietnam and by denouncing grunts as "baby-killers" and "rapists."

"Yes; quaint and curious war is!"

0

Old Man.   Army slang for a commander.

The term was used only if the guy were competent and likable... but if he were competent, liking him would come naturally to grunts.

The concept "old" had nothing to do with chronological age. In Nam an infantry platoon leader was typically in his early to mid-twenties and a company commander in his mid to late twenties.

They were the "adult supervision" for the grunts who typically ranged in age from nineteen to twenty- one.

OPFOR.   Pronounced OP-for

Acronym and abbreviation for Opposing Forces.

In other words, "enemy," bad guys," and other more picturesque but less socially acceptable terms.

This is not an expression used in Nam. In my AO, we just referred to the enemy as "dinks"

OPFOR came into use during the final phases of the Cold War, during the Regan Administration, when, for reasons never explained to me, it became unacceptable to refer to the putative enemy against whom all our planning, hopes and despair was aimed, as the "Russkies," the "Reds," the "Commies," "Ivan."

OPORD.   Pronounced OP-ord.

The OPORD was a formal, written document representing the delusions of out-of-touch staff-weenies, REMFs and lifers, which was not to be taken seriously by grunts ... if possible.

This is an acronym for "Operations Order," which was also known as the "Five Paragraph Operations Order" because it packaged and sorted bullshit and delusion into five standard paragraphs.

1. **Situation** — what's going on; who are the bad guys; how bad are they; who's on our side; where am I?
2. **Mission** — delusional and fantastical description of expectations
3. **Execution** — an even more delusional and fantastical description of how these delusional and fantastical expectations are to be achieved by the grunts mentioned in paragraph one.
4. **Service Support** – an oxymoronic fairy tale about lifers, ash, trash, cabbages and kings.
5. **Command & Signal** – "Wave bye-bye, boys! I'll be here if you need me!"

The archive OPORD was usually re-written after victory for the historians or shredded after defeat to protect the guilty; "I told the old man this wouldn't work!"

The best advice I was ever given about OPORDS was stated to me by one of my Fifth Army mentors,

> "Every plan becomes obsolete the second that the first soldier steps across the Line of Departure. Everything after that is an aspect of leadership called 'Chaos Theory'."

P

P38.   The P38 was C-Rat can opener, an absolute miracle of army ingenuity. This thing didn't break, rust, need sharpening or polishing, and always did what it was designed to do ... open C-Rat cans.

Grunts became very attached to their P38s often wearing them around their necks on a chord like some sacred talisman; they were the "green scapulars" of gruntdom.

The only maintenance required for a P38 was occasionally holding it over a match flame to kill the nasty Viet-Microbes.

Palace Guard.   This described a unit being assigned to firebase security after the bunkers were built and before the lifers, wire, and sandbags arrived.

Palace guard meant sleeping in a hootch, minimum digging, hot A rations and coffee, not humping the boonies except for occasional patrols without rucks.

As close to heaven as possible in Nam ... at least until the lifers showed up with the sandbags and wire.

Pay Grade.   Military pay grades were used by the army to determine wages and benefits.

Pay grades are divided into three groups, Enlisted (E); Warrant Officer (W); and Officer (O).

Enlisted Pay Grades

> E1 = Private Trainee
> E2 = Private
> E3 = Private First Class
> E4 = Spec. 4, Corporal
> E5 = Spec. 5, Sergeant

E6 = Spec. 6, Staff Sergeant

E7 = Sergeant First Class, Platoon Sergeant

E8 = First Sergeant, Master Sergeant

E9 = Sergeant Major, Command Sergeant Major

Pay grades were often used in lieu of rank to describe someone's position in the army food chain. But they were only used when talking about someone, never when talking to someone; e.g.

"Who's the new platoon sergeant?" (refers to a position in the TOE)

"Sergeant Smith." (title of any sergeant)

"He an E7?" (pay grade, refers to the authorized pay grade per the TOE; and a rank = Platoon Sergeant)

"Naw, he's an E6!" (refers to the pay grade) "A shake 'n' bake!" (Refers to source of rank, perceived competence and expected life span).

If you can follow this, you're ready to join the S1 section!

There was a correspondence between pay grade, rank and title, but it wasn't ironclad. Under the tradition of there being no rank among sergeants, all sergeants were called "sergeant."

But, unless you were nuts, drunk, high, or all three, you called an E8 wearing a diamond between his chevrons and three rockers "First Sergeant" or "Top."

If the E8 were a Master Sergeant (no diamond), you would just stay the hell out of his way; there was nothing to be gained in socializing with an E8, and much to be lost.

Also, you called an E9, "Sergeant Major" (three chevrons up, three rockers down with a star, or star and wreath in the center).

The first time you screwed this up, was the last time you'd screw this up (refer to the movie, *We Were Soldiers,* the "Good morning, Sergeant Major" scene in front of Infantry Hall, for the details concerning this protocol).

A real mystery were the so-called "specialist" ranks.

These were descendants of the old WWII Tech ranks meant for soldiers who were more technician than leader. But, for some weird and wonderful reason infantry E4's were Spec 4's (Specialist 4th Class) not Corporals. The only way you could become a corporal in the infantry was by being busted down from sergeant.

Due to a "personnel shortages" after Tet '68, I was promoted from PFC (Private First Class) E3 to Sergeant E4, or "Acting Jack." I was entitled to wear a sergeant's stripes (which grunts did not do in the boonies) and be addressed as "sergeant" (something else that would make one nervous out in the boonies). I also got a squad leader's (E6) slot, but not the money.

The army, like most bureaucracy-centric organizations, will, under great pressure, allow an individual to skip a level or two in the hierarchy of authority, but not in the hierarchy of pay.

But, what the hell! If we were in it for the money, we'd have joined the mafia, not the army ... essentially the sort of same work but better clothes, better hours, better working conditions, more money, and a great opportunity to get into witness protection program instead of a VA hospital.

Peanut Butter Frag.   This was a grunt's idea of a really funny joke.

Here's how it worked: take a can of C Rat peanut butter, unopened; toss said can into a fire; wait for the peanut butter to get white hot and expand to the point where the can explodes; sit back and watch the fun.

Thousands of dollars in MPC have changed hands betting when the thing would explode and which FNG would wish he had kept his shirt on ... I have a few peanut butter scars myself.

Phantom Jet.   A grunt term for Manna from Heaven or, to quote a contemporary song, "Judy in the Skies with Napalm."

This is the McDonnell Douglas F-4 Phantom II, a two-seat, twin-engine, all-weather, long-range, supersonic interceptor fighter/fighter-bomber.

The bad guys would never see this one coming! It flew so fast that they heard it only after it passed them, at which point they were beyond hearing.

The Phantom provided a veritable smorgasbord of nasty surprises for close air support — bombs, napalm, missiles, canon shells, and bullets.

Any zoomies who flew, serviced, cleaned, changed the oil, or got within a hundred feet of one of one of these puppies drank free when in the same AO as grunts.

####////TOP SECRET///

Phoenix Program.   Everything I think I know about this I learned from a Hollywood movie! That's my story, and I'm sticking to it!

Official government policy states that the so-called "Phoenix Program" was a paranoid fantasy of leftist journalists and Hollywood film writers. Through this mythical "Phoenix Program," the CIA financed PSYOP missions, assassinations, and other war crimes.

If you knew anything about this, the government would have to kill you. So, if you're alive to read this, *ipso facto* bibity bobity boo, proves that the program never existed!

The existence of this program was vigorously denied, especially by the CIA guys — "Skip," "Biff," and "Scooter" — who, although never there, mission briefed and debriefed army LRRP and Hawkeye teams in Nam.

It never happened ... understand ... never happened.

Burn this book after reading! Then buy another copy! Repeat if necessary!

####///TOP SECRET///

Phonetic Alphabet.   This is the army version of the A B Cs ... more accurately, the "Alpha, Bravo, Charlies."

The phonetic alphabet described names that the army assigned to the letters of the alphabet.

A Alpha	H Hotel	O Oscar	V Victor
B Bravo	I India	P Papa	W Whiskey
C Charlie	J Juliet	Q Quebec	X X-ray
D Delta	K Kilo	R Romeo	Y Yankee
E Echo	L Lima	S Sierra	Z Zulu
F Foxtrot	M Mike	T Tango	
G Golf	N November	U Uniform	

The alleged purpose of this system is so the letters and numbers can be understood by those who transmit and receive voice messages by radio or telephone regardless of their native language.

So, theoretically someone from Georgia, PFC Foghorn Leghorn, say, could understand someone from Brooklyn, SP4 Bugs "The Bunny" Walkowicz:

> "Hey, Y'all! Ah say this hee-yah's Romeo Foxtrot Two Two, over, y'all"

> "Nyahh ... Yo! Romeo Foxtrawt Tooh Tooh, Victah Deltah Tree Tree, Go or What!"

The phonetic alphabet can be used to create unique and wonderful army acronyms; e.g.:

- Grunt = 11B = "One One Bravo"
- Viet Cong = VC = "Victor Charlie" (or just "Charlie" to his friends and intimates)
- Landing Zone = LZ = "Lima Zulu"
- Cluster F*#k = CF = "Charlie Foxtrot"

Pop Quiz: What does "Foxtrot Uniform Bravo Alpha Romeo" mean?

Piasters.   Also called "pi" which is pronounced, PEE.

This was a slang term for the denomination of Vietnamese currency, "The Coke Girl wants 50 pi for a can of beer," or the currency itself, "Are you talking piasters or US?" The actual denomination of Vietnamese money was "Dong," from the Vietnamese, *dong tien*, "money."

This was typically a lower form of negotiable currency in Nam, above C-Rats, cigarettes, tropical chocolate bars, and personal services, but below the greenback (very rare) and MPC (not authorized for possession by indigenous personnel ... yeah, right).

The typical water point exchange rate was 100 pi (mot tram dong) to $1.00 MPC, but could vary wildly on payday, when pi was pretty worthless in any Saigon bar, or when the army decided to change the MPC currency, in which case a few hundred piasters could buy back a bushel basket full of MPC from your local, black-market rep.

Piss Tube.   A piss tube was a field-expedient, grunt urinal.

In the boonies, a grunt would just use a tree or dig a little hole, but on a firebase the basic requisites of sanitation had to be observed in a place where flush toilets were not an option and port-a-potties hadn't yet been invented.

So, to accommodate #1, grunts would go outside the bunker line, but inside the wire, and dig a dry well — a trench three to four feet deep, filled with stones – on which they'd stand a couple of the tubes used to ship and store mortar or artillery rounds, open on both ends, and cover the stones with at least a foot of soil ... *et voilà* ... piss tubes.

Since #2 was burned, a grunt couldn't #1 and #2 in the same place — it made the #2 too hard to light.

For #2, a fifty-gallon drum was cut in half and coated with diesel fuel. Periodically, the contents of the drum were doused with diesel and burned ... preferably down wind of the mess hall. This was a detail custom made for FNGs.

Then there was the day that the FNG coated the #2 barrel with MoGas instead of diesel. Along comes a poor, unsuspecting grunt who decides to have a smoke while he's doing his business ... BOOM! ... second-degree burns in a perfect circle around his butt. It got him out of the field for a couple of weeks, but I have no idea how he explained the scars to his wife when he got back home.

The fact that the facilities were outside the bunker line meant that a grunt really didn't want to go at night. If he had to, he'd better make really sure that the guys on the bunker line knew he was out there. And he would take his shit paper and his weapon, because he might find himself squatting next to some NVA sapper with irritable bowel syndrome. Most grunts just grit their teeth and waited for the sun to come up ... grunts really wanted to avoid a meeting engagement with their pants around their ankles and critical elements of their anatomy in their hands ... really bad form.

Piss Up A Rope. This was a metaphorical expression describing the attempt to accomplish anything futile, like reasoning with a lifer. Also "Pissing into the Wind."

In a sense, grunts in Nam spent most of their time pissing up a rope. Even the least gifted of us understood clearly that was the essence of the grunt's role in the US strategy in Nam:

They attack us; we kick the crap out of them; do a body count; we wait for them to recover; they attack us; we kick the crap out of them; do a body count; we wait for them to recover; repeat as many times as necessary until you DEROS.

Despite this, grunts kept doing duty.

Grunts would willingly piss up a rope if they felt the cause were worthwhile. Nathanael West's novel *Miss Lonelyhearts* explains it this way:

> "Man has a tropism for order. Keys in one pocket, change in another. Mandolins are tuned G D A E. The physical world has a tropism for disorder, entropy, Man against Nature ... the battle of the centuries. Keys yearn to mix with change. Mandolins strive to get out of tune. Every order has within it the germ of destruction. All order is doomed, yet the battle is worthwhile."

If the cause were worthwhile, albeit futile, grunts would attempt it anyway. "We the unwilling, led by the unknowing, do the impossible for the ungrateful."

The best illustration I can offer for this phenomenon is, dead or alive, grunts refused to leave buddies behind on the battlefield. On the civilian side, rescuers and first responders are told to abandon victims if the situation is potentially deadly to the rescuer — there's no point in making a bad situation worse. But grunts willingly took casualties to recover their dead, wounded and missing.

The police, firemen, and other rescuers in the stairways of the World Trade Center Towers on 9/11 acted like grunts, not civilians. May God bless them and keep them.

The grunt experience in Nam in a nutshell:

>"All order is doomed, yet the battle is worthwhile," or

>"Go piss up a rope!" ... "No problem, sir! How high, Sir!"

Point Man.　　　　This was the first grunt in a column of grunts crashing through the bush.

This was typically a guy whose name you didn't bother learning.

It was a good position to be in if a grunt wanted to meet interesting and exotic people who were armed to the teeth, competent in mayhem, and had really bad attitudes.

Actually, I preferred walking point.

Either I wasn't one of God's brightest lights, or I felt I had a better chance seeing what I was walking into. I remember one day we were out on a platoon sized recon patrol and were working with some scout dogs. We were climbing a ridge, and I came to a point where I couldn't see over the lip of ridge in front of me. So, we sent the dog up. After a few moments of silence, the dog burst down the ridge past us, yelping. I looked back to the LT and he pointed me up over the ridge, where the dog had run from. I image the expression on my face at that moment was quite priceless.

Here's a piece of advice. If you're part of the column of grunts crashing through the bush and you see a scout dog running back down the column, yelping, followed by the point man who is also yelping ... follow them ... quickly.

Police Call.　　　　Not 911, but a formal, liferesque process for picking up litter, real and imaginary.

This was one of the favorite rituals of lifers who believed that all terrain was mocking them by concealing cigarette butts and gum wrappers.

Police call was also described as "Asses and Elbows" ... and that's all I care to say about that ... you don't ask and I won't tell.

Poncho. This is not the Cisco Kid's sidekick, but grunt-speak for "raincoat."

A poncho is a large, rubberized sheet with a hole poked through the middle with a hood and draw string for your head; it was designed to be used for a raincoat.

Grunts didn't use their ponchos to keep dry ... a totally futile effort during the rainy season ... but they used them to build hootches to sleep in.

Wearing a poncho in the monsoon only kept the wet and heat in next to your body, which produced some interesting and bizarre life forms on your skin, none of which were friendly or pleasant.

Poncho Liner. This is rare proof that even army contractors could sometimes get things right!

A poncho liner was a blanket made of some secret, magic, space-age material that was light and kept a grunt warm even when it was wet ... which was just about always during the monsoon.

Grunts developed a deep and meaningful commitment to their poncho liners. Some had pet names and were given presents on anniversaries and special occasions. This was a grunt's "bush-wife" because sleeping with it on a full air mattress, with an M16 between the legs, was the closest thing to "grunt-bliss" that could be achieved in the bush.

The poncho liner is now called the "woobie" by veterans of the great sandbox. No one really knows where this term comes from. The most reasonable explanation it's the result of a child with its blankie who has a somewhat snarky grunt attitude about the relationship. Be that as it may, don't take liberties with another guy's "woobie"; you will get hurt.

Linus' blanket had nothing on a grunt's poncho liner ... I still have mine.

Pop Smoke. An expression meaning to ignite and throw a smoke grenade.

Pop smoke describes the action of deploying an M18 Smoke Grenade, used as a ground-to-ground or ground-to-air signaling device, a target or landing zone marking device, or a screening device for unit movements.

The M18 looked like an OD beer can with a grenade fuse stuck in the top. They came in various designer colors indicated on the top: Red (usually used to indicate something BAD); Green (usually used to indicate something GOOD); Yellow (Can't make up my mind about this); and Violet (Hi, Sailor!).

Now this is VERY important. There was a device referred to as "white smoke" and, when it ignited, it did in fact produce what looked like white smoke. This didn't mean the army was announcing a new Pope had been elected. That's the color of burning white phosphorus.

White phosphorous, or "Willy Pete," will burn through any substance known to man as long as it has oxygen. The white smoke was caused by deploying perpetually ignited particles of very sticky and very nasty stuff, which could not be extinguished unless you could concoct a field expedient vacuum (very difficult without destroying all oxygen-dependent life forms on the planet).

One of the nastiest tricks I ever pulled in Nam had to do with white smoke.

My ranger team was part of a screening force for a brigade firebase. The mentalists in the S2 section divined that a force of NVA were moving in from the west to attack the base. This time, to everyone's surprise, the Houdini Bureau got it right.

My four-man team was inserted right on top of an NVA unit.

What saved our asses was that the dinks got distracted by our insertion bird and tried to shoot it down. Then they put their thinking-pith helmets on, figured out the bird was inserting US troops, did the math – one bird = no more than a rifle squad – and came after us.

They chased us most of that day. They were chasing us close, no more than a hundred meters, up our six, e.g. from behind. We couldn't get enough distance for a safe extraction or for artillery.

At one point, I took a Willy-Pete grenade, "white smoke," replaced the fuse with a timer, hid it under some crushed grasses, and hightailed it out of there. The thing worked like a charm – a pop, a plumb of white smoke, screaming, and cursing.

The white-smoke booby trap convinced the dinks that a six-o'clock pursuit wasn't working for them. They left a few guys in our rear to push us, while the main force moved out to our flank for a parallel pursuit.

We actually spotted their move to our flank. They went down into some low terrain along our right flank.

Our problem was that the dinks were pushing us along a tongue of land, a descending ridge with low ground on both flanks and to the front.

Low ground is bad news when in contact. Commo is lost and, if caught down there, does the old cliché, "Shooting fish in a barrel," mean anything to you?

The terrain indicated that the tongue was formed by two blue lines, one on each flank, converging to our front. Since it was a couple weeks into the rainy season, there was probably water down there.

My assessment was that the force to our rear was pushing us toward the low ground to our front. The parallel pursuit along my right was trying to get ahead of us and would be waiting for us once we descended from the ridge.

The dinks made two mistakes.

The first was letting us see their maneuver.

The second was that the flanking force had put enough distance between us that I had reasonable stand-off for mortars or artillery.

"Romeo Two Six Xray! Romeo Two Six Xray! This is Romeo Two Eight. Fire Mission, over!

"Romeo Two Eight! Romeo Two Six Xray! Fire Mission, over."

"Troops in ravine. Coordinates 98453409. I repeat 98453409. Request Willy Pete, Battery Three, Danger Close."

"Two Eight! Copy! Troops in ravine. Coordinates 98453409. Willy Pete, Battery Three, Danger Close."

"Two Six! Affirmative!"

"Two Eight! Wait one!"

While the arty guys laid in the fire mission, I briefed my guys. I assessed that the pursuit force to our rear was small, somewhere between a fire team and a squad. When the arty came in, I expected them to hunker down, as would we.

As soon as the last rounds came in, we would turn on them, basic meeting engagement drill, two complete M16 mags in their face and frags. Then we would deploy smoke grenades and break for the low ground to our right. We would try to get as much distance as we could then call in an extraction.

As long as 1) the pursuit force to our rear was small; and, 2) they did hunker down when our arty came in; and, 3) we were able to effectively suppress them with small arms fire; and, 4) we made it to the low ground; and, 5) the artillery destroyed or disrupted the pursuit force on our flank: and, 6) there wasn't a whole passel of pissed-off dinks waiting for us in the ravine; and 7) we were able to evade the pursuit, my plan should work.

Any wonder why I don't play the lottery?

Finally,

"Romeo Two Eight! Romeo Two Six Xray! Smoke Out, over."

It was SOP for the artillery to mark a danger close target with an air-burst smoke round.

"Two Six! Two Eight! Copy! Smoke Out, over."

I actually heard the report of an artillery piece to the south. Perfect, I thought, the target is linear running rough north-south.

The smoke round popped exactly where I wanted it, right over the ravine where I suspected the dinks were. I imagine when the snoke round went off right over their heads, it was a 'Aw Shit" moment for my little friends down in the ravine.

"Romeo Two Six Xray! Romeo Two Eight! Splash! On Target! Fire for Effect, over."

"Two Eight! Two Six! Roger! Copy! Fire for Effect! Over."

I heard multiple reports to the south.

I turned to my guys, "Get low! Twelve rounds and we move!"

The artillery whistled in. We heard a Whoomph and large clouds of white smoke puffed up out of the ravine.

"Romeo Two Six Xray! Romeo Two Eight! Splash! On Target! Over."

"Two Eight! Two Six! Copy! On Target! Over."

I yelled, "Count 'em! Twelve!"

Then my "Christmas Miracle." The white smoke from the Willy-Pete rounds was flowing back toward my position. We'd have smoke cover for our move.

When the twelfth round hit, I waited a nanosecond. No more cannon reports. We were covered in white smoke.

"Follow me," I ordered and trotted east toward the ravine. I didn't engage the dinks to our rear. The smoke would mask our movement. The quicker we got to the cover of the ravine the better.

"Romeo Two Six Xray! Romeo Two Eight! Cease Fire! Cease Fire! We are moving! Over."

"Two Eight! Copy Cease Fire! Over."

The smoke was so thick I literally fell into the ravine. No one was waiting for us down there! My guys tumbled in on top me. Quick count; we had all four. We splashed across a small stream, clawed our way up the other side and trotted away from the area.

But, while we were down there, I caught the unmistakable chemical odor of Willy Pete and something else; the best way I can describe it is barbeque.

"Romeo Two Six Xray! Romeo Two Eight! Good job! Crispy critters! We are moving! Over!"

"Roger, Romeo Two Eight! Bird's in the Air! Good Luck! Out!"

Two post scripts to this little tale of daring do.

While we were beating feet away from the contact, I got a call from a call sign I didn't recognize telling me that "the Three wanted me go back and get a body count."

The "Three" would be the battalion S3, at least an O4, a Major.

I refused!

Then a new, very pissed off voice ordered me to go back and get a body count.

I took this to be Mr. Three himself.

I refused!

The pissed-off voice, "Do you know who you're taking to sergeant!"

So much for SIGSEC.

I had a choice. Either I could refuse again, something I was authorized to do under our TSOP, and start a shit storm which my platoon leader would have to handle. Or I could give this field-grade idiot what he wanted.

There was no chance in hell I was turning around and going back down into that ravine to look for the barbeque. So I radioed, "Wait One!"

We kept trotting away from the contact looking for an LZ. I waited a decent amount of time, then radioed,

"Romeo Two Six Xray! Romeo Two Eight! Report Twelve Kilo India Alpha, Zero Whiskey India Alpha. Over!"

There was a brief delay. Romeo Two Six Xray was a ranger on radio duty in the TOC. He was trying to decide whether I went completely dinky dau and had gone back into the ravine to do a body count, or I was bullshitting a REMF.

He made his decision, "Two Eight! Two Six! Copy! Over!"

The second postscript was we captured two NVA on our LZ.

We finally found an extraction point and called it in. Since our bird was already in the air, we almost immediately heard it inbound. Suddenly, two dinks burst out of the wood line, heads and AKs up toward the sound of the chopper.

They walked right into us. We popped up and lowered our m16s on them. They stopped dead; there was less than a meter between us. I thought for a second they were going to go for it, but they lowered their weapons and showed us their hands.

We had them on their knees, and my guys were tying their hands behind their backs as the bird came into sight. We popped smoke and the bird came down on it.

We had not had a chance to radio in this new development. When we stood up our prisoners, the crew chief's eyes almost popped out of his head. For a second, I thought he was going to open up with his M60. I pushed the barrel away and shouted into his ear hole, "Prisoners!"

On the bird, I radioed to the TOC that we had two prisoners. After a bit, the bird was redirected to the 4th Division base camp in Pleiku. We landed, and a couple of MPs took charge of our dinks.

Our bird took off, and we were left standing on the pad. Luckily, we were able to hitch a ride on the afternoon convoy going out to LZ Oasis.

When we got back to our compound, we were met by Floyd, our platoon sergeant. He looked at me with his crooked grin and said, "Twelve?"

I shrugged as best I could in a ruck sack, "Smelled like twelve to me!"

Post-Traumatic Stress Disorder (PTSD). Post-traumatic stress disorder (PTSD) is a mental health condition that's triggered by a terrifying event — either experiencing it or witnessing it. Symptoms may include flashbacks, nightmares and severe anxiety, as well as uncontrollable thoughts about the event.

PTSD wasn't recognized as a legitimate service-related condition during and immediately after the Vietnam war. The condition was referred to as "combat fatigue" or the service member was called "shell shocked." In fact, the condition was thought to be a character flaw of the victim ... "He couldn't take it!"

I was treated for PTSD in the early 1990's. I saw a civilian therapist on my own dime because even by that time having PTSD and seeing a shrink was not a career enhancer in the army.

My symptoms were a sudden onset of inability to make decisions and difficulty handling stressful situations ... again, not a career enhancer in the army.

Also, I was unconsciously suppressing any emotional response to others ... I'd rather puke than cry ... not a good strategy for keeping a marriage together.

After over a year on the couch, I asked my therapist how I was doing. All she'd admit to me is that I "had good coping mechanisms."

Sounds like I morphed from a PTSD victim to a well-briefed sociopath! I can live with that.

Years later, I was reading LTC Dave Grossman's book, *On Combat*, which reproduced the *Diagnostic and Statistical Manual of Mental Disorders* diagnostic criteria for PTSD.

Criterion A: Exposure

1. The person has experienced, witnessed, or been confronted with an event or events that involve actual or threatened death or serious injury, or a threat to the physical integrity of oneself or others.
2. The person's response involved intense fear, helplessness, or horror.

Criterion B: Intrusive Recollection: The traumatic event is persistently re-experienced in at least one of the following ways:

1. Recurrent and intrusive distressing recollections of the event, including images, thoughts, or perceptions. Recurrent distressing dreams of the event.

2. Acting or feeling as if the traumatic event were recurring (includes a sense of reliving the experience, illusions, hallucinations, and dissociative flashback episodes, including those that occur upon awakening or when intoxicated). Intense psychological distress at exposure to internal or external cues that symbolize or resemble an aspect of the traumatic event.
3. Physiologic reactivity upon exposure to internal or external cues that symbolize or resemble an aspect of the traumatic event

Criterion C: Avoidant/Numbing: Persistent avoidance of stimuli associated with the trauma and numbing of general responsiveness (not present before the trauma), as indicated by at least three of the following:

1. Efforts to avoid thoughts, feelings, or conversations associated with the trauma
2. Efforts to avoid activities, places, or people that arouse recollections of the trauma
3. Inability to recall an important aspect of the trauma
4. Markedly diminished interest or participation in significant activities
5. Feeling of detachment or estrangement from others
6. Restricted range of affect (e.g., unable to have loving feelings)
7. Sense of foreshortened future (e.g. does not expect to have a career, marriage, children, or a normal life span)

Criterion D: Hyper-Arousal: Persistent symptoms of increasing arousal (not present before the trauma), indicated by at least two of the following:

1. Difficulty falling or staying asleep
2. Irritability or outbursts of anger
3. Difficulty concentrating
4. Hyper-vigilance

5. Exaggerated startle response

The diagnosis needs to include a history of exposure to a traumatic event meeting two criteria and symptoms from each of three symptom clusters: intrusive recollections, avoidant/numbing symptoms, and hyper-arousal symptoms.

Every grunt I know scores a hundred percent in Criterion A – exposure to horrific events, feelings of intense fear, and helplessness.

And Criterion B convinced me I was in the wrong line of work for recovery; I retired in 1996.

Despite that, I sleep like a baby and rarely have dreams about Nam or being in combat ... although I do dream about being back in Catholic school ... nuns with rulers ... the clacking sound of their giant rosary beads as they sneak up behind me ... a miasma of starch and chalk dust envelops me ... I wake up screaming!

I readily admit to survivor's guilt, "Why him, not me?" And a degree of hyper-vigilance, which may be a residual of growing up in New York City.

My therapy was my children. My responsibility for their care kept me in the game as far as coping with day-to-day life and earning a living.

Also, children are love and life; your child keeps that part of your soul alive and vibrant. Attachment to them and responsibility for them will not allow slipping off into the darkness.

Again, any grunt who has experienced the events listed in Criterion A, e.g., anyone who has seen combat, you need to get checked out. PTSD can lurk in the mind like a time bomb and explode years after the traumatic event.

I was driving to class from work at the beginning of Desert Storm. I was stationed on Ft. Sheridan and was driving down to a night class at Northwestern in Evanston. The news came on the radio and the announcer was describing the opening of the US offensive in Kuwait.

Suddenly, I began seeing pictures in my mind that had nothing to do with what I was doing or what was on the news, and certainly were not enhancing my ability to drive safely. No matter what I did, I couldn't turn them off. I finally had to pull over to the side of the road. I got sick.

It took me a couple of days to sort it out. I had seen something so horrific in Kontum in the spring of 1968 of which I had repressed the memory. I had literally pushed it out of my conscious mind. Somehow, the news report of the combat in the middle east had triggered it. First, as a violent daymare and, after a few days, a literal memory.

I got sick again.

My therapist, who was a radical Jungian, had fun with that at our next session!

The point is, if you have been traumatized by combat, don't let it ruin your life. Get help!

Prick-25. This was slang for the AN/PRC 25 Radio Set.

This was a portable (some guys who had to carry them may dispute that point) VHF FM radio transceiver used to provide short-range, two-way voice communication.

The Prick-25 came with two antennas, the "short stick" and the "long stick." On a good day in the flat lands, a Prick-25 had a range of about ten to fifteen klicks with the short stick. Unfortunately, there were no good days and no flat ground that I ever saw ... except the mud under the rice paddies.

Platoon leaders and company commanders with penis envy would have the RTO hump with the long stick up. This was not an especially good idea since the basic NVA sniper manual states, "In order to shoot an officer, find the top of a radio antenna, drop the aiming point down two - three feet and spray the area liberally."

The Prick-25 was the most potent weapon humped by grunts in Nam because it connected them to all the hardware the Army, Air Force and Navy had ready to back them up. Like the credit card, don't leave home without it ... and have the FNGs hump some extra batteries.

PSYOP.   Pronounced SIGH-op.

This was an acronym for "Psychological Operations."

This was army jargon for "A Mind F'ck" or "Winning their hearts and minds." Carrot and stick, I guess.

PSYOPs were the source of millions of leaflets dropped by thousands of aircraft, then policed up by lifers, used by grunts in the shitter, and burned by FNGs with the shit ... a basic army ecological cycle.

Punji Stake.   This was a type of booby trap used by the bad guys.

Punji stakes were spikes, made of sharpened wood or bamboo, placed upright in the ground waiting for some poor unsuspecting grunt to run up on it. Most punji wounds were in the foot or lower leg, but they could be real nasty if a grunt fell on top of one.

Punji stakes were sometimes placed in a camouflaged pit, a "Punji Pit." When the bad guys were in a really nasty mood (which was pretty much always) punji stakes would also be placed in the sides of the pit pointing down making it impossible for a grunt to remove his leg quickly without severe damage.

Punji stakes were not meant to kill but to wound in an attempt to tie up a unit by forcing it to evacuate the casualties — "Kill one and knock one out of the fight; wound one and knock three out of the fight."

Punji stakes were also an attempt to lower morale, but what the bad guys didn't understand was that punjis only served to piss most grunts off.

Some grunts actually saw them as an opportunity for a short vacation. Unlike getting shot, blown up or ripped up by shrapnel, this was not usually a life-threatening wound. But it was a ticket to a nice clean medical facility staffed by female nurses who would coo, cater, and look like angels while you lazed between clean, white sheets, and ate three hots a day after a hot shower.

Thank you, ladies! Love you all! Why you didn't accept my many proposals of marriage has confused me to this day.

Punji stakes were rumored to be coated with chicken shit which, if it got into a grunt's blood stream and remained untreated, would cause him to re-enlist and turn into a lifer with each full moon.

Push.   Slang for a radio frequency, or freq (pronounced "freak").

Operational pushes were assigned on a daily basis in the CEOI, usually two for operations, "Command & Control," and two for ash & trash, "Admin Log." The military frequency band ranged from 30.00 to 75.95 MHz in 50 kHz steps.

Knowing key operations pushes was like gold for grunts in the field. For example, if you had the aviation frequencies, a couple cases of Cs could get you a helicopter ride out of the boonies, which beat the hell out of humping out on leather.

Once, while working LRRPs near the coast, we obtained a few interesting Navy pushes and discovered the wonders of ice cream machines and the main batteries of the USS New Jersey.

PX.   Pronounced PEE EX, an acronym and abbreviation for Post Exchange.

The PX was an army Walmart, a place where soldiers could go to buy assorted and sordid stuff, like civilian clothes, candy, cigarettes, dirty magazines, comic books, fishing equipment, living room furniture, appliances, paperbacks ... a little piece of capitalist enterprise plopped down right in the middle of Nam.

For a grunt to find a PX, he had to travel up the army food chain. The closest PX to us was on the 4th Division base camp, Camp Enari.

This posed two obstacles for a grunt: 1) How to get back there; and 2) Camp Enari was the capital of REMFdom in the AO.

There were a couple of ways of getting to the rear. Getting shot or injured ... risky, at best ... or "having an appointment" ... or just passing through on the way to someplace else.

Once a grunt figured out how to get back to base camp, then he had to figure out how to go undetected by the REMFs and Lifers for whom

Camp Enari was their natural habitat. This was somewhat like treading shark-infested waters in a meat-suit.

The basic disguise required clean jungle fatigues with all patches, nametags, insignia of rank affixed; a regulation "Charlie Brown" baseball cap; a clean shave; a GI haircut; and shined boots.

When in Lifer-Land, look the part!

This was especially essential when entering the PX complex ... think of this as the kill zone of a chicken-shit ambush. REMFs, Lifers, and even MPs waited there hoping to detect and eliminate any grunt who had the audacity not only to be out of the field, but actually attempt to access the amenities reserved for charter members of the Army, BIG A!

There was a separate building in the PX complex on Enari called the Class VI store ... booze, beer and soda. This was theoretically available to all members of the armed forces with a few interesting catches.

First, a grunt had to infiltrate undetected through the lifer kill-zone.

Second, a grunt had to be carrying his "ration card," which indicated the limitations on the joy juice that could be purchased over a period of time.

Third, a grunt had to present his military ID card, as if being in a full Liferesque outfit in the middle of a combat zone was enough to establish his bona fides.

Fourth, a soldier had to be at least eighteen to buy beer and at least twenty-one to buy booze.

I was on Enari during May of 1969 passing through on my way for my 30-day extension leave. I got delayed because of a mix-up with my orders, so I got stuck there for a couple of nights.

For whatever reason these things happen, I got a yen for a rum and coke ... Bacardi dark, real Coca Cola, ice cubes, and a frosted glass. I didn't dare hope to find a slice of lime.

I decided to hop on over to the Class VI and purchase the ingredients ... not the ice of course. A friendly cook agreed to share a few cubes in return for my sharing the rum.

I passed through the lifer kill zone with minimal problem other than a couple of the PX Commandos bracing me that my uniform was "unauthorized." I guess my cammies and headgear weren't working that day ... the enemy could see me.

One REMF asked if I ever shined my boots; I told him no; shoe polish might soften the water-tight, rock-hard substance the leather parts of my jungle boots had morphed into after surviving two rainy seasons in the boonies.

I wonder what the REMFs would do if they detected the Chi-Com 9mm automatic I was carrying under my blouse. Weapons tended to make Base-Camp Commandos faint.

I finally arrived at the Class VI store where I discovered they actually had stateside shopping carts, just like the A&P! I probably stood staring at the things with my mouth hanging open for a few minutes. Finally, I grabbed one, found a case of Coke ... $2.40 MPC on the legit market ... and a fifth of Don Bacardi Dark Fine Cuban by-way-of-Puerto-Rico rum. Then I queued up for check out,

When it was my turn, I presented the babysahn at the cash register with my military ID and ration card. She looked at them, scrutinized me, and said, "You please 'scuse me ti ti, sargie." She took my documents and went into an office behind the counter.

This was not a good sign! I wondered if she had detected that I did have enough REMF-Club Bonus Points to be shopping there.

Worse, I heard a voice behind me say, "What the f' now!"

I turned to see an army master sergeant standing behind me balancing a couple of cases of beer and a bottle of bourbon in his arms.

The bad news, he was in a lifer-suit.

The good news, he had a 1st Division combat patch, a ranger tab, and a CIB with two stars – World War II, Korea, and a previous tour in Nam.

I shrugged and gave him my best "I don't know what the f's going on" grin; then said, "You want to put your stuff up here, master sergeant?"

The master sergeant plopped his boodle up on the counter and favored me with a positive-sounding rumble, the closest one could expect to a thank you from a very senior infantry NCO.

He asked me, "Who you with?"

"K-75, master sergeant," I said.

"Heard rangers were reactivate," he said. "Good move on the army's part. I was with them at Pointe du Hoc ... Normandy ..."

The arrival of our babysahn interrupted him. She had come back out of the office accompanied by a REMF in his lifer-suit, a Spec-5 by his collar tabs, holding my ID and ration card with the ends of his fingertips as if he could catch some contagious disease from them.

"You cannot purchase liquor, Sergeant ... uh ..." He looked down at my ID card for a long second "... Sergeant Gleason. You can take the soda but the rum stays."

"Why not?" I countered. "There's room for it on my ration card?"

The SP5 storekeeper gave me a look people normally reserve for cockroaches on kitchen counters. He sighed in a way that reminded me of my eighth-grade nun when I blew a catechism question.

"MACV regulations specify that a service member be at least twenty-one years of age to purchase liquor," he sniffed.

I was stunned.

The army can send a grunt into combat at eighteen but won't let him buy booze until he's twenty-one!

I was just about to protest saying I had been in country over thirteen months in the field, eating shit, and getting my ass shot off ... blah ... blah ... blah ... when I noticed the MP, who was permanently stationed at the counter to take care of uppity grunts, was giving me the I-dare-you-to-say-one-more-word look.

Then, next to me, I heard the master sergeant explode, "This is bullshit!"

He gave the MP his "I-dare-you-to-open-your-f'ing-mouth" look, then turned back to the storekeeper. "Can I buy the rum?"

This was of course a rhetorical question coming from a combat experienced E8 to a pencil-neck E5 shopkeeper.

The master sergeant tossed his ration card at the SP5 who barely glanced at it.

"Of ... of course, master sergeant!" the storekeeper stammered. I swear I heard the REMF's heels click together.

The master sergeant included my rum with his bottle of bourbon. "Separate bags," I heard him tell the babysahn who was packing the order.

Then to the SP5, "Is there anything in your precious MACV regs that say I can't give a gift to another NCO?"

The store keeper mumbled, "No, master sergeant ... not that I'm aware."

The master sergeant gave the MP another hard look. Then he handed me the bag with the rum in it. "Enjoy, sergeant! Lift one for me and for the rangers!"

Then he marched out of the shop.

To this day, every time I taste a Bacardi *Cuba Libre*, I think of that guy!

PX Commando.   A PX Commando was a soldier who festooned his khakis and Class A's with every minor ribbon, award, and badge for which he was entitled (or not) that could be purchased at a PX.

When the army awarded a significant medal, like a Bronze Star, Air Medal, or Purple Heart, the ribbon came in the same presentation box as the medals themselves. Minor awards, like the National Defense Ribbon and now, the "I-Survived-Basic-Training" ribbon, could be purchased over the counter at the PX.

One of the common decorative practices of the PX Commandos had to do with weapons qualification badges.

When a soldier qualified with a weapon, the army awarded a qualification badge based on the level of achievement: expert, sharpshooter, marksman. Additionally, the weapons or weapons system was identified by a small, metal, rectangular indicator which was affixed to the bottom of the badge: "Rifle," "Pistol," "Slingshot," etc. The badge was affixed and centered, just below the upper pocket line on the left side of the uniform.

A PX Commando typically wore multiple qualification badges or a single expert badge with multiple weapons identifiers affixed.

After I had retired, I ran into a PX Commando in the Atlanta airport: one-stripe E2; infantry-blue plastic backings on his enlisted brass; infantry-blue cord on his right shoulder; National Defense and Army Service Ribbon above his left pocket; and below those, an expert qualification badge indicating every weapon the army has ever used: "Rifle," "Automatic Rifle," "Pistol," "Bayonet," "P38," "Belt Buckle," "Musket,' "Paper," "Rock," "Scissors." The kid looked like he had built a ladder reaching down to his waist!

Bless him! Going home on his first leave after infantry training in Benning trying to impress the hell out of the girl-next-store and cast deadly fear into the hearts of Jodies everywhere.

I distinctly remembering doing much the same thing on my first leave home after AIT. I even wore an infantry-blue ascot with my khakis! The only reaction I got from my girlfriend was the question, "Why blue? It's not your color."

When PX Commandos went out on pass, they tended to load their uniforms up with PX gewgaws – usually after they got outside the gate – until they resembled Christmas trees.

This was a way of drawing the attention of the local army-town talent in the GI bars around post, like a peacock spreading his tail feathers. The ladies of Bar Corps knew AR 600–8–22, Awards and Decorations, better than most Sergeant Majors, so the PX Commandos weren't fooling anybody.

"Ohhh ... Private Snuffy ... how could you have so many medals after just four weeks of basic ... you must be ... special!"

These fine ladies also knew how much a recruit got paid down to the penny. So this attraction only lasted for a few champagne cocktails.

R

Ration Card. A US Military Assistance Command Vietnam (MAC-V) ration card was issued to each soldier upon arriving in country. The purpose of this document seemed to be to limit grunts' access to wine, liquor, tobacco, and PX goodies so the REMFs didn't run out.

Actually, I don't know of a single grunt who drank wine in Nam, except for those crazy rice wine parties in the Montagnard villages.

> "What pairs best with ham and lima beans ... a red? White? MD 2020? What about a crisp little blush?"

Ration cards served no purpose at all in the boonies, the usual habitat of grunts in Nam ... no PX, no Class VI stores. So, grunts had them tucked away somewhere in a wallet with pictures of mom, dad, Marylou, a few folded MPC bills and piasters, a military ID card, all wrapped in a brown, plastic, water-proof C-Rat supplement bag and stuffed into a water-proof bag at the bottom of a ruck sack.

Besides, the army issued grunts tobacco with C-Rats and in SP Packs. Beer and soda usually arrived on the last supply bird of the day and, if a grunt were fortunate enough to get to a beer hall on a base camp, ration cards were not required ... sweet three-point-two oblivion.

Telling by the availability of US beer and cigarettes from Nguyen's Water-Point Mobile Groceries, a significant portion of these goodies were being siphoned off into the black market long before they got down to the army retail level. In fact, the only reliable supply of BA-30's, army flashlight batteries, in the boonies was from these water point capitalists in the big straw hats!

So, other than providing REMFs another opportunity to bust a grunt's agates in the rear, ration cards were pretty useless to a grunt.

Redball. For Generation Z readers, this was not an energy drink!

A redball, also referred to as a "Hardball," was a major, paved road, so named because on army maps it was represented by a red line. Minor, unpaved roads were black lines, and trails – mythical as well as real – were represented by broken black lines.

In my old stomping grounds, the II Corps AO, there were two major redballs: Highway 14 which ran north and south connecting the cities of Dak To, Kontum, Pleiku and Ban Me Thuot; and Highway 19, the "Beach Road," which ran from Pleiku, over the mountains to Ahn Khe, then down "Happy Valley" to the coast.

Calling Highway 14 "paved" was at best a wistful fantasy. The French probably paved it back in the 1950s then just left it to rot. The mortar and rocket fissures along the roadway didn't improve the driving experience.

The only worse roadway I've ever experienced is the BQE in New York City that runs between Queens and Brooklyn; that thing eats semis.

Despite its condition, Highway 14 was the major logistical route in the highlands. The army and the NVA fought constantly over control.

In Quang Duc province, Highway 14 swings west and closely parallels the Cambodian border. In September, 1968, my infantry unit was part of a task force blocking the NVA from making incursions over the border to interdict the highway.

I was on the battalion firebase just outside a small village called Duc Lap. We had built a chopper pad just outside the wire, which we were using to supply our units out in the boonies.

The LZ was within a few dozen meters of the TOC, so when the brass flew in on their Loaches, they had a short walk to the Cave of Winds. In fact, since it was the rainy season, the REMFs had us lay a sandbag path so the field-grade ponces wouldn't spoil their shoe shines.

A problem we had was the supply choppers had to come in crosswind, so the birds couldn't carry full loads. A supply run that should take a single sortie was taking two or three. So, one of the chopper drivers, a senior warrant, and I went to see the S3, the operations guy.

The rotor-head explained the problem to this Maestro of Mystic Maneuvers and Pompous Procedures. He said we should relocate the landing pad to the north end of the firebase where the birds could land into the prevailing winds and carry full loads. I informed Major Disaster that I had specked out the terrain and we had plenty of flat ground and good clearance to build a pad. He said he'd take it up with the Battalion Commander.

A couple hours later, one of the staff lackies searched me out and told me that relocating the helicopter pad was a no go. When I asked why, I was told it would be too far a walk from the TOC for the Brass ... after all ... it was the rainy season.

REMF.   Pronounced REMF.

This is an acronym for "Rear Echelon Mother F'er"; a general term for all pernicious, un-grunt forms of life in the army.

REMF is not an assignment, branch of service, or MOS. It's a state of mind. On the civilian-side, terms like "empty suit" or "sociopath" might be used.

Indications of REMFism included the idea that one was actually entitled to eat three hots a day, sleep on a bunk out of the rain, sleep entire nights without having to pull guard, have a club to drink cold beer and other forms of chilled alcohol, have access to hot showers, sleep without boots, wear clean, pressed uniforms with patches and insignia of rank properly attached.

But someone could have all this and not necessarily be a REMF.

Once someone began siphoning off needed supplies before they could get to the field ... extra field jackets, batteries, flashlights, etc. ... only letting C-rats and ammo get through, cutting orders to promote oneself to sergeant and to award oneself a CIB, believing the need of the logistics system for neat and complete paperwork prevailed over the need of grunts in the field for mission critical supplies, then, one was entering the magic realm of REMFdom.

Let me tell you a story I've entitled, "The Clean Lieutenant Goes on a Visit."

During the summer of 1968, the "Summer of Love," we were on a firebase near Ban Me Thuot during the rainy season. We were wet, cold and grumpy as one is likely to become when living underwater without gills and webbed feet.

One day, a slick landed at the firebase and out jumped an amazing sight — a seemingly, newly-minted, clean, 1st Lieutenant — wearing spotless, tailored, and smartly pressed fatigues on its body, a regulation "Charlie Brown" baseball cap with a Silver Bar on its head, highly polished boots on its feet, a shiny, black attaché case in its hand, and Finance Corps insignia on its collar.

This apparition skipped and dodged across the landing pad, avoiding all the puddles and mud, and walked over to the company TOC.

A few minutes later, our platoon sergeant collected us up for a "meeting." Again, an amazing occurrence! Two wonders in one day! A clean lieutenant and a "meeting."

We were a little nervous and fidgety sitting around grouped in the open, so the clean lieutenant got right to the point. He had our lieutenant, who was not nearly as clean, pass out some IBM cards and some stubby No. 2 pencils while the clean lieutenant spoke.

"Good morning, men! I'm Lieutenant Fuzz (an alias) of the Finance Corps, and I need to take just a few minutes of your time to get some paper work straightened out for you. Your platoon leader is giving each of you a copy of an IRS form which we need in order to process your pay properly. When you get the form, I'd like you to ... Yes, soldier! You have a question?"

"Yes, sir! I thought we didn't pay federal tax in Nam."

"That's correct, soldier. But you have to fill out this form so that the IRS knows where you are. Now once you get the form ... another question?

"Yes, sir! Are you saying that one part of the government doesn't know where another part of the government stashed us?"

"It's not quite that simple ..."

"I don't see the point of this, sir! Why doesn't somebody from the army just walk over ..."

"Men! Under federal law, filling out this form is mandatory! Failure to do so within thirty days of arriving at your duty station could result in a fine of $10,000 and up to ninety days in jail."

"Sir! Would that be a jail in Nam or in the States?"

"Soldier! I don't see ..."

"Sir! Would the ninety days be good time? I mean would it come off our tour?"

"That has nothing ..."

"You get three hots a day in jail, don't you, sir? I mean, that's a law, isn't it?"

"People! Let's get back to ..."

"We give ourselves up, sir! Arrest us!"

"What ... What ..."

"Sir! We're not filling out this f'ing IRS form! We're cheating on our taxes! We're criminals! Take us to jail!"

"I can't ... Lieutenant! Can you get your people under control here!

Our lieutenant was laughing so hard, he almost wet his already wet trou. Meanwhile, we rushed the clean lieutenant in an effort to surrender ourselves to him *en masse*.

"Take me! Please, sir! I'm a criminal! I've got to pay for my crimes against the IRS. Take me to jail!"

The clean lieutenant and his IRS forms were gone on the next bird out.

In a grunt's esteem, any REMF certainly ranked above a civilian by his willingness to serve, but at times one step below civilian by his efforts to make an impossibly horrible situation just that much worse.

I was sorely tempted to remove this entry or tone it down a bit because I am loath to insult anyone who served in Nam and did his (or her) duty while putting his (or her) life on the line. In a sense, as long as the bad guys were tossing 122mm rockets around and sneaking into base camps with satchel charges, even REMFdom wasn't all that safe.

But, then I remembered the perverse human condition known as "denial." No one reading this would ever acknowledge that it describes them. For them, the REMF will remain a mythical creature created by the minds of paranoid and malcontented grunts. In other words, not *moi*!

And I'm okay with that. Hell! I've even forgiven Jane Fonda! Well ... almost!

Red Leg.   This could mean two things to a grunt.

If the guy was from Cincinnati, it was the name of the hometown national-league baseball team, so named so that Senator Joe McCarthy was not tempted to investigate a town that called its baseball team the Reds.

To the rest of us, it meant artillery guy. The branch color of the artillery was red (Sorry about that, Uncle Joe) hence the designation.

Artillery batteries were deployed down to the infantry battalion level. So, my infantry battalion had a battery of 105's in direct support and deployed onto our battalion firebase.

Somewhere, in the great obscure cloud called brigade and division planning, we also had artillery batteries in "indirect support," usually 155's or better ... meaning any number of infantry battalions competed for their attention.

Red Legs were okay as far as grunts were concerned. First, they were out in the boonies, embracing the same suck we were. Second, they were good to trade with.

The artillery battery was rich in things unavailable to grunts, like BA-30's, flashlight batteries, and unused artillery charges, useful to heat water as long as you didn't mind going through life without eyebrows.

Reple Deple.   Pronounced REP-il DEP-il.
This was an acronym for Replacement Depot.

This was a centralized, in-country, collection point for all arriving FNGs. Its formal purpose was to adjust the FNGs to the climate, provide an in-country orientation, conduct specialized weapons and combat training, and coordinate the assignment of replacements.

Its informal goal was to scare the crap out of the newbies, as if that were difficult.

Just arriving in Nam was enough to ensure their little pee-pee's wouldn't function for a month ... there was nothing like that blast of hot, humid air that hit a replacement in the face when he walked out of the plane to say, "Welcome to Hell!"

One of the favorite "scare" tactics used in the Repl Depl was to have the FNGs sort through the uniforms of casualties to see if any of the stuff was re-usable. Most of the time all the nasty bits were out of the clothes before the FNG sorted through them, but not always. There's nothing like sorting through clothes full of some poor grunt's bits and pieces to see if the unit patches were reusable.

Another favorite scare tactic of the REMFs was telling the FNGs "war stories."

"You poor bastards! Your orders just came through for the 4th Division! I heard they're really catching shit outside Kontum! They ran out of body bags up there!"

After a couple of days of this treatment, the FNGs were willing to burn shit or polish some REMFs brass for the next twelve months in order to avoid going up country.

I was going through the Repl Depl in Long Binh coming back into country after a thirty-day leave. Because I was clean, healthy-looking, and had a new uniform on, a couple of permanent-party REMFs mistook me for an FNG and started in with the war stories.

"Where you headed, Sarge?"

"75th Infantry ... LRRPs"

"Oh, Shit; those guys are always catchin' shit!"

"No shit!"

"Oh yeah! The dinks pay five hundred bucks just for the head of a LRRP."

"Yeah, that's right; couple of weeks ago a bunch of them went out and never came back; nobody knows what happened to them. You're screwed!"

Ah! It was moments like that when a grunt appreciated being back among his own.

Report of Survey.   This is a formal investigation concerning the loss, damage, or destruction of government property.

An appointee, referred to as the "survey officer" recommends either to assess the loss of the property unavoidable through accident or authorized use, or to assess liability against the individual responsible for the property through negligence or willful misconduct, i.e. you signed for it, now you have to pay for it!

Reports of Survey for infantry units in Nam pretty much all had the same result, loss or destruction due to combat.

This is why a company commander, who signed for everything a line company owned, for which he was fiscally responsible, depended on the good will of his first sergeant and supply sergeant.

I've heard rumors that a running list of missing stuff was kept and, every time something got blown up, the list of missing stuff was written off as a "combat loss" due to that incident.

Just rumors, mind you.

The rule back in the old Brown-Boot Army was, "you break it, you buy it."

My first squad leader in Nam destroyed an armored personnel carrier during a drunken joyride in West Germany. The report of survey found him liable for the APC by virtue of misconduct and assessed him the entire cost of one M113.

He was given two choices: either write the government a check for the APC or re-enlist and pay it off paycheck by paycheck. He chose the latter. The Army said thanks and sent him to Nam.

When I was an officer in the old Black-Boot Army, the reg had changed; an individual could only be assessed the equivalent of one month's pay on a report of survey.

Despite this, a commander still had to endure the dreaded "change-of-command survey".

When a new company commander was appointed to a unit, he and the outgoing commander did an item-by-item survey of every article for which the outgoing commander had signed when taking over the unit. Any discrepancy came out of the outgoing commander's pocket.

This included every mess kit; trouser, fatigue, medium/regular; boots, pair, combat, leather, black; socks, pair, woolen, OD; shirt, T, white on the company books.

Granted, none of these items were that expensive *per se*, but a guy could get nickeled-and-dimed to death real quick!

I heard rumors of guys visiting a local Army-Navy store and buying up sets of surplus fatigues, steel pots, mess kits, and other sundries to make up for supply-room shortages on the cheap.

Just rumors, mind you.

R&R.   This was an abbreviation for "Rest and Relaxation," "Rest and Recuperation," "Rampage and Riot."

R&R was a one-week per combat tour, fully paid, and doesn't-come-off-your-leave-time vacation for soldiers in Nam.

R&R centers came in two flavors, in-country and out-of-country.

Out-of-country R&R centers were located in places like Taipei, Sydney, Singapore, and Honolulu (for married guys and virgins).

Grunt requirements for an R&R center typically included:

1. anyplace but Nam
2. no one shooting at you competently (the Huks outside Manila in the Philippines sometimes shot at you, but rarely competently)
3. a place to sleep out of the rain in a bed with your boots off
4. three hots a day
5. inexpensive booze and cold beer
6. availability of female companionship
7. no lifers (or the ability to completely ignore them, with which the beer and booze helped)

There were actually "in-country" R&R centers, like Vung Tau, which were cleverly disguised as MACV operations centers.

These places were pretty much reserved for REMFs. Grunts rarely got to go there except when the resorts got overrun by the NVA, in which case grunts would go in, make the place safe for the REMFs, and leave without so much as a thank you or a cold beer.

Rock 'n' Roll.   A type of music favored by boomers and an expression used to describe firing a weapon, usually the M16, in fully automatic mode. In other words, putting as many bullets down range as possible as quickly as possible, as long as possible.

"Rock 'n' Roll" will get the bad guys' heads down, but a grunt is not going to hit squat after the first couple of rounds pull the weapon off target. And this will probably burn up all a grunt's ammo before the bad guys get tired of playing. Then it becomes ... yes, you guessed it ... a fist fight ... that is, a fist fight for the grunt ... the bad guys still have ammo.

Good fire discipline, the ability of preventing premature ballistic non-ejaculation, requires that only one grunt in each fire team fires on automatic.

Each burst of automatic fire should be short, about three rounds per burst. That way the weapon stays trained somewhere in the general neighborhood of the target.

The rest of the riflemen fire on semi-automatic; that is, one bullet at a time.

In a fire fight, grunts typically fired semi-automatic rapidly over their sights. That way the ammo lasts until the fire fight's over. The M16, which was mostly plastic, made a lousy club.

For my civilian readers, in a firefight in jungle terrain, a grunt rarely had clear targets. He may see movement, detect the source of enemy fire, or be directed to fire into a specific zone in order to provide suppressing fire.

So, the point of fire control is to lay down a good volume of fire into a specific, restricted area in order to establish and maintain fire superiority over the bad guys.

Even if the fire is not hitting anyone, believe me, if rounds are snapping around their heads, they're not going to be gawking around looking for grunts or the maneuver element attempting to get around their flank.

Running out of ammo in the middle of a fire fight is really a bad idea. So, stay off the rock 'n' roll setting! That stuff only works in Arnold Schwarzenegger movies where weapons never have to be reloaded and Arnold never gets hit.

The exception to the rock 'n' roll, fire-discipline rule is immediate action for close ambush or meeting engagement, in which case grunts light up the bad guys until they're gone — the bad guys and the ammo.

A typical point man practice was to take two thirty-round magazines, tape them bottom-to-bottom with the rounds in each facing in opposite directions, load one of the magazines into the M16, chamber a round, replace the chambered round in the magazine, and put the weapon on "Safe."

If the point man ran into the bad guys, he simultaneous found cover, slammed the M16 selector switch into "Auto," and hit the trigger until the bolt locked back. Then he reversed the tandem magazines, locked and loaded, hit the trigger until the bolt locked back.

If he was still around after all that, he did what everybody else was doing — went forward, went back, dropped down, whatever. Hopefully, by that time, his buddies were providing some suppressing fire, grenades, and smoke.

The chances of a positive outcome for a point man in a "meeting engagement" were not good, but the whole point of walking point was to avoid such things.

Oh Yeah! If you're somewhere down the column when all this hits the fan, and you see the point man run past you screaming, follow quickly. Have I said this enough?

Round Eye.   This expression describes anything "American, not Vietnamese (or East Asian)."

It usually applied to people, not things. When it applied to things it usually differentiated between "good" "valuable" and "bad" "worthless."

I know ... sounds pretty "racist" doesn't it ... well, in a war, if the worst thing happening between opposing sides were name calling and hate speech, it would have been a much happier experience for many.

Some Asians were quite taken with the size of our noses; *da bi dz* "big nose" was one of the first Chinese expressions I learned.

Hell, being mistaken for Jimmy Durante was a damned site better than getting shot at!

RPG.   A hand-held, anti-tank, anti-personnel, anti-anything, Soviet missile launcher.

The launcher is a wood-wrapped, steel tube, which was easy to recognize since the missile protruded from the launch tube. So, it was also called a "Dink Hard On."

Like any rocket, the RPG was very dangerous, and grunts hated them. Unlike artillery and mortars, a grunt couldn't hear it coming. And, since it was a direct fire weapon, it was very hard to duck.

Bad guys carrying RPGs were known to have quite a difficult time surrendering.

RTO.   This was an abbreviation for "Radio Telephone Operator" (but there were no telephones).

This was the grunt who carried the old man's Prick-25. Sometimes referred to as the old man's "jeep driver" or "Xray."

Xray was typically the go-to guy when grunts wanted to know what was going on since he typically took the old man's calls. So, this was a job with a lot of prestige.

It was also a job with an uncertain future since the bad guys knew that the guy near the radio, or under the antenna, was the leader and tended to spray a lot of 7.62 shorts in that direction.

Ruck Sack.   This was the fundamental piece of grunt luggage. It's what put the hump into hump.

Technically, it was called the US army ALICE pack, "All-Purpose Lightweight Individual Carrying Equipment," with Frame and Shoulder Straps.

This was where a grunt kept his "stuff": three days of C- Rats (nine meals); a few hundred rounds of various ammo — 5.56 mm in magazines for the M16, 40 mm for the M79, a few belts of 7.62 mm for the M60 ... and if you're an FNG ... an 81mm round or two for the mortars and an M72 LAW; a couple pair of socks; foot powder; a claymore and a few trip flares; insect repellant; a few bags of Kool Aid; writing material and ballpoint pens; cigarettes; field sweater or sweat shirt; poncho; poncho liner; air mattress; a couple plugs of "chaw"; an instamatic camera and couple rolls of film wrapped in a C-Rat Accessory Pack bag; transistor radio; lighter; shit paper; e-tool (or for the FNG a pick or a spade); flashlight; album of snapshots from home or a plastic-wrapped picture of the "girl you left behind;" a couple of quarts of water in canteens or two-quart water bags; iodine pills for water purification; big bottle of aspirin; battery for the Prick-25; batteries for the camera, flashlight (the infamously scarce BA30) and the transistor; candles; smoke, Willy Pete and frag grenades; machete with scabbard; bottle of salt pills.

While humping, grunts looked a lot like a long line of muddy, wet, olive drab snails. Walking bent over (which was the only way you could move under a ruck) was also an effective strategy for climbing muddy mountains on all fours.

For some strange reason defying sense, gravity and basic geography, grunts seemed never to go down a hill ... only up.

When a grunt actually got to go downhill, the ruck and gravity proved a challenge. If a grunt tried to descend while walking upright, the ruck would cause him to pitch forward and take out everyone below him ... I've seen this happen ... it doesn't make the perpetrator very popular with his down-hill mates. The only effective way for a grunt to descend was by sliding down on his ass using his heels as brakes.

Standing straight up, even on level ground, would typically cause a grunt to fall on his ass, if it could be found under all the equipment, and, like the proverbial turtle, he couldn't get up without help.

Rules of Engagement. The "Rules of Engagement" (ROE) determined when, where, and how force, especially the deadly kind, could be used.

For grunts, this was who they could shoot, when and where.

The "kill them all and let God sort them out" principle was not legal, moral, or permissible.

In general, this was the deal (Hollywood filmmakers and leftist journalists, please pay attention):

- If someone were shooting at a grunt, he could shoot back.
- If the target were identifiable as enemy combatants — uniforms, equipment, activity, location, etc.— a grunt could engage (army euphemism for "shoot").
- Fire could not be directed into or near civilian areas unless it could be established that such fire was mission essential and/or would preserve the lives of US personnel, allied personnel, or civilians.

Violate these rules and a grunt stood a good chance of a ten-to-twenty-year R&R in Leavenworth ... which meant a roof, a bed, three hits a day and lots of interesting new friends.

Grunts, like most people, did the right thing for either one of two reasons: either they understood it was the right thing to do and did it; or they understood that not doing it would get them into a world of hurt.

Most grunts believed that harming civilians was wrong.

Like most Americans, grunts saw themselves as the "good guys," the "cowboys with the white hats." They were in Nam to help the Vietnamese, not harm them. It was not consistent with a grunt's cultural values to harm the innocent.

Granted, in an insurgency it was difficult at times to determine who was a "civilian," but in general, grunts would not only avoid harming civilians, even at the risk of their own safety, but they would also dis-courage others from harming civilians.

For grunts who didn't see it that way, there was always the threat of a good ass-kicking, prison, or both.

S

Sad Sack.   A characterization for an incompetent and sloppy soldier. AKA, a Snuffy.

The characterization derives from a comic strip, and later a comic book (not a "graphic novel") created by George Baker during World War II. Sad Sack was an incompetent and shamming buck private, a "GI Everyman," who experienced the absurdities and humiliations of army life.

To be clear, not every unsightly soldier was a sad sack. Most grunts would not pass muster on a formal army post or even in an in-country basecamp. Typically, their uniforms were dirty and torn, boots unshined, hair a bit shaggy, couple days growth on the chin ... but they weren't sad sacks ... just check the condition of their weapons.

Here's a parable I took to heart as a company commander later in my career,

"The Legend of Private Snuffy."

Word comes down from brigade that the Brigade Commander is going to inspect the unit at reveille. As part of the inspection, the BC is going to ask the troops MOS-related questions. In fact, a friendly on brigade staff sent down a list of the colonel's typical questions.

So, the company commander has his platoon leaders and NCO's drill all the troops on the expected questions.

Squad Leader: "Snuffy, what's the maximum effective range of the M16A1 rifle?"

Snuffy: "I don't know, sergeant."

Squad Leader: "It's 416 meters, Snuffy! 416 meters! Repeat that! 416 meters!"

Snuffy: "416 meters, sergeant!"

Squad Leader: "Good job snuffy! So, tomorrow at reveille, when the brigade commander asks you what the maximum effective range of the M16A1 rifle is, how are you going to respond?"

Snuffy: "416 meters!"

Then ....

Platoon Leader: "Snuffy, what's the maximum effective range of the M16A1 rifle?"

Snuffy: "I don't know, sir."

Platoon Leader: "It's 416 meters, Snuffy! 416 meters! Repeat that! 416 meters!"

Snuffy: "416 meters, sir!"

Platoon Leader: "Good job snuffy! So, tomorrow at reveille, when the brigade commander asks you what the maximum effective range of the M16A1 rifle is, how are you going to respond?"

Snuffy: "416 meters!"

Finally ...

Company Commander: "Snuffy, what's the maximum effective range of the M16A1 rifle?"

Snuffy: "I don't know, sir."

Company Commander: "It's 416 meters, Snuffy! 416 meters! Repeat that! 416 meters!"

Snuffy: "416 meters, sir!"

Company Commander: "Good job snuffy! So, tomorrow at reveille, when the brigade commander asks you what the maximum effective range of the M16A1 rifle is, how are you going to respond?"

Snuffy: "416 meters!"

Comes reveille ...

Brigade Commander: "What's your name, soldier?"

Snuffy: "Private Snuffy, sir!"

Brigade Commander: "Private Snuffy, what's the maximum effective range of the M16A1 rifle?"

Snuffy: "I don't know, sir!"

Brigade Commander: "Why don't you know, soldier?"

Snuffy: "No one ever told me, sir!"

Brigade Commander: "Captain, why doesn't your trooper know the maximum effective range of his weapon?"

Company Commander: "No excuse, sir!"

Brigade Commander: "You bet there's no excuse, captain! You report to me at my headquarters at 1500 hours this afternoon so we can discuss your career!"

Saigon Tea.   This had nothing to do with Lipton's.

A saigon tea was the drink of choice of bar girls. "Hey, GI ... you buy me saigon tea?"

If the babysahn were drinking it, it was literal tea on the rocks. The professional ethics of bar girls didn't permit them to drink alcohol while on duty hustling GIs.

The price of a saigon tea was equivalent to the best 12-year-old scotch in a mid-town Manhattan bar X 5 (or a seven-ounce cup of beer at a major-league baseball game).

That is, of course, unless a GI were drinking the saigon tea. In that case, the price was about the same, but now the drink had morphed into something we called in my native land a "mickey finn."

> "Good night sweet prince: And flights of angels sing thee to thy rest!"

I wonder if the commies changed the name of this, too?

> "Hey, Comrade Barkeep! Me and Comrade Babysahn'll have two Ho Chi Minh City Teas, *s'il vous plait*."

Salute.   Theoretically, a military greeting courtesy rendered between two soldiers.

The subordinate, the lower ranking of the two soldiers, initiates the salute and holds it until the superior returns it. Also, a verbal greeting accompanies the salute, "Good afternoon, sir!"

> Enlisted salute officers and warrants.
> Officers salute officers
> Warrants in a good mood salute officers
> Enlisted do not salute enlisted

That's the theory anyway.

In Nam, salutes were not rendered in the field, unless you really hated the guy! Doing so would identify officers and leaders to enemy snipers. Think of Bugs Bunny holding a sign over Daffy Duck, "Shoot Me!" so Elmer Fudd would get the message.

The protocol on the 4th Division Base Camp, Camp Enari, was confused. A grunt could get his ass handed to him either for saluting or not saluting.

Sometime during my second tour my policy was not to salute anyone under the rank of major. My thought was company-grade officers couldn't do that much damage to me and the world would be a much better place with a few less field-grades screwing things up.

At the end of my third tour, I was on Enari out-processing for my discharge from active duty ... I actually became a "civilian" in Nam. I was hustling around various division staff-weenie offices getting signatures and initials on my forms when I walked past a 1LT. I gave him the proper greeting, "Good Morning, LT!" but didn't salute.

LT Fuzz tried to brace me, "Soldier! Don't you salute officers ..."

He had to stop there. I was still wearing the standard ranger field uniform: camouflaged "tree" battle dress, no insignia of rank, no badges, no patches, black beret, and a pair of faded, scuffed-up boots that had seen more time in-country than the ponce who was addressing me as "soldier.".

I specked him out. Clean, pressed fatigues; polished boots; clean shaven; regulation "Charlie Brown" baseball cap with silver bar; 4th Division patch left shoulder; no combat patch right shoulder; infantry insignia and black bar sown on collar; no CIB. This guy almost glowed!

FNG or REMF, I decided, or both.

I had a choice. Since I was wearing no insignia of rank, a uniform consistent with a special operations unit, and I had less than 24-hours left on active duty, I could either not inform the good LT of my enlisted status and / or indicate I didn't give a damn about his offended prestige.

Or I could just screw with his head.

I chose the latter.

"No! I don't!" I told him, turned, and walked off to my next administrivia stop.

Also, never make the mistake of saluting a senior NCO.

Not only will it not be returned, but you will get your butt scorched, "You don't salute me, smackhead! I still have to work for a living!"

Salute Report.   This was the name and format of an immediate, informal, field, contact report.

The report was usually given right after the standard radio message, "Shit! Shit! Shit! Contact! Contact! Contact!"

S - Size of the enemy force
A - Activity of the hostiles
L - Location; where they're at
U - Unit designation, patches, insignia of the bad guys
T - What time you made their acquaintance
E - Equipment; what stuff they're carrying

This was the basis for all observations made on recon patrols, LR-RPs, or when you hit the shit. I can still do this one in my sleep.

One of my worst SALUTE reports was given during one of my last LRRPs. We were working an AO called "Happy Valley" out of Camp Radcliff. We were sitting on a reputed high-traffic infiltration trail up from the coast. We had hunkered down for the night in some dense foliage about half-way down a ridgeline overlooking the trail.

Sometime right before BMNT, my guy on the radio shook me awake.

"Movement," he breathed into my ear.

"Where?" I breathed back.

"All around us!"

When I shook the cobwebs out of my head, I knew he was right. They were right below us, and there was a lot of them. They were making no effort to be stealthy. In fact, they were taking a break. I could hear conversations in Vietnamese, smell commie-cigarette smoke, food cooking, BO, dinks crapping out, and nuoc mam breath.

I prayed none of them came up the ridge to pee into our bushes ... or worse!

I was pretty sure they didn't know we were there; we were still breathing. But they were too damn close to report contact.

They stayed in place through BMNT, and then they moved out east toward the coast.

As soon as they were out of sight down the trail, I reported the contact.

"Romeo Two Five Xray! Romeo Two Eight! Contact!"

"Two Eight! Xray! Go!"

"Company sized element moving on foot eastbound from my location along designated trail; OD and khaki fatigues, red collar insignia, some pith helmets; bad breath and body odor; time immediate; equipped with light-infantry small arms."

"Copy, Two Eight! Are you still in contact?"

"Negative contact! They've moved off! Will follow and advise."

We did follow the dinks for a few klicks. Unlike the stealthy jungle warriors of repute, they left a trail wide enough to drive a truck down. We paralleled it along the high ground so we wouldn't stumble on to any rear security element.

Once we were satisfied that they were staying on the trail, we handed it over to the zoomies for follow up, while we got our butts well out of napalm range.

"San Francisco"   A tune by Scott McKenzie.

"If you're going to San Francisco / Be sure to wear some flowers in your hair..."

This was one of the three required songs to be played by any USO show or Filipino NCO-Club band, along with "The Green Green Grass of Home" and "We Gotta Get Out Of This Place."

This probably had something to do with the fact that a lot of guys shipped through the Oakland army Depot. So "San Francisco" meant "going home" and not any affection for hippies ... except for hippy girls, of course ... grunts would forgive the female race just about anything ... except Jane Fonda, of course ... well maybe even Jane as Barbarella in the Orgasmatron.

Satchel Charge. This was the tool of choice for NVA sappers and a hell of a way to wake up ... or not.

The satchel charge was a combat demolition device made up of a charge of dynamite or plastic explosive, a carrying device or wrapping similar to a satchel, and a triggering mechanism.

NVA sappers would attempt to infiltrate though the perimeter of a firebase and use satchel charges to destroy artillery, mortars, ammo, bunkers, and people ... pretty much in that order.

It was a one-way trip for them and they pretty much knew it. So, dealing with these guys was as tricky as a death wish and twenty pounds of C4 can be.

For the sapper, surrender wasn't an option, but taking a few grunts for company on that journey to the great workers' paradise in the sky was. And grunts knew it.

SEA Hut. Abbreviation for a Southeast Asia Hut; pronounced SEA-hut.

This is not a seafood restaurant or an anchovy-infected pizza delivery service that guarantees arrival in one hour.

The SEA hut was a 16-by 32-foot wood-frame building with a metal roof, extended rafters, screened-in ventilation, whose floor was raised off the ground. Its principal use was for barracks, administration offices and storage on permanent basecamps.

SEA Huts were usually a sign that the surrounding terrain was infested with lifers and REMFs.

A notable exception was my LRRP platoon. We were housed in SEA Huts, with individual cots, foot lockers, and electric lights! After nine months of sleeping in a poncho-hootch spooning with two other grunts, this was in my opinion five-star accommodation.

The fact that the SEA Hut had a high profile and because the floor was elevated off the ground, the sandbag walls didn't offer much protection, made me a bit nervous at times. But, to make up for its tactical deficiencies, there was usually a cooler with iced beer and soda in the center aisle.

Hey! Sometimes you just have to make compromises with your choices!

Section 8.   A nutcase.

The term comes from Section VIII of the World War II–era United States Army Regulation 615–360, concerning the separation of service members from the military. Section VIII provided for the discharge of those who were deemed mentally unfit for military service.

In other words, all of us grunts after a couple of weeks in the boonies. Of course, we were "functionally nuts," so the army wasn't sending us anywhere.

My favorite Section 8 story is told in Joseph Heller's novel, *Catch 22*.

Yossarian, a bombardier flying missions over enemy territory during WWII, asks the flight surgeon whether the surgeon believes the Yossarian is crazy.

The doc agrees saying Yossarian is the craziest guy he knows.

Yossarian then asks whether the army air force discharges the insane under Section VIII.

Again, the flight surgeon agrees.

So, Yossarian asks, would the doc discharge Yossarian.

The flight surgeon says absolutely, but Yossarian would have to request formally a discharge under Section VIII.

Yossarian says he'll make the request.

The doc says requesting to be discharged from duty as dangerous as Yossarian's would be a sane act, therefore disqualifying Yossarian from discharge under Section VII.

There was only one catch and that was Catch-22, which specified that a concern for one's safety in the face of dangers that were real and immediate was the process of a rational mind.

Orr was crazy and could be grounded. All he had to do was ask; and as soon as he did, he would no longer be crazy and would have to fly more missions. Orr would be crazy to fly more missions and sane if he didn't, but if he were sane he had to fly them. If he flew them he was crazy and didn't have to, but if he didn't want to he was sane and had to. Yossarian was moved very deeply by the absolute simplicity of this clause of Catch-22 and let out a respectful whistle. (Chapter 5)

Grunts practiced a kind of "baseline" insanity among themselves.

This was the condition that allowed a grunt to leave a relatively safe bunker and run toward a firefight because all his buddies were.

This was the condition that caused grunts to attack through the kill zone of a known ambush site because they had to get to their buddies pinned down on the other side.

This was the condition that caused a grunt who was safe back in the rear to find a chopper to take him back out to the field the second he heard his buddies were in the shit.

This was the condition that caused a grunts to break cover to retrieve their dead and wounded.

Most would call these acts insane; we knew them as love.

Many years after leaving Nam, I was taking a road trip with my oldest daughter, who was in grad school studying for her doctorate in psychology.

I asked her what the word "psychotic" meant explaining I heard it often in the manner of an insult, "Don't go out with her! She's psychotic!" Or "Don't take that assignment! The commander is a psycho!"

My darlin' daughter, being a grad student, delivered a thirty-minute lecture on the meaning and implications of psychotic and psychosis.

I finally interrupted her saying, "If I understand what you're saying, we're all nuts."

"Pretty much," she agreed.

After being so enlightened, I no longer classified people by those who were sane and others. I looked at them as "Insane and Realizes It" and "Insane and in Denial."

Shake 'n' Bake.   Sometimes the term was used to describe an officer commissioned through OCS, but for the most part in Nam a "shake 'n' bake" was a graduate of the army NCO academy, who usually came into country as an E5 or E6 FNG.

The NCO academy concept was created to address the need for NCO leadership in Nam. Most grunt enlisted leaders in Nam were more junior in rank than their assigned responsibilities demanded, at least according to the army TOE. For example, the TOE designates a squad leader as an E6, Staff Sergeant; I had a squad as an E4, "Acting Jack."

Sometimes, these misguided shake 'n' bakes thought that the stripes bestowed upon them in the States had more authority than experience and expertise in combat. Although the army rank and organizational structure granted legitimate authority to these individuals, for grunts "competence" was the essential source of all authority. A grunt leader had to demonstrate the skills required for keeping his guys alive and sending the bad guys to the "Great Rice Paddy in the Sky."

Also, a leader had to "take care of his guys." In gruntdom, a squad leader took care of all aspects of the welfare of the squad. If a grunt believed that a leader wouldn't do this but would knowingly throw him to the wolves, even to get a legitimate job done, there was going to be trouble before long.

In a sense, the relationship between the leader and the led, when leadership worked right, was a combination of trust and friendship. That's a tall order for any leader, but damned near impossible for an FNG with stripes and an attitude.

Most of these shake 'n' bakes were scared to death when they got in country. Not only were they in harm's way, like the rest of us, but they were assigned leadership responsibility by rank and position over a bunch of grunts who had forgotten more about combat than the shake 'n' bake could have ever learned in the States.

For grunts, the "FNG rules" applied regardless of rank. For the "shake 'n' bake" — the good ones, anyway, and there were plenty of good ones — they listened, watched and learned. They learned how to do the job, stayed alive, and kept their people alive.

For the others, there were always plenty of jobs in supply and the mess hall.

Sham.   This was a verb meaning "to temporarily avoid work and responsibility through cunning means."

In other words, getting off the line for a few days despite the vigilance of the lifers. Anyone who did this was called a "shammer," and anyone who was recognized as being especially adept at this was called a "sham artist."

Shamming should never be confused with "shirking," which was avoiding duty at the expense of other grunts, or the refusal of an 11B to join (or re-join) his unit for any reason. For this grunts had no respect or toleration.

Let me try to illustrate the difference:

After the firefight where my helmet got killed, I was medevacked back to division. I had a slight head wound caused either by bullet fragments, helmet fragments, whatever I hit on the way down, or all of the above.

No big deal... a couple of stitches, a little antiseptic, some Brass Hat hands me a Purple Heart and shakes my hand... but then the doc said the magic words, "We're going to keep you overnight for observation. We want to make sure you don't have a concussion."

So, since my unit's now sitting on a firebase pulling palace guard and doesn't miss me, and I'm back at division in a nice cozy hospital, lying in a bed with clean sheets, eating three hots a day, surrounded by female nurses, with a piece of paper that says, "Restricted Duty—no field duty and no work details," the right answer when the doctor asks, "How you feeling this morning, sergeant?" is "I feel fine, sir, lying down. But, when I get up to go to the latrine I get really dizzy!"

Repeat that until the doc figures it out and throws your ass out of the hospital!

As long as my buddies in the field don't need me for a couple of days, there's no problem stretching a two-day treatment into a six or seven-day mini-vacation.

That's grunt-approved "shamming."

"Shirking" on the other hand is "avoiding duty" or deliberately not being where you're needed or supposed to be. And there were guys in Nam who shirked.

Lifers were infamous for it. Some senior NCOs, who were supposed to be squad leaders and platoon sergeants, found ways of staying out of the field for their entire tour.

Some guys claimed racial, political or even religious reasons for not going forward. These guys usually congregated in a base camp which created a curious and disturbing mix of army rigor and revolutionary nihilism.

Base camps became at times more like dysfunctional communities than army bases. This was one of the reasons grunts avoided them—not only were they full of REMFs, lifers and shirkers, but they could be dangerous!

I was passing through a divisional base camp on my way back to the field. I just happened to be there at the beginning of the month, payday; so, I collected my roll of MPC, sent a couple of money orders home and decided to have a couple of beers at the NCO club before heading back out.

I remember being cautioned about a spate of "muggings" every payday. I thought it curious and really didn't take it seriously. Muggings happen in New York, not Pleiku.

On my way back to my billets, I got jumped. I got hit in the head and rolled into a ditch. The guys who jumped me made a couple of mistakes.

First, they didn't knock me unconscious... I saw stars, but I also saw them coming down the side of the ditch after me.

Second, they brought knives to a gun fight. I had a nice, little Chicom 9mm pistol in my belt that I kept for emergencies. So, I let loose on them. Luckily for them, rolling down a hill in the dark after being sapped on the head did nothing for my marksmanship.

I don't think I hit anything, but I definitely cleared the place out. I didn't see any bodies, blood, or bits when I pulled myself out of the ditch, but I didn't look too carefully.

I didn't want to explain the situation to the Military Police or lose my 9mm, a primo war trophy. So, I got back to my billet, spent the night in base camp and got the hell out of Dodge bright and early the next morning. In the boonies, you at least know who your friends are.

I've read a couple of apologia for some of the politically motivated shirking that was going on in Nam. I don't want to enter that debate, but I will share a story about a guy who refused to shirk despite his ideology.

During my last days with a line unit, I was in charge of company "TOC Security." I had a small rifle squad and our job was to make sure no sappers got close to the old man or his RTO.

Part of any company headquarters was the "head medic," the senior medic for the company. In Nam, medics didn't wear Red Crosses on their helmet or arm bands — this made too good an aiming point for the bad guys — but they did carry weapons for personal protection — usually an M16 or a 45. Although they weren't expected to take part defending or attacking anything, they had to be there to care for and protect casualties.

So, the medics went everywhere grunts went, and sometimes didn't have the luxury to stay under cover when a grunt got hurt. Grunts had all the respect in the world for their medics, even the ones that fleeced them blind in poker games.

One night, when we were in a night laager, I noticed our head medic wasn't carrying a weapon. I thought he had put it down somewhere and had walked away from I t... not a recommended practice in the boonies.

So I asked him where it was, and he said he didn't have one. I thought he was bullshitting me; no one goes to the field without a weapon—that's just crazy.

He told me he didn't carry a weapon because he was a conscientious objector; he refused to use deadly force against anyone.

So, I asked the next logical question, "What the hell are you doing in Nam?" He said he had been drafted and felt that it was his duty to serve his country.

When he declared himself a conscientious objector, "CO" in army-jargon, the army, with its perverse sense of irony, assigned him to the Medical Corps and sent him to Nam as a field medic. He said he really had no problem with being a medic in the field, because he was helping out in a way he believed appropriate.

I was flabbergasted! When I looked at this guy, I thought I was seeing that fine line between heroism and insanity.

I'm sure that if he had wanted to, he could have avoided Nam altogether or at least have gotten an assignment in one of the rear areas. Hell, I didn't think a base camp was safe without a nine-mil, and this guy was walking around the boonies with no protection but his medical bag.

From that day, Doc became my special project; he went nowhere unless I was with him. The company commander wasn't pleased that I was giving a CO so much attention, but I wasn't that fond of the company commander.

Shithook.   A not-so-affectionate name for the Boeing CH-47, a large, two bladed, heavy-lift helicopter with a loading ramp in the rear and a cargo hook in its belly ... hence the second half its name.

The first half of its name had to do with its prop-wash. One of these could flatten an acre of hootches in seconds.

Transcript of an actual radio transmission:

> Grunt on the Ground: "This is Alpha Sierra Two Six; the shithook is inbound to my location.
>
> Helicopter Pilot: "This is a Chinook, not a shithook!"
>
> Grunt on the Ground: "If you were down here eating all this shit, you'd call it a shithook too!"
>
> Helicopter Pilot: "We roger that, Two Six."

The arrival of a shithook at a fire base was usually welcomed with great affection by grunts as an indication something good was coming in — packages, mail, beer— or something good was going out — them.

Shit Sandwich.   This was a metaphorical expression used to describe any person or situation that's not optimal. In fact, to use a modern expression taught to me by my kids, it's when something really "sucks."

Q: What's the difference between a lifer and a shit sandwich?
A: The bread!

This concept was often used to differentiate between life and army life, as in, "Sometimes life hands you a shit sandwich; in the army you're not authorized bread."

This expression has been replaced in modern grunt parlance as a shit show.

Short Round.   This expression had two potential meanings.
First, it was any armament that was distance challenged.

Second, it was a nickname describing the runt of the grunt litter and one of the stock characters in a rifle squad. This was a little guy you didn't burden with the M60 or the M79.

The expression also described an artillery or mortar round that didn't quite make it all the way to the intended target ... hopefully it made it out of the perimeter, but not always.

It was always a good idea to duck somewhere when the artillery was doing its thing. Artillery rounds are a "for whom it may concern" thing once they leave the tube.

Short Timer.   This was a grunt nearing the end of his combat tour, usually in the last month of a twelve-month tour.

The danger of being a short timer was that, for the first time since he was an FNG, a grunt actually became conscious of the possibility of surviving his combat tour. The desire to stay alive for these last few weeks began to interfere with his ability to function properly as a grunt. In other words, his desire to live began to interfere with his duty.

A short timer was known to be nervous, reluctant to go on patrol, even get out of his bunker. He was probably the only grunt who slept in the bottom of a bunker in a flack vest and helmet.

A short timer feared that he had used up all his Mojo to become a somewhat inauspicious and ill-fated individual. Since nature loves irony, what better than to let a guy see the finish line before squashing him?

If lightning were to strike anywhere in the Corps area, it would hit the short timer.

If a tree fell in the forest, it'd fall on the short timer.

In a bird in flight dropped a load, it's fall on the shot timer.

Watch any WWII movie: the short-timer is the bomber pilot on his last mission over a "soft" target who takes the picture of his sweetheart out of his battered hat and tells his co-pilot about his plans to get married and raise a family ...

BLOOM!!!

Melancholy Music!

Roll Credits!

The End!

Grunts never stood too close to a short timer.

Short-Timer Stick. A swagger stick, often carved with service dates, sweetheart's name, home town, "FTA" and various other obscenities, carried by an overconfident short timer daring fate to squash him.

Sick Call. A formation, usually held after reveille of personnel requiring medical attention.

In the army, there was a stigma attached to sick call. In fact, there was a Jody call based on it, "Close your eyes and bow your head / There I see the walking dead."

I imagine this attitude was based on some macho myth that real men don't get sick. In fact, there was an unwritten rule in the army, "Officers do not go on sick call."

I know I never did!

I stocked up on GI Gin and learned minor surgery techniques from a field manual.

Sign / Counter Sign.   This was a two-word code, which changed every twenty-four hours, which was used to challenge unknown parties and verify friendlies.

The first word was the "challenge" given by the challenging party; the second word, the "counter sign," was a verification given by the challenged party.

If you got it right, you didn't get shot.

Under the rules of engagement, all unknown parties had to be challenged in some manner before they could be shot at unless one could verify their unfriendliness by other means: uniform, equipment, nuoc mam breath, or they were actively trying to kill you.

Please notice the flaw in the flow of this procedure.

The brainiacs in the S2 section, Military Intelligence (forget it ... it's too old a joke for even me to use), would try to come up with word combinations that were not culturally obvious. So instead of "Apple Pie" and "Base Ball" they'd use "Apple Ball" and "Base Pie."

Also, under the mistaken impression that East Asians, like the actors who played the Japanese parts in WWII movies, had trouble pronouncing their L's and R's, the sign counter-sign combinations often used words full of these letters in a cleverly futile attempt to unmask the devilishly cunning NVA sappers.

So, if "Lolly Really" came back sounding like "Rorry Learry" you had a problem ... Learry!

Intel was always paranoid about the enemy stealing the countersigns, so grunts were encouraged to be careful, and clever, when challenging unknowns in the dark. The following is an actual dialogue between an FNG on a bunker line trying to bring an LP through the wire after dark:

> FNG on Guard Duty: "Halt! Who's there?"
> Voice from out of the Darkness: "The LP, idiot!"
> FNG: "Lollipop?"

Voice from out of the Darkness: "Roar!"

Silence ...

FNG: "Who played 2nd base for the Brooklyn Dodgers in 1949?"

Silence ...

Then ...

Voice from out of the Darkness: "How the F#%k should I know!

FNG: "Advance, friendly!"

Actually, it was Jackie Lobinson.

Years after Vietnam, I was participating in a company-in-the-defense ARTEP during April at Ft. Drum NY, the only part of the State of New York above the Arctic Circle. We had been dug in for eight days during which the temperature never got above 40 degrees (Fahrenheit, unfortunately) and never stopped raining.

One afternoon, a slick landed behind our position and out jumped the brigade commander in his sharply starched and pressed fatigues, spit-shined boots, steel pot with airborne chinstrap, aviator sunglasses, corncob pipe, and a line of camouflage paint on each cheek. (I swear! I couldn't make this up even if I had imagination).

He told me, "Just ignore me, lieutenant! I want to talk to the men."

So, like any sane company-grade officer, I ignored him by sticking close to him as he walked along the company perimeter.

Finally, he came to one of my more promising young NCOs, a Puerto Rican kid from New York. The sergeant was sitting on the edge of his fighting position, watching some frogs mate. The hole had filled with ice water days ago.

I imagine the kid was trying not to slip into hyperthermia by day-dreaming about sunny beaches, salsa, and *Cuba Libres* in a cabana.

When he spotted the colonel, instead of challenging him, the kid jumped up, rendered a smart salute, and greeted the colonel, "Good Afternoon, Sir!"

The colonel returned the salute, but said, "Why didn't you challenge me, Sergeant?"

The kid replied, "I recognize you, sir!"

Great answer, I thought!

But the colonel, being one if those people who always had to find something wrong to beat a subordinate into submission with, responded, "How do you know I'm not a Russian who looks exactly like me?"

The expression on the sergeant's face was pretty priceless and, luckily, he didn't agree with the colonel's logic and shoot him out of hand.

I also learned that the Spanish word *tonto* wasn't restricted to the Lone Ranger's sidekick.

SitRep. Pronounced, SIT-rep; an acronym for "Situation Report."

This is army jargon for telling your six what's going on.

Actually, belaboring the pun too much, there were some lifers whose credibility would have improved if they did periodically tell their sixes what the hell was going on (or vice versa) (See, "Six," below, for an explanation of what just happened!)

The shortest Sitreps were made by special ops units in the fields and LP's. At night, the control station would call over the radio:

"Romeo Two Eight! Romeo Two! This is Romeo Two Six Xray! If your sitrep is negative, break squelch twice."

The responding station would just key the radio handset twice to confirm nothing was happening, or a "Negative Sitrep."

Six. This potentially meant one of two things to a grunt: his boss or his ass, with no necessary relationship.

"Six" referred to the boss for reasons that make sense only under the assumption that the US army wanted to make it easy for the NVA to read its signals.

Any "roll-your-own" call sign that ended in the numeral "6" designated a leader; for example, a call sign like "Echo Foxtrot Two Six" typically designated the second platoon leader. So, any leader was referred to as "six."

"Six" also referred to a grunt's metaphorical "ass" which was also a metaphor for his well-being, as in the expressions "Watch my six!" or "I got your six!"

This is probably based on using "clock directions," based on the old analog, numbers-and-hands clocks that we boomers are so fond of.

Generation X, please pay attention to tis.

"12" is straight ahead; "3" is directly to the right; "9" is directly to the left; and "6" is ... are you ready for this ... behind!

SKS.   This was an abbreviation for *Samozaryadniy Karabin Sistemi Simonova*, a Soviet semi-automatic carbine firing a 7.62 round from a ten-round internal magazine. It was pretty effective out to around 200 meters.

These rifles were pretty down-scale for the bad guys. They were usually found in VC units while the front-line NVA units carried the AK47 and its variants.

The SKS came sometimes equipped with a very nasty "icepick" bayonet; very scary, but if you got close enough to see it you had a lot of other things to worry about ... like all of the 7.62-shorts cracking around your head.

Slick.   What you thought you were in civilian life before the army got hold of you.

Also, the is the grunt term for the UH1 Iroquois, a small cargo helicopter.

In Nam, this was the basic grunt air-taxi taking them swiftly and stealthily somewhere to surprise the bad guys who rarely were there or, if they were, surprised.

The arrival of slicks at a firebase had an ambiguous reception by grunts.

One slick usually meant something "good" — food, packages, mail, beer — unless the slick contained a steak dinner, a chaplain and a staff weenie.

Many slicks arriving at a fire base meant grunts were about to go somewhere they didn't want to go, but many slicks on an LZ in the boonies usually meant a ride home.

SNAFU. Pronounced SNA-foo.
This is an acronym for "Situation Normal, All F'ed Up."
This is the highest rating possible for an army (or civilian) operation properly planned according to the FUBAR principle, and it's the standard level of achievement for all army operations.
For a grunt, just another day in paradise!

Snake Eater. A not-so-affectionate nickname for an army Ranger.
This refers not so much to their culinary habits as to their general attitude about life, NVA, and the rest of God's creation.
But it could also refer to eating habits. For this, I offer two pieces of advice: 1) it doesn't taste like chicken, and 2) cook it until it's "well done" — it kills the taste and detoxifies most of the venom.

SOL. An abbreviation for "Shit Out of Luck." Essentially what a grunt has been since he arrived in country.

SOP. Pronounced Ess Oh Pee
This is an acronym and abbreviation for "Standard Operating Procedure;" also referred to as a TSOP, "Tactical Standard Operating Procedure," for units that wanted to appear "strac."
Essentially this is a unit's standard and permanent FUBAR statement describing a procedure or set of procedures to perform certain standard operations or functions or reactions to designated expected events, e.g., "Immediate Action Drills".

The SOP was supposed to offer guidance where official doctrine was lacking, extremely broad, or just not too damned relevant. The SOP was also used to provide practical detail to official doctrine or to explain how it was to be implemented ... or sometimes the old man was making it up as he went along.

Most SOP's were obsolete or irrelevant, but a unit had to have them to pass an inspection. Look around any lifer's desk (in the army or in the private sector) and you'll find a bunch of three-ring binders designated "SOP," "Policy," "Procedures," etc.

Ancient proverb: "You will never find wisdom or anything useful in a three-ring binder."

Souvenir.   Pronounced, SUE-vah-near.

This was pidgin for "give" from the French, *souvenir*, "to remember;" or the English "to pay good money for a bunch of worthless trash and trinkets, bring them home from an exotic, foreign country, and find out nobody wants anything to do with a ceramic water buffalo with a thermometer on its butt, engraved 'Souvenir of Vietnam'."

"Babysahn, how much for beer?"
"50 pi, GI; MPC 50 cent!"
"You souvenir me?"
"What! You dinky dau, GI!? You numbah ten cheap charrie!"
If you understand this, you've read too much!
Stop!
Save yourself!
You're ready to DEROS.

SP Pack.   This was a "supplement" pack, an A-ration (real food) supplement containing cigarettes (we knew smoking could kill; we just weren't very concerned), candy, paperback novels and writing paper, etc.

The SP pack is often blamed for hooking grunts on tobacco, tropical chocolate, and Matt Helm novels.

Spad.   This was the Douglas A-1 Sky Raider, a propeller-driven single-seat attack bomber used by the Navy, Air Force and something called the VNAF (Viet Nam Air Force) for close air support.

When this puppy showed up, it was always a bit of a shock for grunts, because it made them think either that they were suddenly in the wrong war or that the US had run out of jet aircraft.

Despite that, the Spad was much loved for the scunion it could bring with its four twenty-millimeter canons and 8,000 pounds of ordinance, including bombs, napalm, rockets, and kitchen sinks. This baby humped ordinance like a grunt.

Unlike jet aircraft that seemed to have a relationship with its target like a hooker with a leper ... zip, boom, and gone ... the Spad seemed to make love to its target ... it kept working until everyone was satisfied and having a good smoke.

Spooky.   Also called "Puff the Magic Dragon" ... another interpretation of the expression I'm sure Peter, Paul and Mary detest.

This was the AC-47, an Air Force C-47 Skytrain modified by mounting three 7.62 mm General Electric miniguns which fired through two rear window openings and the side cargo door on the left side of the aircraft.

Spooky's primary function was close air support for grunts and we loved ... I say again ... loved these guys! Why? Read this,

> "Coverage given by a Spooky was over an elliptical area approximately 52 yards in diameter, placing a projectile within every 2.4 yards during a 3 second burst."

In other words, "Scunion;" "Holey Bad Guys;" "Blow Smoke;" "If you got 'em, light 'em;" "Grease Gun;" "We find 'em, you kill 'em;" etc. etc. etc.!

These guys loved their work ... and they did it soooo well.

SSDD.   This is an abbreviation for "Same Shit Different Day."

This is an articulation of SNAFU resulting in FUBAR which deconstructs the essential inexpressibility logocentrism of army planning (*v.*

Jacques Derrida. *On Grammatology*); or, just another day in the magic kingdom known as gruntdom.

Staff.   Also called "The Cave of Winds."

In theory, army staff consists of officers and enlisted personnel that provide a "bi-directional flow of information between a commander, subordinate commanders and staffs and subordinate units."

The purpose was for planning operations, providing accurate, timely information on which command decisions are based, and managing administration and logistics.

At battalion level and above, staff was divided into five "specialties" or "sections":

> **"S1"—Personnel and Administration:** The S1 is the head clerk ruling a world of paper, typewriters, obscure regulations, ciphers and symbols, paper clips, mimeograph machines and carbon paper. The S1 is usually the old man's "adjutant," kind of a private secretary with an attitude.

> **"S2"—Intelligence and Security:** This is the center of the oxymoron known as "military intelligence." The S2 was also in charge of time and weather... how would you like to have that job during the monsoons?

> **"S3"—Operations and Training:** In the military pecking order, the S3 was #3 after the XO and the old man. He was the king of FUBAR and SNAFU, developing and coordinating all OPORDS.

> **"S4"—Logistics and Supply:** This is the "King of Ash & Trash." He's the unit juggler — transportation, maintenance, supply, mess, combat trains, all belonged to the S4. This was not a job for the weak, faint of heart, the short of patience, with a complete lack of a sense of humor.

> **"S5"—Public Affairs:** This was the "minds & hearts" operation; more accurately the bag man for the futile efforts to make them like us ... the good guys, that is.

The XO, (Executive Officer), was typically the "Chief of Staff" who had to orchestrate and coordinate all the staff functions and weenies ... which explains why XO's were never in a good mood.

Grunts were not compatible with staff weenies. The only perceived benefit of being close to staff was pulling palace guard and sharing in the hot chow and other amenities that seemed to magically appear whenever staff was nearby.

The fact that the staff-weenies were usually too busy to screw with the grunts on the bunker line was not missed. Other than that, grunts just avoided them like the black syph and referred to them simply as a "bunch of S'es living in the Cave of Winds."

Stand Down.   Theoretically, this was a short, in-country holiday for an entire unit.

The stated purpose of the stand down was to get a unit off the line for a few days to relieve some of the stress and strain of humping the boonies, living like animals, and constantly running into bad guys.

The real purpose was to take care of the unit ash, trash and administrivia. It gave the lifers a chance to straighten out the grunts, making them "strac" à la lifer.

The infantry battalion to which I was first assigned in Nam was part of a division task force, meaning it had no fixed AO of its own but got sent anywhere in the division AO where the shit was hitting the fan.

Also, the battalion was the division's "step child;" it was never part of the division's traditional organization but had been "taken over" from another division. Many in the unit thought they weren't treated as well as the rest of the division's "children;" like "Cinderella," we got to clean up all the division's shit.

But, after we probably had been on the line a bit too long up around An Khe and Kontum during the initial stages the Tet'68 counter offensive, our step-division finally brought us onto its base camp.

The unit was a bit "rough," even by grunt standards. Everyone was filthy, unshaven, long-haired, pissed off, and not too sure whose army they were in — a veritable lifers' nightmare.

The first day, the division played it smart. They quarantined the entire battalion by putting us in tents in the dead space between the bunker line and the actual cantonment area. We were advised not to go wandering around the base camp looking for the PX or the "Class Six" store (army-speak for liquor store).

After some poor misguided REMF Major wandered into our encampment insisting somewhat vigorously on being saluted and being treated somewhat insensitively by some grunt NCOs, the word actually went out to the rest of the division to stay the hell away from us.

"Soldier! Don't you salute officers!"

"Only if I want them shot by some sniper."

"Sir! Right!"

"Right"

"Sir!"

"What?"

"When's the last time you shaved?"

"Don't remember!"

"Sir! Right!"

"Didn't we do this already?"

After that, our old man, a first lieutenant looking as filthy and rough as we did but whom we respected as a grunt and would follow to hell if he asked us, told us to stop picking on the REMFs.

That first night, the division drove deuces loaded with hot food and cold beer into our encampment and just left us alone. The noise died down by 10 PM; we were in no shape to handle beer and really needed the sleep.

The next day, division didn't play it as smart.

Stand down, although potentially beneficial and pleasurable for grunts, is actually a demonstration of REMF power, who take an entire unit off the line in order to catch up with their paperwork.

For the entire day, we went from admin station to admin station confirming facts already in our 201 files.

"Yes! I'm still male."

"Yes! My birth date hasn't changed so I'm really nineteen."

"Yes! I'm still here!"

Also, there was a feeble attempt at providing basic medical services with the caveat that no condition that would prevent a grunt from going back to the field could be diagnosed.

"Yes! Your teeth are rotting out of your head. But, under MACV directive, 11B's are authorized halitosis."

"That's the worst case of jungle rot I've ever seen. Thank God you have two feet!."

"I've never seen anything like that before! Take a couple of aspirin and see a real doctor when you get back to the world."

The division did accomplish getting us cleaned up, shaved, groomed, and into somewhat clean and serviceable jungle fatigues. We at least were beginning to look like something that a lifer would recognize as soldiers.

But this is how things went seriously wrong.

That night the division threw a party for the entire battalion in the EM club. There was beer, music, beer, a USO band, beer, females in the USO band, and beer, and beer.

At one point, guys thought it a good idea to pour beer over each other's heads ... somebody thought the alcohol would kill the cooties, I imagine. Soon, the beer was ankle deep in the club, and we were getting a bit rowdy, but contained, because no one seriously considered leaving the club. In fact, a few guys were crapped out on their tables.

But the REMFs at division panicked. They closed the club and tossed about five hundred drunk grunts, who were not ready to end the party, onto the streets of the base camp in the middle of the night.

So, we continued to celebrate.

So, division sent in the MPs, who were no match for a bunch of grunts, who were used to tangling with the NVA on a regular basis.

At one point, I remember a grunt human wave attack through a cordon of MPs against the division swimming pool. I'm not sure what the purpose of that was ... we probably thought a bath was in order and someone said chlorine would kill the cooties ... but it seemed to make sense at the time.

The next morning, at Oh-Dark-Thirty, division had the entire battalion on choppers flying out to an AO called "anyplace but here."

My company wound up on a jungle-covered hill somewhere in the deep, deep boonies digging holes and chopping down trees while we tried to deal with the hangovers.

We were never invited back.

Stand To. This is a routine action in which fighting positions are occupied at a hundred percent strength in the morning from BMNT, "Begin Morning Nautical Twilight", until full light, and in the evening from full light until EENT, "End Evening Nautical Twilight."

For those who are as in the dark (yes! A pun) about these terms, as most grunts were, "nautical twilight" is defined as the time when "the center of the sun is more than 6° below the horizon but less than 12°" as opposed to most civilized concepts of dawn and twilight, not ironically called "Civil" time, when the center of the sun in less than 6° below the horizon ... in other words, you can just about see the top of the damn thing ... as in, "Goooood Morning, Vietnam!"

Stand-to was based on the theory that these are the most likely times for the bad guys to attack.

The practice of stand-to is said to originate with tactics dating back to the French and Indian War, when armies on both sides (the French as well as the Indians, I guess) would use BMNT and EENT to launch attacks.

This seems to be a compelling demonstration of the currency of army tactics during the Vietnam war.

Unfortunately, the bad guys were well aware of this theory, and only a moron (and morons were pretty much extinct by the second phase of the Tet counter-offensive in 1968) would attack a US firebase during stand to.

Stars and Stripes. Again, to a grunt in Nam this could mean two things.

First and foremost, the American flag, Old Glory. Come to attention, salute, and try your damndest not to die for it today and be shipped home under one.

Second, *US Pravda*, the propaganda sheet of the US Armed Forces.

According to itself, *Stars and Stripes* is financed through the Department of Defense, but its content is independent and protected by the First Amendment right of Freedom of Speech.

Right! As my daddy used to say, "Money talks; bullshit walks!"

Stars and Stripes rarely talked to grunts. Either the content was irrelevant to our situation ... "Hey, Sarge! Says here Hitler's still dead!" ... or it addressed issues far above our heads.

"Hey, Sarge! *Stars and Stripes* says the president claims we're winning the war!"

"Great! Did he mention what inning we're in?"

A grunt's best use of the paper was as a supplement to the army's stingy allocation of toilet paper ... three squares a day per soldier, just like chow.

Starlight Scope. The AN/PVS-2 Starlight scopes were first generation passive night vision devices that used ambient light to amplify images.

Grunts didn't see these very often out in the field because the army considered the technology highly sensitive and classified. To get one, a grunt would have to sign his life away, as if he hadn't already by enlisting in the infantry.

The Starlight scope was a "passive" night vison device meaning it did not use an active, infrared light source to illumine a target, which could be detected, but the dingus enhanced the light from natural sources, principally the moon, to illumine targets.

The Starlight scope would have been an excellent tool for night security ... bunker guard, LPs, night patrols ... so the army of course rendered the tool almost inaccessible to grunts.

First, the army wrapped the Starlight scope with a plethora of scary, ultra-secure restrictions that no grunt in his right mind wanted to get tangled in.

> "Just sign these seventeen forms, sergeant ... leave your wallet, your poncho liner, and your left testicle with us ... and tell us again where your parents live in the states."

Second, there weren't many of these to go around. I think my infantry battalion had a few, which were left in the security area of a secret supply room somewhere in the rear.

Third, the batteries were never available when and where the Starlight scope was.

Other than that, it was a great piece of technology.

I was able to get my hands on one while I was pulling Hawkeyes with the rangers. Before taking it out on a mission, I tested it in basecamp.

As far as seeing targets in the dark, it was first rate.

Everything was illumed in a green glow, like the space-aliens in a cheap sci-fi flick. Also, nothing had any depth, a two-dimensional portrayal of nightlife in glowy-green way before the disco craze.

As far as being able to use it to aim a weapon, forget about it! No crosshairs, couldn't see the rifle-sights, could not judge range.

So, I wrote it off as an interesting novelty but not worth jeopardizing my career and my testicles to risk taking it out into the field.

Steel Pot.   The basic and, according to lifers, the only authorized headgear for grunts in the field.

Based on weight as a factor of its utility, grunts preferred boonie hats. Who am I trying to kid? Grunts wore boonie hats to stick it to lifers.

The Vietnam-era army "steel pot" had a number of components: the chin strap, the head band, the helmet liner, the steel helmet itself, the camouflage cover, and the elastic band to hold it on the helmet.

A favorite trick of grunts in the rear was to wear the liner with the commo cover over it while ... usually the lifers caught on to this one real quick. But, the other day, I was watching one of the old 1950's nuclear mutant monster movies, *Them*. It's the one about the Los Angeles being devoured by giant nuclear-mutant ants from Las Vegas ... a classic!

The hero was played by an actor named James Arness, who later became famous as Marshall Matt Dillon in the TV series, *Gunsmoke*.

Arness was a big guy ... someone you wouldn't mess with unless it was unavoidable. In the movie, he's leading a crew of army guys attacking the giant ants in the LA sewer system ... credible when you consider the setting ... and there's this six foot-something, broad shouldered hero-type running around the sewers with a tommy gun, wearing a helmet liner on his head.

He looked like a six-foot, OD, circumcised pecker! The giant nuclear-mutant ants must have died of hysterics! "Run guys! Here comes the pecker!"

The condition of the camo cover was a way of visually determining precedence in the grunt food chain.

FNGs wore nice clean and bright camo covers, but guys who'd been around awhile wore faded, dirty, torn covers, which were usually decorated with various mottos and symbols of their discontent. Favorites were "FTA," the peace symbol, sports team logos, flowers, "SF" meaning San Francisco meaning DEROS, "Dig Here" was always popular with the airborne guys, Ace of Spades, girlfriend's name, poker chips, shamrocks, skull & crossbones, etc.

Since a steel pot couldn't stop an AK round or a serious piece of shrapnel, gave no protection from the sun, gave a grunt's head an unmistakable target profile and a migraine, and weighed a lot, their perceived utility was reduced to:

- Expressing one's inner discontented artist
- Boiling water for coffee, tea, and minor surgery
- Holding water for shaving or washing various critical body parts
- Soaking feet (when puddles and mud weren't readily available)
- Preparing C-Ration stews, various casseroles, pâtés, ham & lima bean *fois gras,* and the like

- Mixing boat drinks, or creating something drinkable out of after-shave and canned OJ
- Portable latrine for those times when leaving a bunker was not advisable
- Smashing small to medium sized bugs, amphibians, and reptiles (the M16 was advisable for the large critters)
- Protecting the testicles during mortar attacks when a bunker, hole, or ditch wasn't handy
- Carrying insect repellant, shit paper and a first aid kit in the elastic band
- Tapping M16 magazines before loading.

... only a few of which required actually wearing the damned thing.

Strac.   An acronym that somehow translates into having one's shit together, being well trained and prepared, having "all your shit in one bag."

In general, a "good" thing if one remembers the term was defined very differently by grunts and lifers.

For a lifer, "strac" meant highly polished boots, straight gig lines, clean & pressed uniforms, short haircuts (high & tight), daily close shaves, regular formations, work details, regular police calls (ass holes & elbows), etc.

For a grunt, "strac" meant clean and serviceable weapons; well-positioned, deep and well-fortified fighting positions; well-practiced immediate action drills; clean potable water that didn't taste like bleached iodine; at least enough Cs for three meals a day (but hot food was much better); dry hootches; air mattresses that didn't leak; dry poncho liners; at least three hours of uninterrupted sleep a night, etc.

Sweat Bee.   This is another charming example of the Vietnamese fauna,

The sweat bee was bug attracted to the salt in human sweat and who shows its appreciation for the feed by stinging the back, arm, face, or whatever part of the grunt that fed it.

The name "sweat bee" refers to members of the Halictidae, a large family of bees that are common in most of the world except Australia and Southeast Asia, where they are only a minor faunistic element".

Obviously, whoever characterized these guys as a "minor faunistic element" never had to dig a bunker, trench a perimeter or fill sandbags in Nam.

> "Do be a dew bee; don't be a sweat bee ... do bee do bee do!" A Grunt impersonating Frank Sinatra impersonating Miss Francis of Ding Dong School

T

Ti Ti.　　Pronounced, Tee Tee.

This was pidgin for "little," "a little bit," from the French, *petit*.

This term was often used to designate the squad "short round" or a lifer's manhood, e.g., "GI! You boocoo ti ti."

Tiger Stripes.　　A uniform camouflage pattern favored by ARVN Ranger, special ops units, and LRRPs, who had fashion sense.

Tiger stripe fatigues were also worn by some US special ops units, but most grunts favored a pattern that was later called "woodland," but in Nam, grunts referred to these uniforms as "trees."

Special ops guys could be divided into "tigers tripes" and "trees," based on what they wore in the field. Once the choice was made, grunts rarely crossed over.

For example, while in the LRRPs, since I wore "woodland" pattern fatigues and beer was my hallucinogen of choice, I could have been classified as a "tree juicer" — kind of Tolkienesque in a somewhat perverse way.

Since this is an entry with "tiger" in the title, it's a good place to talk about the real thing. And, yes, Elizabeth, there are tigers in Nam.

For grunts, tigers were a subject of myth and horror.

Grunts rarely, if ever, saw them. No tiger in its right mind would get near a bunch of armed grunts, and for a tiger (and most NVA), grunts were easy to avoid (and grunts rarely had any complaints about either situation).

A common "grunt-tiger-rumor" in the Highlands went something like this:

> "Tigers ate the dead and wounded left on the battlefield, and once they had tasted human flesh, even human flesh

impregnated with nuoc mam, that's all they wanted to eat. So, they would stalk grunts, wait until dark, charge into a night laager and drag out some chubby GI for a meal (chubby = FNG; grunts lost their baby-fat after a couple of weeks of C Rats, humping, cigarettes, and stress)."

Sitting in the world, reading this in the safety of your living room (or bathroom, if that's your preference) this story doesn't sound very frightening. Try thinking about this crap while sitting in the dark on a night laager in the middle of a real jungle, when the moon is down, not being able to see the end of your nose and being the only one around who's awake. Is that a bit more nerve racking.

So, when grunts were having a bullshit session, there was usually a story about a unit who had a couple of guys dragged out of the perimeter by tigers "never to be seen again."

I'm probably one of the few people who has actually seen a tiger in the wild. Luckily, when it happened, I wasn't wearing any underwear or I would have had a real laundry problem.

Here's how it happened.

I had just joined the LRRPs and was out on one of my first missions. In the highlands up near Cambodia, a LRRP team was typically assigned a four-square-klick area: go in, poke around, report what's going on and get the hell out.

Now recon patrols try to avoid contact with the bad guys. Tactically, the point is to find them, report, and leave without them knowing. Personally, when there are only four grunts and hundreds of bad guys, meeting engagements rarely have happy endings for the grunts.

Based on the terrain and enemy activity, LRRPs usually had two routines for working an AO.

The first, which was highly popular with many, was to get into the AO, find a good spot for observation, and hunker down there for a few days. Believe me, if four LRRPs were sharing an AO with a company or two of bad guys, the last thing the LRRPs wanted was to do the NVA a favor by crashing around the bush ... that sort of crap was reserved for Hawk Eye missions.

The other method of covering an AO was the "tourist" approach. The LRRP team humped though every inch of the AO examining every hill, dale, stream, ridgeline, nook, cranny, and wait-a-minute bush looking for bad guys.

My first team leader was a country boy from someplace down in southern Georgia with an unpronounceable name and overrun with alligators even in the winter. And he was a "tourist."

He dragged us over every hill and into every dale in our AO. We probably went only a couple of klicks in "map distance" since, in the mountains, for every hundred meters you go horizontally, you go five hundred vertically.

Late in the afternoon of the first day, we were moving west just below a ridgeline through some fairly clear terrain; the sun was in our faces. I was walking point, when I detected movement about a hundred meters out coming right at us. Because the terrain we were moving through was open, we were pretty much exposed -- caught with our "pants down" – but we still executed a hasty ambush drill.

I was out front of the team trying to identify the threat ... the movement sounded like multiple humans walking ... not a good sign in the boonies when you knew there are no friendlies around.

Whoever was out there, I caught a glimpse of them when they passed between me and the sun. I saw multiple figures walking upright and got the impression of brown clothing — again not good news since the NVA often wore khaki.

I signaled to the team pointing to where they would break out into the open in front of us and aimed my M16 at that point.

They continued to come right at us. When the first one broke into the open, I held fire because I sensed something wrong in the way it moved. I raised a closed fist, "Hold Fire!"

By the time the second figure broke cover I realized I was looking down my rifle sights at a couple of orangutans!

The good news, they weren't NVA!

The other news, orangutans are very territorial and the head monkey was not pleased to see us.

One of the cardinal rules we had in the LRRPs was, "Don't piss off the monkeys." We had an entire team sent to the hospital by a bunch of pissed off monkeys, who actually beat the rangers senseless and bent their M16s.

So we didi mau'd a klick or so out of their way.

Just before sundown that evening, we found ourselves leaning up against our ruck sacks at the edge of a large clearing. We were feeling pretty relaxed and were experiencing a "Walt Disney" moment. The birds were fluttering about singing and, in the clearing, Bambi and his family were calmly munching grass — a pretty good sign that no one was around.

Then the deer froze and, after a few moments, fled into the forest.

"I wonder if they smelled us?" I asked.

The team leader wet his finger and held it up in the breeze. "Naw!" he said, "Wind's wrong. Must a been somethin' else"

Oh great, I thought, "somethin' else," in an area full of pissed-off monkeys and NVA.

We had humped ourselves into exhaustion, almost ambushed a pack of grumpy monkeys, and now "somethin' else" is spooking the deer. This mission kept getting better and better.

Observing Roger's Rangers Standing Order #8, "When we march, we keep moving 'til dark, so as to give the enemy the least possible chance at us", we used "Ending Evening Nautical Twilight," the time between sundown and full dark, to move about a klick and find a nice snug place for the night.

We found some thick brush and burrowed our way in. "Somethin' else" wasn't going to get close to us without making a hell of a lot of noise. Just to seal the deal, we placed claymores around our little nigh laager.

The moon was down that night; I literally could not see my hand at the end of my nose. Although I was with three other guys, I felt totally alone in the dark. The only sign that there was anybody else near me was the muffled sound of the radio breaking squelch for the sitreps.

Sometime during the night, I heard movement in the dark. The first thing I noticed was that the insects had stopped singing. Then I heard something moving toward directly toward our position.

Now even a city boy like me can tell the difference between a human and an animal moving through the bush in the dark. This was an animal. It was too big to be human and no human would go crashing through the bush in a combat zone like this thing did. And it was making a bee line right at us.

None of us made a sound. I felt a bit exposed. I was the guy this thing was going to step on first. I couldn't see to shoot and, surrounded by that much brush, I didn't dare toss grenades in the dark.

I was fumbling through my equipment to find the "clicker" for the claymore I had put out somewhere in the dark... where exactly ... I hadn't a clue, which was okay because in the dark, I wasn't sure where my claymore was in relation to the approaching critter.

The thing continued to come right at us ... and by "us," I mean me.

By the noise it was making, I thought it was huge ... it had to be a water buffalo or an elephant (Yes, there were those in Nam too). My irrational fear was that it was going to step on me ... not the most noble way to go.

It's impossible to judge distance in the dark, but the thing seemed to stop moving around ten meters from me. Then silence ... absolute and seemingly eternal silence.

Then a sound came out of the dark like the explosive moaning of an asthmatic steam locomotive, three or four times.

Then this city boy knew what was out there in the dark! I had seen it in a movie when I was a kid. It was a f'ing nuclear- mutant, LRRP-eating MONSTER! And it was right next to me in the dark!

Then it just went away.

The next morning, following Roger's Rangers Standing Order #15, "Don't sleep beyond dawn. Dawn's when the French and Indians attack," we had moved about a klick away from our night laager by the time the sun was up.

But our "monster" had piqued the team leader's curiosity. So, we circled back around to where we had spent the night. The team leader nosed around the brush for a while, and then called me over.

"See that?" he said pointing to the ground.

I looked down and saw nothing but dirt. So, I said,

"Yeah! What do you think that is?"

"Tracks!" he said, "Cat tracks!"

Now again, being the city boy, when someone says "cat" to me, I envision a "pussy cat," the kind that says "meow" and rubs up against my leg for attention. So when the team leader decided to follow the "cat" tracks, I wasn't particularly concerned.

Well, follow them we did, for about half a day.

In the early afternoon, we were following the trail (which I had yet to detect) along a small blue line through a bamboo thicket. Then we heard it … about a hundred meters in front of us … roaring … repeated and seemingly ill-tempered roaring!

Now I was a city boy in denial.

I now understood we're not creeping up on a pussy cat, but my frame of reference for the jungle variety of cat is based on what I've seen on TV and at the Central Park Zoo.

On TV, the Jungle Jim wrestles with these things with a knife and wins; they're no bigger than large dogs.

And the ones I had seen in the Central Park Zoo seemed pretty lethargic, hanging out, yawning, napping in the sun, waiting for feeding time.

So, I'm still okay with this scenario; no panic yet … denial… denial … denial!

We were getting close to the critter, so the team leader put us into a line; four rangers abreast anchored on the team leader, who was following the trail along the blue line.

I was on the tail end of the line. As we were moving through the bamboo thicket, I was more concerned with not getting out in front of the rest of the guys (not the smartest thing to do since it might put me between a target and three armed and nervous rangers) than I was with what was hidden in the brush in front of us.

So I kept looking over to my left to make sure I was still directly abreast of the team. That is, until I looked to my left and realized that not only had the rest of the guys stopped moving, but they all were staring at something behind me ... did I say staring ... I mean looking with an expression of abject shock and horror ... eyes the size of tea saucers... mouths hanging open ... little drops of drool creeping down their chins ... did I mention whatever was terrorizing them was behind me?

Like in an Abbott and Costello movie, oh so slowly I turned until I spotted what had caused three combat-experienced rangers to go into a state of shock.

A tiger!

A tiger standing about fifteen meters behind me.

Now another piece of bad news!

Tigers are not the size of large dogs. This one was the size of a small pony. On all fours, it came up almost to my chest.

The only good news — the tiger was looking away from me.

Not for long!

No sooner had two sequential thoughts formed in my panicked brain - 1) Shoot it! And 2) No! My bullets are too small and will only piss it off! - when the tiger turned its head and looked right at me.

I can't even begin to describe what it's like to go eyeball to eyeball with a tiger, other than, "Tiger, Tiger, Burning bright / In the forests of the night" doesn't even come close!

I fell right over on my ass with a seemingly useless M16 clutched to my chest at port arms.

Luckily, the tiger wasn't in the mood for socializing, or dining, and disappeared into the bush before my butt hit the ground.

The rest of the guys ran over to me. I heard voices seemly many miles away saying, "Why didn't you fire."

I could only point to where the tiger had been and stammer, "T... t... t... t... tiger... b... b... big... eyes... eat... gone..."

We never spotted that "cat" again, thank God!

During the day, it was nowhere to be seen. But every evening around dusk, it let us know in no uncertain roars and growls it was around, we were in its territory, and not pleased with our company.

And that, my dear readers, is why I never wore tiger stripes ... professional courtesy!

TOC.   Pronounced, TOK.

This is an acronym for "Tactical Operations Center."

The TOC is a command post that usually includes a small group of "specialty" staff personnel who guide tactical elements (aka "grunts") during a mission.

On the company-level, the TOC is pretty much the old man, the head medic, and the RTO. On the battalion and brigade level, it's the old man, and his operations (S3) and intelligence (S2) elements and a bunch of radios and RTOs.

According to tactical doctrine, the location of the TOC was never to be revealed to the bad guys, but in Nam they always knew where it was ... find a firebase with a company or two of grunts on palace guard — it's the place where all the helicopter traffic is and where the smell of bacon and coffee comes from every morning — then locate the tent or bunker with all the radio antennas sticking out of it.

Also, tactically the TOC was to be kept separate from the Combat Trains. The "official" reason was to disperse unit assets. The "real" reason is that no one ever wanted two infantry Majors in the same location; the cat fights could be messy and nasty!!!

The TOC was a prime target for the bad guys.

Since their marksmanship with mortars and rockets left a lot to be desired (by them, not us), they would sometimes send sappers in. For this reason, and also the fact that there is nothing to be gained getting too close to the bosses, grunts would tend to avoid the TOC, especially after dark.

A quick comment on NVA marksmanship.

Although most 11C's (grunt mortar guys) would sneer at NVA accuracy with their 82mm mortars, you have to remember that the US mortar guys could put HE round on a dime at two klicks in less than three rounds. So meeting that standard wasn't easy.

But, when the NVA were shooting their 122mm rockets, the ultimate in a "for whom it may concern" weapon, they didn't have to get too close to do damage. Anything in the neighborhood was a hit. Besides, grunts couldn't hear these things coming, unless they heard the explosion from the launch, and 122's were hard to duck.

Luckily for grunts, the bad guys usually reserved the big stuff for the juicy targets, like base camps and logistics centers.

Even being a REMF in Nam had its risks. Although grunts never got along with REMFs, they took their chances with the rest of us and did their duty ... at least their version of it.

A 122mm rocket attack on a logistics center was the cause of my being classified MIA, possibly killed, a second time.

While I was with the rangers, my former infantry battalion was pulling palace guard on a logistics base near Pleiku.

It was Summer of 1969. The NVA was beginning to recover from its debacle in Tet '68 and the US had kindly assisted them by not bombing of their supply lines along the Cambodian border. So they had some ordinance to throw around and were becoming feisty again.

I had a couple of days between missions, so I went down to Pleiku to visit a couple of buddies. We went over to a club for a few drinks.

The guy I was with was boasting that he was "dating" the Vietnamese barmaid. I didn't take him too seriously — guy talk, I thought — but I should have. The barmaid slipped me a "mickey;" two drinks and I was absolutely plastered.

I remember announcing to anyone who cared that I had had enough and staggering out to the latrine, where my body relieved itself of the toxins and I passed out.

While I was somewhere in dreamland, the bad guys hit the base with a bunch of 122's.

After the smoke cleared — literally — the grunts on the base did a headcount and of course I was missing — no one thought to look in the latrine because only a moron would go there during a rocket attack. No one had considered an unconscious moron.

I came to a lot worse for the wear around 2 AM (that's 0200 Hours grunt standard time). I had no idea what had happened while I was out.

I staggered around in the dark and found the tent where I was supposed to sleep. I noticed that the lights were still on, and no one was in any of the bunks.

Strange, but I was hurting too badly to try to figure it out, or even wonder about it. So, I just got into my bunk and pulled my poncho liner over my head.

A few minutes later a grunt came into the tent and sat on the bunk next to mine. And much to my horror, he felt it necessary to unburden himself to me (although it soon became obvious that he didn't know it was me under the poncho liner).

"Man! What a kick in the ass! Getting it like that!"

"Urrgh!" (That was about all the speech capability I could muster at that moment).

"Yeah! A guy does a full tour in the boonies and gets his ass greased in a base camp!"

"Urrgh!"

"Shit! Goes to show you ... get out while you can. You go extending a tour and you're just asking for it."

"Urrgh!"

"Yeah! A real f'ing shame. We probably won't find enough to stuff a body bag."

"Urrgh!"

"Hey! Did you know Sergeant Gleason?"

It was right at this point that I realized that I was involved in this conversation more than I had thought. I sat up.

"Gleason! I'm Gleason!"

The grunt reacted as if I had punched him; not much experience in witnessing resurrections, I guess.

I spent the rest of the night, and most of the next morning, getting my ass chewed out for not being dead ... best ass-chewing I ever took considering the alternative.

TOE. This is an abbreviation for "Table of Organization and Equipment."

TOE is a model and the authorized structure of an army unit from the number of personnel, their position and grades, to how many pairs of socks are authorized for each snuffy.

This is just what it sounds like ... the Org Chart of Gruntdom, and a list of everything grunts were supposed to and were entitled to have.

Now this is an important distinction. Just because grunts were supposed (or in army-speak, "authorized") to have something doesn't mean they actually had it ... blame it on the supply chain.

For example, grunts were authorized to have flashlight batteries, BA30's in army-speak, because they had flashlights. But, since BA30's powered every portable radio in base camp, the batteries rarely made it all the way out to the boonies where the grunts and their flashlights were.

Now, if grunts were to ask for ("requisition" in army-speak) something that made perfect sense for them to have but the TOE didn't specify that grunts are authorized to have it, the grunts were SOL, e.g. "Grenadiers are not authorized to carry 45s under the TOE; if the bad guys get too close, beat them over the head with your M79!"

This is where the grunt informal logistic processes of "barter" and "reallocation" came into play. It was kind of a "Robin Hood" thing: "Take from the REMFs and give to the grunts."

This is a good place to explain how gruntdom was organized ... at least according to the TOE.

- **The Grunt:** The basic unit was, of course, the grunt—the 11B.
- **Fire Team:** Take four grunts, give an M79 to one, designate another as an "automatic rifleman" and put an E5, "Buck Sergeant," in charge, and you have a "fire team." Fire teams were

formally designated by letter: Alpha and Bravo. Infantry units in Nam were typically so under strength that they weren't organized down to the fire team level.

- **Squad:** Put two fire teams together, put an E6, Staff Sergeant, "Squad Leader," in charge and you have a "squad." Squads were formally designated by number: first, second and third; but mostly they were referred to by the squad leader's last name. "You're in Murphy's squad." This was a grunt's primary "home" with his buddies. From a social-Darwinism perspective, this was the level at which grunts were made, or not. If the squad accepted a guy, he stayed and became part of the "family." If not, the army had to find another job for him in Nam — cook, clerk or "REMF-gopher" were the most common.

- **Platoon:** Three squads, two M60 machine guns, a medic, one E7, "Platoon Sergeant," and a 1st Lieutenant, "Platoon Leader," constituted a "platoon." Platoons were designated by number: first, second and third, or by the name of the platoon leader, except the third platoon which was typically designated the "Third Herd."

- **Company:** Three platoons, an 81mm mortar section, a head medic, an RTO or two, an E8 "First Sergeant," a Lieutenant, "XO" (rarely, if ever, seen in the boonies), and a Captain, "Company Commander," was a "company." Companies were designated by letter: Alpha, Bravo, Charlie and Delta in the Vietnam-era TOE. Most companies maintained a three-platoon structure, but the platoons rarely had more than 20–25 grunts in them.

- **Battalion:** Four "rifle" companies, "Alpha," "Bravo," "Charlie" and "Delta," and an "Echo" Company consisting of a scout platoon and the four-deuce mortar section; a "Headquarters" company for the ash & trash; a section of staff-weenies, S1 through S5; an E9, "Sergeant Major"; two Majors — the "XO" and an "Operations Officer"; and a Lieutenant Colonel, "Battalion Commander."

Infantry battalions were organized with artillery, and command and support elements into "Brigades" and brigades into "Divisions," but this stuff became pretty metaphysical to grunts. The division was identifiable primarily because grunts, at least in the rear areas, wore the divisional "patch" on their left shoulder.

From the grunt point of view, there wasn't much evidence of intelligent life from division level to the president (and at times not even there; for example, one president, LBJ, made the decision to get us involved in Nam and, when another president, Nixon, stopped bombing the NVA supply lines in Laos and Cambodia, the war went from the "mortar attack of the month club" to "Keep digging! Here come the 122mm rockets again!" every night) ... this area of the TOE was commonly referred to by grunts as the "Never Never Land."

Trainee. This is the lowest non-lifer, non-REMF, non-staff weenie form of army life.

Essentially, a quasi-civilian who is being trained to be a soldier, a soldier who is being trained to be an infantryman, an infantryman who is being trained to jump out of perfectly good airplanes and to eat snakes once on the ground; in other words, any soldier in Basic Combat Training (BCT), Advanced Individual Training (AIT), Airborne School, or Ranger School.

This is someone barely qualified to be called "soldier," but not yet qualified to be called an "FNG," which is not qualified to be called a grunt. But, unlike lifers and REMFs, trainees are redeemable:

"What are you, trainee?"

"Drill Sergeant, I am the lowest thing on earth! I am whale shit! I am so dull that I make a hammer seem like a computer! Even my mother doesn't love me, so she sent me here! My girlfriend doesn't love me! She sent me an autographed picture of Jody! Everything I am and everything I hope to be, I owe to my Drill Sergeant, who wishes to remain anonymous for reasons obvious to the casual observer, Drill Sergeant!"

The highest accolade for a trainee was to be recognized as a "soldier" or a "trooper." The first time a drill sergeant called you that ... and meant it ... your chest popped out a few inches and you walked a little taller!

The highest accolade for any soldier was to be accepted as a "grunt" by a squad of combat-experienced grunts. Don't walk tall when that happens; it makes you too good a target!

Like a member of the Jets in the Broadway musical, when you're a grunt, you're grunt all the way, from your first firefight to your last dying day.

That's forever, brother!

Troop Leading Procedures. According to army doctrine, "Troop Leading Procedures" define a sequence of actions taken by a leader preparing to execute a mission.

In theory, these are:

Step 1. Receive the Mission

Step 2. Issue a warning order

Step 3. Make a tentative plan

Step 4. Start necessary movement

Step 5. Reconnoiter

Step 6. Complete the plan

Step 7. Issue the complete order

Step 8. Supervise

In practice, troop leading procedures in Nam worked something like this:

Step 1. Piss off some lifer during stand-down so you and your unit gets kicked out of base camp

Step 2. Get issued the wrong maps

"Hey, LT! Are you sure Central Park is near Pleiku?"

Step 3. Try to get a profile, doctor's appointment, malaria ... anything to keep you off the mission.

Step 4. Get inserted into the wrong AO, so now the maps actually would work if you had a working compass or a lieutenant who knew how to use one.

Step 5. Ignore all radio traffic from any station whose call sign ends in "six"

"STATIC ... Oh Six ... STATIC ... bad copy your last ... STATIC ... higher ground ... STATIC ... bad batteries STATIC ... wet radios ... STATIC...Out".

Step 6. Find a high, comfy hill.

Step 7. Dig in, build hootches, heat up Cs

Step 8. Get forgiven and go back on stand down.

Tropical Chocolate.   The confirmation of a horrible truth! There was such a thing as bad chocolate.

This was a special-formula chocolate that would not melt at the high temperature of the tropics. The formula successfully achieved this goal, but unfortunately the resulting material could not be dissolved by any physical or chemical process known at the time. The secret formula was also known to have devastating effects on lower gastric tract equal to, if not surpassing, Ham and Lima Beans and dysentery.

Tropical chocolate was very helpful in the selection process for nightly LP duty — no one having eaten tropical chocolate was allowed to spend the night in the perimeter.

This was also suspected to be the source of North Vietnamese complaints of the US use of chemical weapons on their own troops.

Along with Kent Cigarettes, tropical chocolate was the only part of an SP pack that had no value on the black market —

"What! You dinky-dau, GI! Me want have babysahn someday!"

Tunnel Rat.   A small, compact, svelte grunt who chased bad guys down into their tunnels and underground lairs with a flashlight, a 45, and a block of C4.

In the hierarchy of grunt psychopathy, the tunnel rat ranked third after explosive ordinance disposal and combat engineer with a bangalore torpedo. Definitely ranked higher than point man and LRRP.

Tunnel rats got a lot of respect, but even grunts believed that — although it was a necessary job — a grunt had to be crazy enough to volunteer for explosive ordinance disposal to do it.

If a grunt were to create a phrase for an impossibly difficult, insanely dangerous but absolutely necessary "thank God you're doing it so I don't have to," job, it would be "tunnel rat."

W

WAC. Pronounced 'whack."

Acronym and abbreviation for the Women's Army Corps.

This was the women's branch of the army during the Vietnam war. The army was at that time segregated by gender; women were found only in the Nursing Corps or in the WACs.

The headquarters of the WAC was Ft. McClellan, Alabama, where, for some perverse reason known only to the gods and to the army, I was stationed for Infantry Leadership School and Advanced Infantry Training (AIT).

This was the only post in my career where men were significantly outnumbered by women.

I learned two important life lessons on McClellan. How to do laundry and women have libidos.

One week while in AIT, I missed the weekly quartermaster laundry pick up. Someone told me that there was a laundromat on the WAC side of the post, so Saturday morning I stuffed all my tighty-whities into my laundry bag and hiked across post to the Forbidden Kingdom.

The WAC side of post was not "officially" off limits to male personnel. Our participation in the secret rites of army femdom was "not encouraged."

I managed to find the laundromat and quickly discovered upon entering that I was "the only man on the island." The place was full of women.

Also, I had no clue how a laundromat operated.

Like the guy in *West Side Story*, I was a victim of my environment growing up. Baby Boomer males were not trained in basic life survival skills – cooking food, shopping, laundry – all this was a complete mystery to us.

So, there I stood, in the middle of the laundromat, surrounded by women, with not a clue about what to do.

Lesson 1, no woman can resist a clueless male in a laundromat.

I was mobbed by eagerly helpful women.

> "First you need to sort your laundry ... colors, whites, delicates ... hee, hee ... you're a guy, you have no delicates ... hee, hee, hee ... whites, hot water and bleach; colors, cold no bleach ... buy your detergent from that machine ..."

In all my life, I had never received so much female attention with so little effort! Why hadn't anyone told me about this before! I had stumbled into laundromat heaven!

My second lesson ... women have libidos!

I realize that in this new age, enlightened by the revelations of the 1960s women's liberation movement, my statement may sound a bit naïve in a chauvinist way. But this was 1967, and I was a product of over twelve years of Catholic education.

According to my upbringing, all post-pubescent encounters between the genders was potentially sinful, e.g. burn in hell for eternity for just thinking about ... well ... you know ... which for a teenaged boy was impossible.

Also, I was taught that women don't like sex!

They only do it, after marriage, to propagate more little Catholics and to keep their sex-fiend husbands from finding it elsewhere and going to hell. "Just tell me when you're done, Sean. I have housework to do!"

There was a dance every Saturday night at the WAC community center on main post, right next to the golf course. Of course, we infantry types were not encouraged to attend. But, since I had been "invited" to go by one of the laundromat Sirens, I duded up in my khakis and dragged a couple of my buddies along with me.

At the hop, the ladies of the WAC entertained us with sad and distressing tales, the trials of having to go through WAC training ... most of which had to do with having no contact with males ... ironic!!!

One young maiden revealed to me some of the field expedients practiced in barracks to alleviate the pressures of enforced army celibacy.

My first giant step toward damnation!

Then she asked me if I wanted to go for a walk on the golf course and "look at the stars."

By this point, I was sure I was going to hell ... at least the army version of it ... Nam ... so, what the hell!

Wait-A-Minute Bush. This was a term describing any one of a number of strange and wonderful Vietnamese bushes and trees that, through the strategic placement of razor sharp and durable thorns and barbs, caused a grunt to immediately halt all movement, including breathing, and re-think his route selection, vocation, and hope of ever having children.

The nastier varieties left their thorns in a grunt's jungle fatigues and flesh so he could enjoy them long after he had managed to extricate himself from the bush itself.

A grunt knew he was having a bad day when he got hung up in a wait-a-minute bush that was also the home of the infamous Vietnamese red tree ant who could strip the flesh from a somewhat dehydrated and emaciated grunt in 9.2 seconds.

A grunt would chew off any body part (except one) to escape these devils.

Warrant Officer. A warrant officer is an army rank above the enlisted grades but below the officer grades. Warrants were highly skilled, single-track specialty guys - technicians and helicopter drivers.

These guys were like senior NCOs on testosterone.

They were typically very good at what they did, so their competence was usually unquestionable, and they were not afraid to get their hands dirty working on stuff. So, it was impossible to hide embarrassing stuff from them.

Also, they were quasi-officers who didn't have to worry about the "gentleman by act of Congress" crap. So they would kick a grunt's ass if he pissed them off.

How technically competent were these guys, you ask? The following is one requirement from the Warrant Officer Qualification Exam:

> "Go into the jungle, collect wood for charcoal and mine iron ore in the neighboring mountains. Design, fabricate, build, zero, and operate a working machine gun with five hundred rounds of ammunition (belted, every fifth round a tracer). Your position will be attacked by an NVA platoon in three hours."

Warrant rank was very confusing in the army social hierarchy. If a grunt called some of these guys "Sir," they'd get pissed and say, "Don't call me that! I still have to work for a living!" Other warrants would give a grunt an Article 15 if he didn't genuflect in their presence.

Most were okay if a grunt just called them "Chief"!

The best way of dealing with warrants was to avoid them altogether, which was pretty easy since the ones not driving helicopters were usually back with the ash & trash, and the ones driving helicopters were usually too busy to worry about the social amenities.

Water Point.   Functionally, this is an army engineer facility to purify and distribute water for drinking.

Water points required access to a body of water, preferably flowing and upstream from any latrines, and a road network for vehicle access. Typically, units in the AO dispatched vehicles towing water trailers to pick up drinking water.

Socially, this was a meeting place of grunts and various Vietnamese underworld characters, who would make Damon Runyon proud.

Economically, this was a drive-through Vietnamese strip mall for beer, soda, trash, trinkets and other shady exchanges.

Although very vulnerable from the point of view of security, the bad guys rarely attacked water points because their black-market percentage was too good ... the vig was about five hundred points on a can of soda. Besides, for many of them this was their day job if they weren't ARVN's.

Imagine: predatory capitalism financing a communist insurgency ... go figure!

Web Gear. A way to describe a grunt's hands and feet during the monsoon season.

Also, a collection of straps, snaps, buckles, belts, and bags a grunt hung all over his body to which "stuff"— about sixty to seventy pounds worth — was attached or packed.

Kind of a grunt Frederick's of Vietnam S&M thing without the sex, the fun, and the baby oil.

"Hey, Sarge! Are these bandoleers me?"

Willy Pete. A grunt term for White Phosphorus, an incendiary weapon made from phosphorus.

Willy Pete was delivered (euphemism alert) by artillery, mortars, and grenades. It was also known as "white smoke" but hopefully played no part in Papal elections.

Willy Pete was one of the nastiest things on the battle field... even grunts hesitated to use this stuff. It consisted of tiny, burning particles of phosphorous that would continue to burn flesh, or anything else they came in contact with, as long as they had oxygen.

The first aid for a WP wound was to smother the wound with mud to stop the burning until the victim could be medevacked somewhere where the medics could pick out the phosphorous particles.

The World. This meant home.

For most grunts, it was a vaguely remembered, mythical place they had left to come to Nam and would return to if they ever got to leave Nam.

This mythical land was reputed to have roofs, beds, clean water, hot chow, hot showers, cold beer, round-eyed women and no firefights (except in Detroit). Here, you could actually sleep the entire night in a bed out of the rain with your boots off and without your M16 between your legs.

The world was rumored to be where the army sent you when you DEROS, but, like heaven, no one ever returned to confirm it.

WTWP. This is an abbreviation for "Wrong Time, Wrong Place," the basic grunt articulation and affirmation of the complex relationship between chance, determinism, and fate. "Wrong time, wrong place, you're screwed."

It's the principle explaining why there's no principle to surviving combat. You can't train for it; you can't plan for it; you can't pray your way out of it ... if you're in the wrong place at the wrong time, you're dead.

In other words, don't waste your time worrying about the bullet out there with your name on it. Worry about all those bullets out there addressed "for whom it may concern."

This is the underlying (un)principle explaining the grunt belief that it's better to be lucky than to be good ... but you better be damned good or your luck won't save you.

A quick story: I was on a firebase just after the rainy season of 1968. The engineers decided to destroy a stock of ammo that had been damaged or was too corroded to be depended on. They dug a hole with a front loader, dumped all the old ammo into it, and set some charges.

We grunts were told to stay in the bunkers but, being kids – I was nineteen at the time – we decided to watch the show.

Besides, I had already had one bunker collapse on me and being buried alive was not on my list of favorite things.

I found myself a nice perch on a storage bunker just behind the bunker line. The engineers called "Fire in the Hole!" and blew the ammo.

It was just as good as the 4th of July.

At least, I thought so until a piece of spent shrapnel smashed a sandbag right next to where I was sitting.

When I say the sandbag, I'm talking about a bag that had been filled with wet mud during the rainy season and then baked in the sun for a few weeks after the rains stopped.

This jagged, smoking piece of metal smashed through a six-inch thick brick inches from where I was sitting. Had I been sitting a few inches to the right, it would have taken off my arm; a little more, it would have split me in half.

I was almost WTWP!

Luck was the difference.

WTWP is the grunt affirmation that, despite every war movie ever made, there are no "feature actors" in the "movie" he was appearing in; fate could screw anyone at any time.

An FNG might think he's in a feature role in this little drama, but there's no assurance he'll still be standing when the credits roll (*v.* John Wayne, *The Sands of Iwo Jima*).

Since we're near the end, this may be a good spot to talk about another way of explaining the difference between a grunt and an FNG ... or any other human being, for that matter.

Earlier, the difference was presented in terms of acceptance —when the other grunts accepted someone as part of the pack, he was no longer an FNG.

There was, however, another way of looking at it.

An FNG became a grunt when something in him died.

There's a scene in the recent TV series *A Band of Brothers* in which a grunt platoon leader tries to explain to a soldier why he couldn't function in combat, why he was acting like a "coward."

> "Your problem is you don't realize you're already dead. Once you do, you can begin to function like a soldier."

Once a soldier realized that he was "dead," that death could claim him at any time, in any place, unexpectedly and suddenly, and that was the essential nature of his condition, then the soldier could go about his duty without being concerned about his survival, something over which he had no control.

Then he became a grunt.

This was not an easy proposition for a nineteen-year-old.

Teenagers are full of life! They're immortal! For them, life has no foreseeable end! They celebrate it! They participate in it through their energy, sports, eating, drinking, sleeping, sex. Life seems to pulsate through their veins.

But life could not be assumed by grunts. They desired it, yes, but they could not cling to it because it could be taken from them at any moment, any unexpected, unjust moment.

What grunts did have were their buddies, their duty, and their enemy.

When grunts went about their business, they could not give a thought for their own survival; that would destroy their ability to function as soldiers facing a competent enemy, who were effectively and competently wielding deadly force against them.

Grunts could depend only on their equipment, their training, their buddies, and luck, but luck would eventually betray them.

They were dead — dead at nineteen.

Once a soldier accepted his "death," and "died" to the world of youth, to the world of a loving family and friends, to the world where he had a lover, a future, children, then he could function in combat.

Only then did he become a grunt.

POSTSCRIPT FROM
THE SECOND EDITION

"Old age hath yet his honour and his toil;
Death closes all: but something ere the end,
Some work of noble note, may yet be done,
Not unbecoming men that strove with Gods."
Tennyson, "Ulysses"

I first read "Ulysses" in high school. I was fifteen, a young naïf who knew it all and would live forever.

The poem meant nothing to me.

I'm sure the teacher explained it to us.

What did I need to know about old age? I would never be old!

Ironically, I was more prophetic than I imagined. Four years later I was in the infantry in Vietnam.

I couple of years ago, I was invited to join the veterans of my Vietnam infantry company at their reunion in North Myrtle Beach, South Carolina: Cacti Blue, A Company, 2nd Battalion, 35th Infantry, 1967-1970.

The organizer, Pat Martin, who had been the company commander's RTO, had tracked me down through our regimental association.

I was strangely apprehensive about attending.

These guys are for me the real deal. No bullshit! No romanticizing! We literally chewed the same dirt together.

I wasn't sure whether my concern was because of the bullshit I had made up in my mind after all these years to somehow euphemize the experience and aggrandize my contribution, or I would get an unflattering view of myself from guys whose opinions I had to respect.

In other words, despite what I had convinced myself about my participation, would I be told I was full of shit. I didn't cut it.

This would be the ultimate performance review of an experience that happened over fifty years ago by authorities who couldn't be questioned.

Our former commander, "The LT" himself, Don Latella, was going to be there!

Was I a grunt?

Was I really a part of this brotherhood?

No worries. We had a great time together, sharing memories, war stories, and not a few beers.

Two things stood out for me.

First, the bond we formed over fifty years ago in Nam is still there.

Second, we still have the fire ... the fire to achieve the impossible against overwhelming odds.

One would think that the horrors of combat and loss would have extinguished our desire to strive.

Our common experiences were the crucible of our brotherhood. They forged an undying desire to achieve, to overcome, to depart on new adventures, to strive with the gods yet again.

So, despite the efforts of my high school teacher, I came to understand Ulysses from my Cacti Brothers.

"Some work of noble note, may yet be done, / Not unbecoming men that strove with Gods."

POSTSCRIPT FROM
THE FIRST EDITION

The first ghost that came was that of my comrade Elpenor, for he had not yet been laid beneath the earth. We had left his body unwaked and unburied in Circe's house ... I was very sorry for him and cried when I saw him. "Elpenor," said I, "how did you come down here into this gloom and darkness?" "Sir," he answered with a groan, "it was all bad luck...." Then I tried to find some way of embracing my poor mother's ghost. Thrice I sprang towards her and tried to clasp her in my arms, but each time she flitted from my embrace as if it were a dream or phantom, and being touched to the quick I said to her, "Mother, why do you not stay still when I would embrace you? If we could throw our arms around one another we might find sad comfort in the sharing of our sorrows even in the house of Hades ..." "My son," she answered, "...all people are like this when they are dead ... and the soul flits away as though it were a dream. Now, however, go back to the light of day as soon as you can..." (Homer. *Odyssey*. Bk XI. Trans. Samuel Butler)

It was many years after I had left Nam before I started my journey back.

Inability to express feelings... lifelessness... "living in Hades" ... had led to a divorce and destroyed a family. But, through this I began to recognize that I was in some manner "dead," and I found someone, a counselor, who could help me find the pathway back to life.

We had worked for some months when I had a dream, a dream that was so vivid that I remember it to this day.

I was back in Nam, but in a large, shadowy barrack room. Although I could see sunlight outside, the room was murky. In the darkness, I could see row upon row of bunks and reclining in each was the indistinct shape of a soldier. Then someone spoke to me, "Get ready! Saddle up! We're going out on patrol." I recognized his voice! I began to distinguish faces: Jimmy, Doc Ambrosio, Jonesy, Spence, guys I knew, friends who didn't make it back. From beyond the room, a voice said, "You don't belong here! You don't belong here..." I turned toward the voice, toward the light. Then I awoke.

This was the beginning of my journey back to life. I will remember my lost brothers forever, but I cannot share their fate. I cannot remain with them.

I must continue to journey into the light, to life.

ABOUT THE AUTHOR

Ray Gleason is a writer, a teacher, a police officer, and retired army infantry officer.

While in Vietnam, Gleason was a rifleman, i.e. grunt, 11 Bush, ground-pounder, with A Company, 2nd Battalion, 35th Infantry ("Cacti Blue"), and he was also a Long-Range Reconnaissance Patrol (LRRP) team leader with the 75th Infantry (Ranger).

During his military career, Gleason was an infantry company commander, an armored cavalry squadron XO, and a division and army-level staff weenie.

Gleason has been awarded the Combat Infantry Badge (CIB), Bronze Star for Valor, Air Medal, Army Commendation Medal, and the Vietnam Cross of Gallantry with Palm.

He still has his poncho liner and P38.

Gleason is an adjunct lecturer in Medieval Literature at Northwestern University in Chicago where he received a Ph.D. in Medieval Literature and an MA in English. Gleason also has a BA in English Literature and European History from Hunter College in New York.

Since retiring from the army, Gleason has served in a number of leadership positions in the telecommunications industry. Gleason also taught literature and leadership ethics at a private high school in Indiana.

Gleason has pitched his hootch in Indiana with his wife, Jan Peyser, a prize-winning silversmith jeweler, designer and entrepreneur. Between them they have six children, seven grandchildren, and five cats.

CPSIA information can be obtained
at www.ICGtesting.com
Printed in the USA
LVHW022153120523
746864LV00010B/91

9 798218 191382